GOD'S WORD
FOR TODAY

✟

Other Books by Dr. O. Hallesby

✠

Prayer

Why I Am a Christian

Under His Wings

Temperament and the Christian Faith

Religious or Christian

The Christian Life

Conscience

A Daily Devotional for the Whole Year

GOD'S WORD FOR TODAY
O. Hallesby

TRANSLATED BY

CLARENCE J. CARLSEN

FOREWORD BY

INGRID TROBISCH

✠

Augsburg
MINNEAPOLIS

GOD'S WORD FOR TODAY

Scripture quotations are from the Holy Bible, King James Version.

Cover design by Cindy Cobb Olson
Interior design by James F. Brisson

Library of Congress Cataloging-in-Publication Data

Hallesby, Ole, 1879–1961.
    [Småstykker til daglig andakt. English]
    God's word for today : a daily devotional for the whole year / O.
  Hallesby : translated by Clarence J. Carlsen : foreword by Ingrid
Trobisch.
       p.   cm.
    Includes bibliographical references.
    ISBN 0-8066-2735-2 :
    1. Family—Prayer-books and devotions—English.   2. Devotional
calendars—Lutheran Church.   I. Title.
BV255.H33513   1994
242'.2—dc20   94-3527
                                                                      CIP

The paper used in this publication meets the minimum requirements of American National Standard for Information Sciences—Permanence of Paper for Printed Library Materials, ANSI Z329.48-1984.   ∞™

Manufactured in the U.S.A.   AF 9-2735

98   97   96   95   94   1   2   3   4   5   6   7   8   9   10

FOREWORD

✝

DAILY renewal is the special gift God wants to give each one of us. Encouragement for the journey and a restful spirit as we push on through the day's joys and chores are a part of this renewal. Hallesby writes, "The peace-filled, victorious, joyful Christian life is possible only to those who have learned the deepest secret of daily renewal: unceasingly to turn to God and receive new power from the realm of the eternal."

God's Word for Today is a timeless book written by a godly man whose teaching brought renewal to the Lutheran Church of Norway. Dr. Hallesby has the gift of expressing deep truths in a simple way so that both adults and children can understand.

As I read these pages I was aware that this was one of the books my father read to my family for our devotions more than a half century ago. I still recall him stopping to look at my mother and comment on a truth which he had just read. Like the story of the wedding at Cana:

"What difference did it make that the two being married were poor when they had Jesus with them at their wedding? Both of them became attached to Jesus in such a way that day that He was permitted to go in and out of their home as long as they lived. Nor is Jesus present in any home without every day, in some manner, changing water into wine."

"The bitter waters of tribulation have been turned into sweet wine. He has not removed our difficulties, but he has transformed them in such a way that we can see His purpose and His grace."

The secret of the daily quiet time is that it brings a sense of security and safety—something which is described in that wonderful German word, Geborgenheit. The prophet Jeremiah says to God's people: "Ask for the old paths, where is the good way, and walk therein, and ye shall find rest for your souls" (Jer. 6:16).

Hallesby writes: "Nothing is so blessed to the soul as this quiet, unceasing fellowship with the Lord. The sense of the Lord's presence which then fills our souls exceeds all else that we can experience of peace and joy, inner satisfaction and security."

Without this daily quiet time I experience a sense of deficit. That "God-shaped vacuum," as St. Augustine puts it, remains an empty place. Instead of rest, my soul is full of unrest—even confusion. I need to listen to God's voice, and in the listening I become confident.

"Take time to meditate. It's the source of power," is a line from an old Irish prayer. I find Hallesby's book an excellent source for both the individual and the family, who want to take time to meditate, to have a breakfast for the soul, as it were. It gives me that sense of security which comes from knowing that I am loved by my Father in heaven. I am then ready to receive orders for the day.

This book, written in the deceptively simple language of distilled wisdom, is a classic for any individual or family who want to begin or end the day listening to the heavenly Father's voice.

Ingrid Trobisch,
Haus Geborgenheit,
Springfield, Missouri

PREFACE

✠

We have many daily devotional books, and many good ones. Some of them, it seems to me, are well nigh perfect models of their kind.

I am not sending out a new one, therefore, because we lack books of daily devotions, nor because I do not appreciate the high standard of excellence of those we do have. However, our experience in connection with family devotions has been that we need to change devotional books from time to time. If a book has been used every day for several years, it is well to let it rest for a while. Then it will have a fresh appeal when we begin to use it again.

Several years have passed now since I began working on this volume. Nevertheless it is with great trembling that I make it public. It is a very difficult task to write brief meditations such as these for every day in the year. Much more difficult than I had thought beforehand. For this reason also I have made use of some older materials. I have thus included several short selections from *Sin and Grace*, especially for the festive occasions.

I look upon family devotions as a vital factor in the edification and spiritual growth of the Church of God. That the home altar has been neglected in recent years in so many of the homes of our land is therefore a tremendous loss. For many years, both in speaking and in writing, I have tried to put in a good word for daily family devotions.

This book is a little attempt on my part to further the cause of daily devotions in the home. It is my humble prayer that God will graciously accompany it on its way into people's hearts and homes.

O. Hallesby
Vinderen, Oslo

PREFATORY NOTE

Devotions for special days and church festivals
that do not fall on the same date every year
will be found at the close of the book.

✠

For of his fulness we all received, and grace for grace.

—JOHN 1:16

THESE words shed divine light upon the year which has just passed.

We have all *received*, it says.

Most of us no doubt are thinking more of the things we have *lost*.

Likely we have all lost something during the year that has gone. Some have perhaps lost *a great deal*. Some have lost money. Others, their health. And still others, some of their dear ones.

During this New Year season you have perhaps often felt how poor you are now and how rich you were at the beginning of last year. Yes, what a change can take place in a home in one year!

Nevertheless our text says: "We all received."

Yes, we all received, even we who lost a great deal. It is this of which God would remind us before we bid adieu to the old year.

We have all received, for God only *gives*. Moreover, He gives to all, both to the evil and to the good. And He gives only good gifts. But He cannot give equally much to all because there are many who will accept only His *temporal* gifts.

We have all received *grace*, it is written further.

Yes, we have all received grace. For all of God's gifts, both temporal and spiritual, are grace. None of us has merited a single one of the gifts we have received.

It is good to bring the old year to a close when we can see that it has brought us grace from God. And it is good to begin the new year when we can see that we are to receive grace. We are not to receive according to our merits. Each day is to bring us new grace and new lovingkindness from God.

"Hitherto hath the Lord helped us!"

Then saith he unto his disciples, The harvest indeed is plenteous, but the laborers are few. Pray ye therefore the Lord of the harvest, that he send forth laborers into his harvest.

—MATTHEW 9:37-38

Now, as then, Jesus stands and looks at the great harvest. Never in the long history of missions have the doors been as open as they are now.

Now, as then, Jesus bids His friends make haste. And the friends of Jesus hear Him as He speaks. Never in the history of missions have we had such a great, many-sided and well-planned missionary program as now.

Now, as then, Jesus says: "Pray. Pray without ceasing."

And the friends of Jesus give heed to what He says. A great united plea ascends to the Lord of missions.

You, too, prayed. And the Lord heard your prayer. He answered you: "In response to your prayer I will send forth a missionary. I will send *you.*"

What did you answer? That you were willing? Or that you wanted *others* sent out to the mission fields? You are not alone in praying thus. That is why there are always too few missionaries.

Or did you receive this answer from the Lord: "I will in answer to your prayer send out a missionary. And since you yourself are too old to go, I will send your grown-up child"?

What did you answer? That you would give up your child? Or that you in your prayer had thought of *other people's* children? Just think, there are believing parents who hinder their children from going out to foreign mission fields.

Or did the Lord answer you thus: "I have heard your prayer about sending forth laborers. But you yourself are too old, and you have no children to send in your place. Send me therefore your money for the time being"?

Most of us are not intended for the mission fields. But Jesus expects that all His friends should *live for missions.*

When that day dawns upon the friends of Jesus, missions will lack neither workers nor funds.

For of his fulness we all received, and grace for grace.
—JOHN 1:16

W<small>E</small> said the other day that in the year just passed we had received grace.

Today we hear that we have received even more, namely, *grace upon grace*.

This is a strange expression. But even stranger are the experiences we have when we receive grace upon grace.

Now and then we all have some experiences that we *cannot understand*.

Did you not have some such experience also last year? I think light will be thrown upon these experiences by these words: *grace upon grace*.

What was it you experienced? Was it spiritual distress? You entered upon a period of spiritual darkness that was so appalling that you thought you would have to give up entirely. Yes, you even thought for a while that you had fallen away from God.

But it was grace upon grace!

It was grace to deal with the self-complacency which had begun to enter by stealth into your Christian life. It was grace to accept grace. It was grace to take your place beneath the cross.

Or was there some unpleasant situation in which you found yourself? It caused you a great deal of distress, and you asked yourself why you had to have such an experience.

But look back upon it now and see if it was not grace upon grace that you experienced! God gave you grace to overcome your self-wilfulness. Grace to become a humble, patient, lowly child of God. And at the same time you received grace to pray.

We *all* received, our text says.

Even you who did not accept. God proffered you His gifts nevertheless.

Of His fulness we have all received. Also you. Think of this grace: you are living today and not lying in the torment of perdition. And what grace that God calls you even today!

Lord, let it alone this year also, till I shall dig about it, and dung it: and if it bear fruit thenceforth, well; but if not, thou shalt cut it down.

—LUKE 13:8-9

HERE Jesus tells us a little of what takes place behind the scenes with the coming of the new year.

In heaven there is conversation about unfruitful trees. There are many such in the orchard of God. They have been standing there since Baptism. For a while all went well. They grew and bore fruit. They lived childhood's innocent life with God.

But then they stopped growing, and there was no fruit. The child had grown old enough to break with God.

Heaven has constantly, each year, tended and cared for the tree. And has expected each year that there would be fruit.

Thus the unconverted are permitted to live in their sins year after year. Under the protection of God, while God calls them.

But then a crisis occurs. That is what this Word of Jesus tells us about today. It becomes a question of cutting down the unfruitful tree. For it stands in the way. The unconverted husband hinders his wife, the unconverted father and mother hinder their children; the unconverted brother hinders his brothers, his sisters, and his companions from being converted.

Then Jesus intercedes for this unconverted person. He still has this way of seeking to save him.

I shudder at the thought that among those who hear these words today are some who at the beginning of this new year really should be cut down. But He has prayed that He might make one more attempt to save you.

Will Jesus succeed in this attempt?

That is for *you* to decide. This year. Now notice carefully the words of Jesus. You are living this year only because He made intercession that you might live. But He added these words, fraught with sadness and seriousness: "If it does not then bear fruit, cut it down!"

12

But godliness with contentment is great gain.

—1 TIMOTHY 6:6

THE stress of economic difficulty darkens many a home. I am not now thinking of the fact that many people are poor and live in very modest circumstances. That in itself need not darken their homes. But I am thinking of this, that many parents do not have the courage to tell their children that they are poor. The children have therefore no idea of how meagre the resources of the home are. And when they see how well their companions are dressed and what expensive amusements they indulge in, they demand the same.

Then many parents do one of two things:

Either they refuse to give their children these things, but do not dare to give the real reasons for doing so—at which the children become irritated and feel that father and mother are doing them an injustice.

Or they give their children these things, though they know that they cannot afford to do so. They would not have their children inferior to their companions.

The family debt mounts, and the unhappiness of both the parents and the home increases. This is, no doubt, the situation in more homes than we suspect.

How entirely different it would be if parents would acquaint their children with their economic situation! Let your children know how much you have to live on for the month or for the year. Figure out for them how much there will be for clothes and how much for amusements.

Yes, some say, but is it not too early to darken the lives of our children with economic worries at their age?

Try, and you will see! You will not deprive them of any of their joys. On the contrary, you will be giving them something very valuable: *a sense of responsibility.* And with it a new *joy,* the joy of helping father and mother make both ends meet.

You will also be giving them something more valuable than amusements and fine clothes. You will be helping them toward contentment. And those who receive a legacy of this kind begin life with a wealth of riches.

13

Love . . . rejoiceth not in unrighteousness, but
rejoiceth with the truth; beareth all things, believeth
all things, hopeth all things, endureth all things.

—1 CORINTHIANS 13:4-7

THE kindly attitude of love has a peculiar capacity for *understanding* others.

This is because the new life of love can never be created
within us until we have learned to understand ourselves and
our own inner defilement of soul.

Those who realize their own sinfulness always become charitable in their judgment of the failings of others. There is
something within them which desires to know whether the
intentions of those who have erred were as bad as they seemed.

In every secular court there is a defense attorney whose duty
it is to indicate all the mitigating circumstances. Is there in
us any such defender who is permitted to express herself and
point out the circumstances which might excuse our neighbor?
So many have dismissed this defender. As a result slander often
flourishes even among Christians.

True love does not only excuse a failing neighbor; it *reproves*
him also. This is undoubtedly love's hardest duty. But it cannot
do otherwise; for it rejoices with the truth.

We Christians of today need to give heed to this aspect of
love. There is very little sincere and kindly neighborly discipline among us.

And there are reasons for this.

There is often a great deal of rivalry among the various
Christian groups. People do not dare to exercise discipline
within their own groups because they are afraid of losing some
of their members. And it is impossible, for obvious reasons,
for members of one group to discipline members of other groups.
Oftentimes they are the subjects of slanderous remarks. Here
is a danger greater than most people suspect.

> Repent ye therefore, and turn again, that your sins
> may be blotted out, that so there may come seasons
> of refreshing from the presence of the Lord.
>
> —ACTS 3:19

Y ES, it is indeed glorious when seasons of refreshing come to us from the presence of the Lord! What a wonderful gift is not a spiritual awakening!

The more I am permitted to have a part in one, the more my heart rejoices in it.

It comes like a gentle breeze and goes from soul to soul, from home to home, from neighborhood to neighborhood.

Sinners without peace, those who have been living on the periphery of the kingdom of God, pass through the narrow gate of repentance and choose to suffer ill treatment with the people of God.

Thoughtless and reckless sinners, who before scarcely ever took the trouble to hear the Word of God, can no longer stay at home, but come to hear.

Hearts, homes, neighborhoods are transformed.

The children of God are as in a dream and can scarcely believe their own eyes. They become childlike and simple in their faith, full of confidence and willingness to sacrifice. They have holy fellowship with one another, a fellowship in which love of one another is pure and strong.

A spiritual awakening with seasons of refreshing has come *from the Lord.*

Let us note this. These things cannot be brought about by *force,* nor can they be *produced artificially.*

But we can *hinder* spiritual awakenings from coming. In many ways, but chiefly by neglecting to pray for their coming.

There are in our cities and communities a few who have taken up this work of intercession. The Lord Himself will make glad your heart and reward you, brother and sister.

Dear friends of God, let us all pray for seasons of refreshing! And let us continue to pray until spiritual awakenings come from the presence of the Lord.

For whosoever would save his life shall lose it: and whosoever shall lose his life for my sake shall find it.

—MATTHEW 16:25

L IFE and death are, beyond all comparison, the greatest mysteries of existence.

I do not know which is the more enigmatic. Here in our passage for today, we have the two mysteries woven together: through death to life.

When Jesus spoke of the mystery of the new life, a teacher of Israel, the noble and pious Nicodemus, was startled.

But when Jesus said that the new birth was possible only through death, through the bloody death of the Messiah, then even His foremost disciple became startled and prayed God to deliver Him from such vain thoughts.

But when Jesus said that all who would share His life must die with Him, His followers forsook Him, one after the other. Only the twelve remained. And not even they understood what He meant.

He who would lose his life shall find it.

This has been Christianity's stumbling-block in all countries and in all ages. Unto the Jews a stumbling-block and unto the Greeks foolishness says the apostle Paul.

To think that a pious Israelite must die and be born again in order to enter the kingdom of God into which he had been circumcised and toward which all his faithfulness in observing the law had been directed! To think that a pious youth must die and receive new life in order to become a Christian!

Here many who would be Christians become startled also. They think that we drive young people away from Christ by such statements.

However, the words of Jesus stand, now as they have always stood: Those who would save their life shall lose it. However, He also says: "Blessed are those who shall find no occasion of stumbling in me!"

It is God who puts to death. But I can withdraw myself. I have the power to save my own life, Jesus says. Buy by so doing I hurl myself into eternal death.

16

And they were bringing unto him little children, that
he should touch them.

—MARK 10:13

Of all the many gifts which God has showered upon us,
none is greater or more precious than our children. He entrusts
us with immortal little human beings, sprung from our own
lives and attached to us by the finest and most tender bonds.
They fill us, too, with a joy which is higher and purer than
any other joy we know.

They set in motion the noblest instincts which we possess.
We love them, and we hope, and strive, and suffer, and sacrifice
for them.

But the greatest of all is that we can bring them to Jesus,
that He may touch them. And to think that we can do this
as soon as they are born!

He receives them in Holy Baptism, takes them to His heart
and fills them with the Holy Spirit, makes them His children
and writes their names in the book of life.

The little one grows and begins to understand what we say.
New joys fill our lives from day to day. Now we can speak with
the little one about Jesus, can see how the little child-heart
spreads like a flower to the sun. Have you ever experienced
greater riches of joy than those which were yours when your
little child folded its tiny hands and prayed its evening prayer,
just as though Jesus were standing at its bedside?

But life is not as simple as all that. Not our life in relation
to our little ones either. As they grow older, it becomes more
difficult to speak with them about Jesus. Their rebelliousness
and disobedience become conscious and wilful. You try to help
your child by disciplining and admonishing it. But you discover
that to rear children is a difficult art, one that you have not
mastered. At times you become fearful as well as weary.

My friend, it is not harmful either to you or to me to feel
impotence in this respect. Do not be afraid. Bring your little
ones to Jesus over and over again. He will bless both you and
them. And: "Let any of you who lack wisdom ask of God!"

17

Forget not to show love unto strangers: for thereby some have entertained angels unawares.

—HEBREWS 13:2

HOSPITALITY is the home with arms open toward a wider fellowship. By hospitality the home circle is extended to include those who in various ways belong to the home by physical or spiritual kinship.

The greater the love of the home, the larger will be that circle which it desires to include.

Considered from this standpoint the Christian home becomes a factor in Christian work. Indeed, it becomes a very important factor. There are aspects of Christian fellowship which can be developed only in the Christian home. That is why hospitality is evaluated so highly in the church of God.

The home needs the communion of saints in its midst. And the communion of saints needs to be brought into the intimate circle of the home.

There are many hospitable homes among the Christian people of our country. They welcome Christian workers and often entertain them for days at a time. God be praised for this hospitality! They open their homes regularly to Christian friends for larger or smaller gatherings in which Christian fellowship is renewed, rekindled, and enriched.

Such homes are divine power stations through which the omnipotence of God goes out to the whole city of community; yes, by means of simple prayer, all the way out to the mission fields.

Hospitality is hindered in many a Christian home because its members have fashioned themselves according to the world and made Christian sociability so expensive and burdensome that they are able only on exceedingly rare occasions to invite their friends.

It is exceedingly important that we overcome our pride and invite our friends to our homes even though the food that is served and all the other arrangements are simple and frugal.

The home will be the gainer. The communion of saints likewise.

Without faith it is impossible to be well-pleasing unto him.

—HEBREWS 11:6

HERE we are told that faith is the decisive thing in the Christian's relationship to God.

It seems to me therefore that "believers" is an excellent name for Christians. Not only because it expresses the contrast between them and those who doubt or deny. But because to believe is life's highest art.

No one else can practice it but Christians.

To *live* in the Biblical sense is to live for God, to live one's life as before Him.

But this is the very thing that is difficult about living. For I dare not show myself to God the way I am.

All heathens know that, no matter how deeply fallen they may be, religiously and morally. Therefore they never approach their deities without offerings.

But Jesus Christ has told us how it is possible for us to stand before God. By faith in Him, my Substitute, I can with confidence appear before Him. That which was between God and me has once for all been removed. On the Chief Corner Stone He has established a place of refuge for all death-sentenced sinners.

I depend upon this. And move thither.

To live in *faith* is an entirely new way of existing. I am, in the first place, in agreement with God that I in myself am lost and therefore have no right to meet God, deserving only to be cast away from Him into eternal perdition.

But I am also in agreement with God with respect to His grace. I have accepted His pardon. And when God Himself is my Substitute, then I have enough, enough for all eternity!

And now I do not expect to be anything else before God but that which I am in my Substitute.

19

> If any man willeth to do his will, he shall know of the teaching, whether it is of God, or whether I speak from myself.
>
> —JOHN 7:17

MOST doubters are of the opinion that they are too intellectual to be able to believe. But this is a misunderstanding. Faith is not based upon *thinking* but upon *experience*. Your doubts therefore arise from the fact that you lack certain experiences. Jesus sums up these experiences in the unique expression: "Do the will of God." He says, as we have seen, that those who will do the will of God shall receive assurance. Now read your New Testament. Yes, but I doubt the Bible, you say. I know that. But you may well skip over the things that you doubt. You will still find enough passages which you yourself will acknowledge to be the *will of God*, eternal and unchangeable. Consider, for example, the Golden Rule.

Do this, Jesus says. Do not only debate, and talk, and wish, and hope, and wait, but do His will, He says. Some entirely new experiences will come to you. In the first place, you will find that you do *not* do unto others as you would that they should do unto you. In the second place, you will find that you *cannot* do it. In the third place, that you do not have the *will* to do it. It is too strenuous and disadvantageous. And therewith you will be convinced that Jesus is right when He says that you are *evil*. You know what is right and true, but you do not care to do it.

Then begin to pray to God.

Yes, but I do not believe in prayer, you say. I know that, but that does not matter. To pray is to speak candidly and confidentially with God. Begin by telling Him that you are a doubter. Then speak with Him about your other daily experiences as you seek to do the will of God.

In a very short time you will become remarkably well acquainted with Him concerning whom you have been in doubt. And when you have experienced that Jesus' teaching about your sinfulness is of God, then it will not be long before the way to the cross of Christ will become both familiar and dear to you.

For I reckon that the sufferings of this present time
are not worthy to be compared with the glory which
shall be revealed in us.

—ROMANS 8:18

HOPE sheds its light upon us also in our suffering. We glorify
God by suffering.

There are always some of His friends in the fires of suffering,
in order that the world may know what the power of Christ
can accomplish. If He some day takes you away from the work
in which you are busily engaged and lays you aside upon a bed,
then look up! Hope is still shedding its bright rays upon you.

Let your remaining powers be employed in suffering quietly
and patiently. When you reach your heavenly home, you shall
see that your heavenly Father has not forgotten the things that
you have suffered.

The star of hope shall shine also in the dark valley of death.
When the earthly house of our tabernacle is dissolved, it will
be because our heavenly home is ready for occupancy. Hope
shines brightly over the death-bed of even young Christians
who die before they have been permitted to use their strength
to glorify the Lord. They shall be permitted to serve the Lord
then! They are simply transplanted to that part of the garden
of God where it is easiest to work and where it is most beautiful.
There we shall serve the Lord day and night.

There we shall also be permitted to serve Him without doing
any harm. While we live here on earth, we often do damage
to the vineyard of the Lord. Oftentimes we trample down some
of the little plants with our hard, uncouth feet. If we could
see all the damage that we have done to our Lord's vineyard
by our spirit, our nature, our thoughts, words, and deeds, and
by the omission of the good things that we have neglected to
do, it would be an exceedingly sorry sight.

Then we would no doubt look forward with greater joy
toward the day when we shall be permitted to serve the Lord
without doing damage to anything in the beautiful garden
of God.

> Whosoever drinketh of the water that I shall give him shall never thirst.
>
> —JOHN 4:14

JESUS knew the human heart. He saw its thirst.

It is sin that has left this burning thirst. Sin has closed our hearts to God. And it is the resulting vacuum within our souls which is constantly crying out for something, knowing not for what it cries.

It turns therefore first to one thing and then to another in the hope of quenching its thirst. People begin with diversion, then turn to pleasure, then to amusements; many even resort to the muddied waters of vice—their souls are so thirsty!

But none of these things help; they afford only momentary relief. Like an anesthetic. But when one comes out of an anesthetic, one is as thirsty as ever, and nauseated besides.

Thereupon many turn to other sources of relief.

They throw themselves into their work. They become useful, even outstanding, prominent in their fields. And their souls feel relieved for a while. "This was something really worth living for," they say.

Whereupon they proceed to fill their souls with love of honor, gain, or the desire for power.

But the more they drink, the more thirsty they become. And while people praise them for their abilities, in dire distress their tortured souls cry out for help.

It is God for whom you are thirsting, my friend.

You yourself have understood this. At least now and then. This has been the worst feature of it, too, as far as you have been concerned. For you would not go to God. You knew that if you did go you would have to live a different life.

As long as you yourself insist upon drinking *poison*, Jesus cannot help you.

But if you this day are willing, Jesus will quench your thirsting soul.

> And the third day there was a marriage in Cana of
> Galilee; and the mother of Jesus was there: and Jesus
> also was bidden, and his disciples.
>
> —JOHN 2:1-2

THE two who were being married that day in Cana were
certainly not rich people. We are told that the family had not
been able to provide sufficient refreshments for their guests.
But what a happy bridal couple they were! And what a never-
to-be-forgotten wedding it was!

What difference did it make that they were poor when they
had Jesus with them at their wedding? What a mighty miracle
He did for them! Still, I do not think that the miracle was all
that interested them. I can imagine that both of them became
attached to Jesus in such a way that day that He was permitted
to go in and out of their home as long as they lived. Nor is
Jesus present in any home without *every day*, in some manner,
changing water into wine.

What a joy that we two who established this home in which
we are now gathered also had Jesus with us at our wedding! What a joy that He has gone in and out among us all
these years!

And then all the miracles that He has performed! As a rule
He has changed water into wine for us also.

We have not been rich either; we have been people of
humble means, like the two in Cana. Our economic circumstances have oftentimes been difficult. It has appeared that the
little we have had could not suffice for all of us. Then He has
quietly added His divine plus, and there has been enough.

Then illness has come, and such other attendant difficulties
as usually accompany sickness. It has seemed to us as though
our entire home and its happiness would be ruined. But then
He has performed a miracle. The bitter waters of tribulation
have been turned into sweet wine. He has not *removed* our
difficulties, but He has transformed them in such a way that
we can see His purpose and His grace.

Today let us thank Him who has given us this home and
made it into such a good place for all of us.

If thou knewest the gift of God, and who it is that saith to thee, Give me to drink; thou wouldest have asked of him, and he would have given thee living water.

—JOHN 4:10

THIS woman thought least of all of meeting Jesus that day. She was simply going her accustomed way to the well after water. Even less did she think of repenting and turning away from her sinful life.

It was Jesus who came to this well of hers, and that at exactly the time when she came to draw water. And it was Jesus who began the conversation.

And He did it, by the way, very simply and tactfully. He began by asking her for a drink of water; and before she knew it she was in the midst of a conversation about the deepest things in life. Whereupon Jesus turned the conversation and began to speak with her about her sins.

Not only did she wonder at Jesus' remarkable knowledge of her most intimate life in sin; but she was stricken in her conscience, confessed her sin, and was saved by Jesus there at the well.

Thus it is that Jesus saves all of us.

He begins, not we. He seeks us. And begins to speak with us. We do not seek a conversation with Him. No doubt we seek rather to avoid it, just as the woman did. But He holds us fast.

He speaks with us during the quiet hours of the night. He speaks with us in church and at other meeting places, even though we may not have gone there to meet Him. It is our salvation that Jesus speaks to us without asking our permission to do so.

But there are some who will not listen to Jesus. They squirm away, as the woman did at first. Is there any one in our little circle here today who has done this? If so, Jesus has a few words to speak to you before we close our brief devotional hour: "If thou knewest the gift of God, and who it is that saith to thee, Give me to drink; thou wouldest have asked him, and he would have given thee living water."

And behold, a woman that had a spirit of infirmity eighteen years; and she was bowed together, and could in no wise lift herself up.

—LUKE 13:11

MANY of the friends of Jesus are in the same situation as this woman.

Once they were elevated to a Christian life which was free, happy, full of praise to God and of testimony concerning Him. Then the spirit of infirmity came. And now they are bowed down to the earth, inwardly bound and condemned, without abiding joy, without a song of praise in their hearts, without a will and without the courage to be a witness unto the Savior.

My dear friend, tell Jesus at once about your condition. Tell Him the whole truth. Show Him where you lost your first love.

Do you now know where that was?

Be honest! Your conscience has no doubt spoken to you about the matter. Remember, you will never become free, you will never be erect again until the inner cause of your ailment has been made known to Jesus.

He must go to the root of the matter if He is to be able to help you.

If you will surrender to Him your secret lust, you will experience His power anew.

You will again be able to walk uprightly. He will again turn your face toward heaven, giving you a heart full of song and praise and the inner desire and power to be a witness unto Him and to serve Him in your daily life.

There is enough of the spirit of infirmity in us to bow us toward the earth each day and to take the joy, power, and courage out of our hearts.

But Jesus is stronger. If He is permitted to lay His hands upon us, He will say to us as He did to the woman: "Thou art loosed from thine infirmity." Then we will receive grace to live as free, exulting, and victorious Christians. Unto the praise of Him whose name we bear.

> And he went down with them, and came to Nazareth;
> and he was subject unto them.
>
> —LUKE 2:51

THE little that we are told about the childhood of Jesus is especially valuable. It tells us that Jesus has entered into our whole life as human beings, has sanctified it and shown us its eternal worth.

No doubt we have some children in our little circle today also. Our Word for today is directed to you especially. It tells us that Jesus, too, was a child. Jesus played, as you do. He ran errands for His father and mother. He went to school. We know that He learned both to read and to write, though the schools of that day were not as good as they are now.

But the most important thing that our Word for today tells us is that Jesus was obedient to His parents. Elsewhere we are told that Jesus *learned* obedience. Dear children! That tells us that it is not easy to be obedient. Of course, you yourselves know a little about this, too. It is often very difficult. You have many unhappy recollections of disobedience. Indeed, you remember certain times when you were so disobedient that you are ashamed even to think about it. Especially when you remember how you grieved your father and mother.

Think how good it is that Jesus died for our sins, for all our sins. When we confess them to Him, He crosses them out of His books up there. And then He casts them behind His back into the sea of *forgetfulness*. A wonderful sea!

Jesus will help you to be obedient to your father and mother and teachers, and to be kind to your brothers and sisters and playmates. He has tried it Himself; He knows therefore how difficult it is for you. And for that reason He will help you day by day.

Come unto me, all ye that labor and are heavy laden,
and I will give you rest.

—MATTHEW 11:28

Not all sinners are weary of sin.

There are many who as yet have no need of a physician.
They sin freely, or at least in relative peace.

I feel sorry for you, my friend. You are in great danger.

To sin is terrible, but to sin unperturbed is even more terrible.

Jesus speaks here to those who are heavy laden. They sin
no longer with joy or in peace. They have been awakened from
their restless sleep. They labor, Jesus says. Yes, they labor more
than others know.

They strive against their sins. Against all their sins; in word,
in deed, in thought, in imagination, in desire.

They labor in prayer. How they struggle and labor in their
prayer chamber! They labor in connection with their reading
of the Word of God. It is almost harder for them to read the
Bible than to pray.

Their lot is indeed a heavy one, heavier than they will
acknowledge to others. In fact, heavier often than they will
admit to themselves.

Jesus says here that He gives *rest*.

But you have become so heavy-hearted and restless since
you began to take refuge in Jesus. You have never been more
restless than you are now.

Indeed! Everything has gone just as it should.

That is the way it must go. Jesus must first make the restful
restless. He has to show you who you are. You have not known
it before. Remember that Jesus preached the entire Sermon on
the Mount before He spoke these words in Matthew 11.

But now you shall receive *rest*. To be saved you need only
be a sinner who would conceal no sin but would cast herself
down at the foot of the cross with it all, placing her whole lost
cause in the hands of Jesus.

Even so let your light shine before men; that they may see your good works, and glorify your Father who is in heaven.

—MATTHEW 5:16

J ESUS has put a precious promise into this admonition. If our life with God becomes real everyday Christianity, then we shall by that very life *win* others for God.

There are many people in our country—and their number is steadily increasing—who, practically speaking, never hear the Word of God and therefore have no other contact with Christianity than that which they gain through the believing Christian men and women employed in their homes, their factories, their stores, or their offices.

You can imagine how they use their eyes. And they have a right to do so.

Young believing friends! You who, in some capacity or other, are employed by unconverted people, God give you eyes to see the work you have to do for God each day. It is your daily life and your daily work that are to win for God these people who are so far away from Him.

It is good that we have pastors. But what of these people who are never present in the pastor's audience?

It is good that we have evangelists. But what of these people who never put their foot inside a place where an evangelist is speaking? Here you have, young friends, work that no pastor or evangelist can do.

Moreover, you certainly cannot do it by *words*. You will soon be instructed to that effect. Then it is good to have God's promise about winning them *without words* by your chaste behavior coupled with fear, by the incorruptible apparel of a meek and quiet spirit which, in the sight of God, is of great price. Do your daily work conscientiously and in love, because the Lord needs it as tangible proof that Christianity *transforms* people, not only on Sundays, but also in their daily life and work.

> Lift up your eyes, and look on the fields, that they
> are white already unto harvest.
>
> —JOHN 4:35

I HAVE meat to eat that ye know not," Jesus said. To do the will of God. To find and to help the lost sheep. Now He had just found one again.

And when the Samaritan woman, leaving her waterpot, fled into the city to tell about the greatest moment in her life, Jesus saw the white fields which stood waiting to be harvested. He saw the great world of humanity, mature in sin and shame like this woman, but, like her, ready to follow the One who could prove to them that He was a real Savior.

This was undoubtedly the most beautiful sight that Jesus ever witnessed here on earth. He must tell it to His disciples at once. He showed them the word of sowing that had been done through the centuries by a faithful God. And He showed them the work to which the white fields now summoned them: "Pray the Lord of the harvest that he send forth laborers into his harvest!"

As there are seasons in the natural realm, so, too, in the kingdom of God. The springing forth of buds and the falling of leaves, the heat of summer and the cold of winter.

In our day we are experiencing a mighty harvest season. Never have the fields been so white, the doors so open, the hearts so receptive.

But we reap where others have sown.

For fourteen years Norwegian missionaries sowed in Zulu-land before the first heathen was won for Christ. Under such circumstances the sowing is done with sighing and in tears. Now we reap what these have sown. By quiet, humble effort our spiritual ancestors brought, in the world of human beings, this ripeness which we now behold with our eyes.

Have you given heed to what Jesus has told you about the fields white unto harvest?

Pray Him that it may become your meat to do the will of God. Then the Lord of the harvest will get what He needs in this busy harvest season: the intercessory prayers, the workers, and the necessary funds.

29

> Love . . . is not provoked, taketh not account of
> evil; . . . believeth all things, hopeth all things,
> endureth all things.
>
> —1 CORINTHIANS 13:4-7

LOVE is not provoked.

Even when it is met with ingratitude and misunderstanding, yes, even with blasphemy and hatred. For it does not seek its own. Only the welfare of others.

On this score we sin a great deal.

How many are there not in our Christian groups who become hurt and offended. And cherish ill-will on this account.

Let us pray God for the love which does not become bitter, does not become envious, does not take account of evil, and does not rejoice in the failings of others.

While souls die unsaved, the friends of Jesus should have other things to do than to become provoked and peeved at one another. Hell laughs, and heaven weeps over such behavior.

Love believes all things.

This is unquestionably the most beautiful aspect of love. It loves, and hopes, and is disappointed. And hopes again. It prays, and weeps, and goes out to seek the lost one anew.

O thou holy love! That thou art from God is at least clear! Such is God. Therefore He found us and won us.

Love believes all things and is never put to shame, says Søren Kierkegaard. On the Great Morning of Surprises we shall see that this also was true.

Hear this, you who love, hope and pray for your prodigal child. You weep so often when you see how hard and cold the heart of your dear one has become.

We are all loved into heaven.

Some must also be *wept* in.

This labor of love it is that the Lord asks of you.

> And straightway on the sabbath day he entered into
> the synagogue and taught.
>
> —MARK 1:21

It was the morning of a holy day, and Jesus had gone to the synagogue with His disciples. He had just spoken.

Suddenly the silence was broken. One who was insane began to cry out. Will-less and unable to restrain himself he gave expression to the evil spirit which works upon all of us. But Jesus stood quietly and bade the evil spirit come out of him. And the man was made whole at once.

When the service was over, they went to the home of Peter. James and John were also invited. Here Peter's wife's mother lay ill. When Jesus heard this, He went over to her bed and took her by the hand. In the same moment the fever left her. And she arose and waited on them.

This went like wild-fire through the city. Before sundown the whole community was gathered outside the door, having brought to Jesus all those that were sick. And He went quietly from one to the other and helped them all, both physically and spiritually.

That night much time elapsed before they could get to rest. It had been a hard day. But even before the others were awake the next morning, Jesus was up. He sought out a lonely place in which to pray.

This was only one day in the life of Jesus.

Think of those who followed Him thus day after day for two years!

What do you think they would have answered if we could have asked them: "What was the most glorious thing you experienced in company with Jesus?"

It is difficult to know what they would have answered. But when I read their accounts in the Gospels, I get an intimation that they would perhaps have answered about as follows: "The most glorious thing we experienced in fellowship with Jesus was that we felt so secure. He cared for us in all things, for us and for all who sought Him."

Dear friends of God! Is not this our experience also?

31

> Pray without ceasing; in everything give thanks: for this is the will of God in Christ Jesus concerning you.
>
> —1 THESSALONIANS 5:17-18

SINCE ancient times prayer has been spoken of as the breath of the soul. This suggests something about prayer that many of us are quick to forget.

Through breathing our bodies are *constantly* being renewed. We *eat* three or four times a day. But we *breathe* all day, and at night, too.

Here we come in contact with an important aspect of prayer. We cannot breathe in the early morning in such a way that it will be sufficient until noon. Likewise, we cannot pray in the morning so as to suffice until noon.

Therefore the apostle says: "Pray without ceasing!"

Indeed, *this* is the secret of the Christian life!

The peace-filled, victorious, joyful Christian life is possible only to those who have learned the deepest secret of daily renewal: unceasingly to turn to God and receive new, fresh power from the realm of the eternal.

Slothful Christians will object that it is impossible to get time for this if one is employed at painstaking work. But, like all pretexts, this is a foolish objection. To breathe does not take any time from our work. And whether we do mental or physical work, it takes no time from our labors to turn our hearts upward for a moment for a brief session with God. Our work will not suffer from this. No one does better work than those who unceasingly pray down upon themselves the blessing of God.

Nothing is so blessed to the soul as this quiet, unceasing fellowship with the Lord. The sense of the Lord's presence which then fills our souls exceeds all else that we can experience of peace and joy, inner satisfaction and security. Adversity and sorrow also lose their poignancy when we share them thus with the Lord.

Be filled with the Spirit.

—EPHESIANS 5:18

Many believers pray for the fulness of the Spirit. But they do not seem to think that their prayers are answered.

For they experience something that they had never expected. They pray for the fulness of the Spirit, but receive instead a fulness of sinfulness. And they do not see that *this* is a fulfillment of their prayer. According to the words of Jesus the Spirit shall convict of sin. Note that this is the *first* thing that Jesus mentions.

The first and surest sign of the fulness of the Spirit is therefore *a sensitive conscience* which feels even the least sin as a bitter pain and desires to become aware of all unfaithfulness and disobedience to the Spirit of God.

This constantly annoying feeling of uncleanness and unholiness is what distinguishes true Christians from those who are worldly and lukewarm and makes them hunger for grace; it impels them at all times to take refuge beneath the cross, there to be continuously cleansed anew in the blood of Christ.

Old sinful habits have by no means lost their power in the lives of those who are filled with the Spirit. On the contrary, because of a conscience made tender, they now feel keenly even the least temptation to sin.

But they have learned a secret way of disarming the tempter. They cast themselves directly into the arms of Jesus and ask Him to remove the power from the temptations which assail them. This Jesus does in many different ways. Most often, however, by giving us a glimpse of the suffering Savior through the Spirit. Thus sin becomes loathsome and distasteful.

It is not to be understood that Spirit-filled souls no longer suffer defeat or fall. They do, alas! But now they know the reason: they are striving in their own strength. And therefore they pray again that they might behold the Lamb of God.

33

And the apostles said unto the Lord, Increase our faith.

—LUKE 17:5

W E see from the Gospels that there was nothing for which Jesus so often upbraided His disciples as for their lack of faith. Undoubtedly there is nothing by which we grieve Jesus oftener than by our lack of faith.

It must wound Him when His children stand at His cross with their daily failings and do not find rest and peace. He hangs there bleeding, in deepest humiliation, and cries out with all the power which the cross possesses: "My grace is sufficient for thee. You need nothing more. God Himself has taken your place. Though your sins be as scarlet, in my blood they shall be white as snow."

And we have nothing else to do but to bow our heads a little more humbly and say: "Lord, increase our faith!"

Or we struggle against the sinful habits of each day, go down to defeat, doubt, or find ourselves regularly in the quagmire of despair. This must without question grieve Him who has said: "Him that cometh to me I will in no wise cast out. I will forgive you without counting how often I have already forgiven you."

You, dear children of God, can you understand why we do not go to Him at once, that He may raise us up and give us fresh courage to begin anew? Oh, yes, we understand why well enough; it is because we can't *believe.*

Or we go about our daily work. And oftentimes it seems such a burden. Partly because it is hard to live and work in a world of sin. Partly because we cannot master our work as we would and should.

What is wrong? We have forgotten to exercise faith. We struggle on from day to day in our own *human* strength. And the *unlimited powers of heaven* are at our disposal. But we do not make use of them.

Those who in childlike faith call down upon their daily life and work the powers of heaven, they can live in the midst of the difficulties and trials of each day with a quiet and cheerful disposition, constantly amazed at what the power of Christ can do.

> While ye have the light, believe on the light, that
> ye may become sons of light.
>
> —JOHN 12:36

IN *the light!* Here we have the Christian life condensed into three words.

Not only to dare to be in the light, but to *will* it, to feel it as a joy to live in the presence of the all-seeing God. That is the great transformation which faith brings about in a human being.

Are you happy to be in that light now?

There was a time when you were. But now? Do you *seek* the light? Do you desire to have your inner life illuminated by the light which pierces even to the dividing of soul and spirit, which discerns the thoughts and intents of the heart? Or have you begun to be afraid of what God thinks about your various plans, thoughts, words, and deeds?

Then seek help! And that at once. Pray that He may work in you a fully surrendered will, causing you to come forth into the light again and to begin to *love the light.*

If Calvary's cross has grown dim to me, the reason is very likely that I have not desired to have my whole heart illuminated. But as soon as I permit the light of God to reveal to me the sin which I have sought to hide, then light falls upon the cross again, and my soul finds rest in His mercy.

The light of God is the best antidote for sin. The oftener we bring our sinful habits out into the full light of God, into the presence of the Lord, the more quickly and the more certainly we will overcome them.

The light is also the best means of furthering our sanctification. The fruits of the Spirit grow in the light. A courageous, joyous, strong and ethical Christian life is developed in those Christians who live their lives each day in the presence of the Lord. They receive courage also to act in accordance with their convictions among other people.

Lord, give us the joy of being children of the light in this world which lieth in the darkness!

Even if ye shall say unto this mountain, Be thou taken up and cast into the sea, it shall be done. And all things, whatsoever ye shall ask in prayer, believing, ye shall receive.

—MATTHEW 21:21-22

Here Jesus draws aside for a moment the veil which separates the visible from the invisible world. He desires to give us a little glimpse into the eternal realm which surrounds us on every hand.

No one can live in the realm of the eternal without *faith.* As soon as faith is present, the realm of the eternal becomes accessible to us. Through the gate known as the *forgiveness of sins* we step into a new environment.

Here we experience remarkable things: new sorrows and new joys, new struggles and new tribulations, new victories and new defeats, new friends and new enemies.

In this realm of the invisible we make new discoveries continually. Not always such great discoveries, but many of them. Both humiliating and exalting.

Now and then we make discoveries which almost take our breath away, namely, when we see what great powers are present in this realm of the invisible. This is especially true when these powers are put at our disposal, when God performs a mighty miracle simply because we ask Him to do so.

In our text today Jesus surprises us by informing us that these heavenly powers are at our free disposal, that we cannot only cause a fig tree to wither, but even cause a mountain to be taken up and cast into the sea, simply by praying that it be done.

And then He unveils faith's secret unto us in these words: *"Whatsoever ye shall ask in prayer, believing, ye shall receive."*

Who among us can hear these words without being ashamed of our lack of faith? However, we can, as the disciples did, make supplication to Him in our poverty, to Him who is the originator and perfecter of faith: "Lord, increase our faith!"

36

For the word of God is living, and active, and sharper than any two-edged sword.

—HEBREWS 4:12

IT is exceedingly hard for many of the children of God to read the Bible every day. They do not cease reading, but their reading becomes such a dull and heavy task that they are afraid it is of no avail. They do not seem to derive any benefit from it.

My friend, do not permit yourself to become thus confused, provided you in simple faith and prayer make use of your Bible each day.

It may be that you misunderstand Bible reading somewhat. It is easy for you to think that it is you who are to strive in one way or another to draw spiritual nourishment from that which you read.

No, it is the Holy Spirit who is to make the Word you read food for your soul.

Remember that He must perform a *miracle* every time you read the Bible if it is to become bread unto your soul. And He is glad to perform this miracle.

When you pick up your Bible, therefore, fold your hands in a childlike way and ask Him to perform the miracle, whether you read much or little.

And when you have done this, read with confidence and assurance that what you read enters into your soul as spiritual food.

Do not sit there with nervous questionings as to whether it becomes food, and food enough, unto your soul. The people who think too much about the food they eat and their digestion weaken their digestive powers and develop a nervous stomach.

No, gather your thoughts about the Word as you read. And thank God for the eternal truths which have coursed through your soul. The Spirit will see to it that the Word does its work within you, even though you do not always know *what* it works.

For every one that doeth evil hateth the light, and
cometh not to the light.

—JOHN 3:20

W HEN Adam and Eve had sinned, they hid themselves from
the face of the Lord among the trees of the garden.

It may seem childish that they really tried to hide from God.

And yet it is this very thing that all of the children of Adam
and Eve do, following the example of their parents.

The unconverted really do nothing else all their lives but
seek to hide from God.

God calls: "Where art thou?"

And they hear when God calls. But they hide themselves.
And there are many trees in the garden. There are diversions
and amusements, lust and vice, and all sorts of feverish activity,
both mental and physical.

If you could look into the hearts of all these various types
of people, you would see how many of them are seeking a
hiding place in these things, away from the living God and
their own disquieted conscience.

But no one can escape God. The time is coming when we
must all come out into the light.

Come out of your hiding place, therefore, O mortal! Come
voluntarily, before you are forced to come out into the divine
light which will become your eternal anguish.

Jesus calls you again today.

Not to frighten you. But to tell you that He loves you and
misses you. The sinful life which you are trying to conceal and
which holds you back every time you try to cast yourself upon
the mercy of God, for this He has in His boundless grace and
mercy made full atonement on your behalf.

Your debt is all paid, and it will be wiped out the very
moment that you come forth into the light and confess all.

Why do you tarry?

> And in the fourth watch in the night he came unto
> them, walking upon the sea.
>
> —MATTHEW 14:25

J ESUS had crossed over to a desert place. However, even a desert place becomes very active when Jesus is there. People assembled from all directions. He spoke to them and healed their sick. Toward evening He fed five thousand men, besides women and children.

Enthusiasm was running high. This was a Messiah according to their own hearts. The disciples were no doubt confident of victory. It appeared now that He would at last begin His mission in earnest, that all might see who He was.

Whereupon Jesus suddenly withdrew Himself. He vanished. Not even His disciples were permitted to accompany Him. They had to go in the boat alone.

Jesus had gone up into a mountain to pray. He tarried there a long while.

The disciples had worked hard throughout the night. The weather was fearful. And now in the dawning light they saw some one come walking on the water. It must be a ghost! We are told that they cried out. But then they heard the voice of Jesus: "Be of good cheer; it is I; be not afraid!"

All their fears vanished. Peter became so bold that he also was going to walk upon the water. And all went well with him for some distance. Then a huge wave came directly toward him. He became frightened and began to sink. But he cried to Jesus, who caught him by the hand and lifted him up again. After Jesus had reproved Peter, they both joined the others in the boat. Then the storm ceased. And they all fell down at the feet of Jesus and worshipped Him.

Yes, what does it matter that we must face both storm and darkness, if Jesus comes walking on the waves and says: "It is I!" How blessed it is when the tribulations of the world and our own unbelief humiliate us in such a way that we, like the disciples, fall down at the feet of Jesus and worship Him!

But straightway Jesus spake unto them, saying, Be of good cheer; is it I; be not afraid.

—MATTHEW 14:27

Wᴇ noted yesterday a few of the things which the disciples experienced that remarkable night on the Sea of Galilee. But we are all out on a greater sea, upon the great and stormy ocean of life. Oftentimes the voyage may be pleasant. But at other times it may be exceedingly dangerous, with darkness, head winds, and a storm-tossed sea. It seems as though our little boat must be swallowed up.

How suddenly can not a storm blow up! Did you not know that fine old sailor? How through decades of hard work he had accumulated a little capital, sufficient so that he and his wife might have a carefree old age? And how he lost every cent as a result of a bank failure?

Or look at that young lady over there with the heavy, black veil over her tear-stained face. She is coming from the grave of a young man. There all her beautiful dreams lie buried.

Or watch him sitting there in the wheel-chair. A victim of influenza, lame and crippled for life.

A mother prays for her sick child and is permitted to keep it—but mentally unbalanced for life! Or look at that mother, too, who was also permitted to keep her child. And the boy is neither mentally diseased nor physically disabled. But how he tortures the life out of his mother by his ungodly life!

A friend of mine buried his wife and three children within the space of twenty-three months. "It seemed to me that they might as well have buried me also," he said. Although he had a house and home, woods and fields, money enough.

But it is even worse when Jesus vanishes from our sight. We cannot understand His ways. We doubt and we murmur.

Then Jesus calls to us out of the darkness and in the storms: "It is I! It is I who have brought it all to pass. It is I who come to you in the form of suffering." And as soon as we recognize His voice we are saved.

With desire I have desired to eat this passover with
you before I suffer.

—LUKE 22:15

IT is sad to think of all the believers who for one reason or
another neglect the Communion Table.

There are some people who as a matter of principle do not
partake of the Sacrament of the Altar. But aside from them
there are not many Christians among us who openly despise
our Lord's precious Supper.

But they neglect it, nevertheless. They seldom go to Communion. Many, because they do not deem themselves worthy.
Alas, what damage has not the thought of the "unworthy"
communicant wrought in the church of Christ!

When we go to the Table of the Lord, only that is required
which is always required when we draw near unto God: that
we turn to Him in our helplessness with sincere hearts, that
He may save us from our sins. This Table is a Table of *grace*.

Here He waits to impart, freely and without merit on our
part, the riches of His grace to all poor, empty, and anxious
souls. Here He waits to warm the cold-hearted, to quench the
thirsty, to satisfy the hungry, to strengthen the weak hands
and to confirm the feeble knees.

Whenever you come to His Table, He enters quickly and
unnoticed into your soul and body and does His hidden but
blessed work.

Go to the Lord's Table therefore as often as it is set where
you are present. Never sit as an on-looker when other children
of God go to Communion. Go and commune and praise the
Lord who gave you also this opportunity.

> "Thus may we all Thy word obey,
> For we, O God, are Thine;
> And go rejoicing on our way,
> Renewed with strength divine."

> Walk by the Spirit, and ye shall not fulfill the lust
> of the flesh.
>
> —GALATIANS 5:16

JESUS is come that we might have life and have it *abundantly*.
He saves us, not that we should enter into heaven after a life
of *defeat*, but that we should be *victorious*, unto the praise of
His glory who purchased victory for us at such a great price.

This is the way the disciples understood Jesus. It is true that
they tell us that never in this life will we be able to rid ourselves
of our old flesh, whose mind is enmity against God. But the
apostle tells us in our Word for today that if we walk by the
Spirit we shall not fulfill the lusts of the flesh.

There is a great deal of weak and emaciated Christianity
among us, the kind that simply marks time and never makes
any progress in sanctification. Old character failings are carried
along from year to year. Our good deeds, which Jesus expects
should shine before others, are conspicuous only by their absence.

There is some striving against sin. But, as is the way of the
world, only against those sins which are "dangerous" because
they deprive people of their good name and reputation.

My friend, do you know that you are asleep and on the way
to spiritual death? Have you not read of the thorns and thistles
which gradually choke the good seed? What is your will? Shall
the thorns or the good seed be permitted to live in your heart?

But what shall I do? you ask. I have neither the power nor
the will that I should have. I am like a lame person unable to
rise.

My friend, you have forgotten that there is something known
as the *grace* of God.

Cast yourself down before the God of grace. Confess your
lukewarm will-lessness, and He will forgive you for this terrible
sin for the sake of the precious blood of Jesus.

Moreover He will give you that grace which is known as
the Spirit of God. And when you begin to walk by the Spirit,
you will not have to fulfill the lusts of the flesh.

For ye died, and your life is hid with Christ in God.

—COLOSSIANS 3:3

ALL life has a hidden side.

It is that to which we refer when we speak of the mystery of life. Divine life, too, has its hidden side, its sacred mystery.

Life itself is always hidden; it is never bared to the eye of another person. That which we see in other believers is only the fruit of the hidden life; we see it in their ways, their words, their acts, and in the things they suffer.

It is beautifully true that sincere Christians live far richer lives with God in their hearts than any other person knows anything about.

Do not forget that when you see children of God. Oftentimes they may appear dry and withered. They may often seem very cold and reserved, something which is harmful both to themselves and their surroundings. But, when you see this, do not forget that within this less fortunate outer shell these children of God oftentimes have a rich and fine kernel of tender and intimate fellowship with God.

In this inner, hidden world we struggle, we suffer, and we go down to defeat more frequently and disastrously than others may ever suspect. Here the open wounds of our conscience smart. Here we blush because of our lukewarm and worldly heart. Here we tremble in unspeakable agony. Here we often find ourselves held fast in the slough of despond.

But here we also experience unspeakable *joy.*

Here we have not only our great Tabor-seasons; here we experience also the lesser, yet blessed, gleams of grace that come to us in our daily lives. A little word of consolation, and our souls are permeated through and through with a hidden power. Or an answer to prayer, perhaps in connection with some little thing, but doubly precious to us because it shows us how God cares for us even in the little things of life. Or little victories over ourselves. Oftentimes so small that we dare not mention them to others. But to us they are precious and indispensable, binding our hearts to God in grateful joy.

> So is the kingdom of God, as if a man should cast
> seed upon the earth; and should sleep and rise night
> and day, and the seed should spring up and grow, he
> knoweth not how.
>
> —MARK 4:26-27

WHEN the Lord hides His face, our hearts feel empty as far as the workings of God's grace are concerned. Selfishness and worldliness fill every fiber of our souls; our regret at having sinned seems cold; faith seems to have disappeared from our hearts. We are slothful in prayer and the Word of God seems dry and distasteful to us. We feel as though all has been lost and that the Spirit of God has forsaken us.

Then our blessed Savior comes and tells us that what we are experiencing is not dangerous, but the contrary. He says that we are experiencing a sound and good growth.

That which we are experiencing is the shedding of the leaves. But when the leaves begin to fall, the fruit is ripe. Yes, but where can the Lord find any fruit in me? you say. Well, the Lord sees better than you. He can see both growth and fruit where you can see nothing.

In the first place, there is the *sense of sinfulness.*

You have no doubt had a sense of sinfulness ever since you became a Christian. But never as now. The same thing has happened to you as happened to Peter when he fell on his face before Jesus. Did Peter see his growth at the time? No, but Jesus did, and said: "Fear not; for henceforth thou shalt catch human beings!"

So also with you. As a result of your humiliation you have become not only more *precious* but also more *useful* to the Lord. Go forth now with no confidence in yourself but with much confidence in Him, and you shall see! God gives grace to the humble, grace also to win souls for God. No one is more irresistible than a person who is humble.

In the next place, you grow more *patient.*

When those who are like condemned criminals have been pardoned at the cross of Christ, they never demand a place of prominence among others. Rather, they feel put to shame by the confidence and love shown them by others.

> I dwell in the high and holy place, with him also
> that is of a contrite and humble spirit.
>   —ISAIAH 57:15

No one can become a Christian without first having been made contrite of heart.

It is *God* who makes us contrite. But it is a difficult task, even for Him. In fact, it must be considered a mighty miracle when God makes the hard-hearted contrite.

How God does it, I cannot say. This is the miraculous element in spiritual awakenings, their mysterious content.

Although we cannot explain the miraculous element in spiritual awakenings, we can nevertheless experience it. And we all experience it in the same way. We experience what the prophet puts in these words: "The Lord is at hand." The Lord lays hold of sinners and quickly brings them into His holy presence.

So divine is God that sinners need only to experience God, to be in the presence of God, to have their hearts of stone crushed.

In the nearness of God we become *isolated.* Though we sit in a large audience, we cannot hide ourselves in the multitude. God is speaking to *me.* In God's presence we become *small.*

We feel how far we are away from God. Here at last is One speaking to me with whom debate is out of the question and with whom there can be no compromise. All I can do is to listen and to give heed.

In God's presence we feel *sinful.*

We have come into the super-light of heaven, which, to begin with, seems absolutely unendurable. We see our past sins, the lesser as well as the greater, in a painfully clear light. We see our *inner* sins, a bottomless and boundless sea of impurity and iniquity.

Behold, our hearts are now contrite. We have no excuses to offer; we make no objections to what God has to say to us.

Moreover, now we sinners *surrender* to God. Unconditionally, making no demands of any kind.

And whatsoever ye do, in word or in deed, do all in the name of the Lord Jesus, giving thanks to God the Father through him.

—COLOSSIANS 3:17

Here is a word to those of us who desire earnestly to practice *everyday Christianity.*

Most of us have a tendency to live a double life, a *worldly* and a *religious.* To make matters worse, we cannot really reconcile the two either; they come in conflict with each other. Those who see us on Sunday at church services have difficulty in recognizing us on Monday morning when they meet us at work or at our place of business.

Ours is not everyday Christianity until we do *everything* in the name of Jesus, until we desire to do nothing but that which can stand the test of the light of God, until we will do nothing except the Lord go with us.

What a joy to know that He will go with us in *all* that we do, even in the smallest and most routine tasks. If we do these things in the consciousness that it is His will that we should perform these little, ordinary tasks, our whole life will become a worship of God. Then every day will be a holy day, and there will be something of a halo about our most commonplace duties.

"Giving thanks to God the Father through him," says the apostle further.

Here is another side of everyday Christianity. In all that we do we should thank God. That is, our whole life should be one continuous giving of thanks to God.

We should thank Him in our *hearts.* "Singing with grace in your hearts unto God," says the apostle in the preceding verse. We should also thank Him in *words,* that both God and people may hear it. And we should thank Him in *deed.* Everything that we do should be like a quiet clasping of the hand of God in gratitude, as though we were saying: "Wilt Thou accept that which I now do? It is a little thankoffering in appreciation of Christ who has saved me and in so doing has brought me all this unmerited joy!"

46

Said I not unto thee, that, if thou believedst, thou
shouldest see the glory of God?

IT was an unspeakably trying time for Martha and Mary. First
this, that Lazarus became ill. However, they knew that
Jesus had healed many sick folk. Therefore they sent to Him
in all confidence only this brief message: "He whom thou lovest
is sick."

But, strangely enough, Jesus did not come. Lazarus grew
steadily worse. Of course they could not think of Lazarus as
dying. Jesus was not far away, and He could heal him with
only a word. However, Lazarus died.

And the sisters felt hurt. Why did Jesus treat them thus in
their hour of distress? Had He not helped *all* who asked Him,
even the heathen? It was all so incomprehensible to them.
Both of them met Jesus with the upbraiding words: "Lord, if
thou hadst been here, my brother had not died."

But Jesus had *reasons* for doing what He did. In the first
place, He wanted to help Martha. It was difficult for her to
find time to listen when Jesus spoke. But now busy Martha
had time. Now the Lord did not have to *ask* her to sit still and
listen. She came of her own accord as soon as she heard that
Jesus was in the vicinity.

Since that time there has been many a busy Martha who
would not be still before the Lord until sickness and tribulation came to her with this message: "The Master is here and
calleth thee."

He had also another reason. The sisters had asked Him to
heal Lazarus. Jesus would do *more* than they asked of Him. He
would *raise Lazarus from the dead.*

Your trials and your sorrows are incomprehensible to you.
And you have prayed the Lord unceasingly that He would
remove them from you. But He has had something greater in
mind. He will reveal to you His *glory.* If you will only believe.

47

Let both grow together until the harvest.
                                    —MATTHEW 13:30

THERE is a peculiar note of sadness in this parable of the wheat and the tares.

With a few powerful strokes Jesus portrays the disappointments to which His great work of saving souls is subject here in this world, and will be to the very end of time. The field is the world. He who sows the good seed is the Son of Man. The good seed means the children of the kingdom. The tares are the children of the evil one. The enemy who sowed them is the devil. The harvest is the end of the world.

A mighty drama!

When the servants saw the havoc that had been wrought, they wanted to proceed at once to gather up the tares. But the householder said: "No, for then you will damage the wheat also. Let them grow together until the harvest."

Indeed! The disciples of Jesus no doubt often felt a desire to do away with the worst enemies of the kingdom. When the Samaritans closed their city and their homes to Jesus, James and John asked for permission to bid fire come down from heaven to consume these sinful people. But Jesus said: "Ye know not what manner of spirit ye are. For the Son of man came not to destroy people but to save them."

It is possible for us also to observe how the enemies of God blaspheme the Lord and lead people astray in large numbers, until we too wish that God would strike them down.

But then He dismisses us with these words: "I am not come to destroy people. Let them stand until the harvest. And pray for them, that they might be saved. They, too, have an immortal soul for which I have died."

However, He does take note of our inner distress and comforts us by saying: There is a time coming when I shall put all my enemies under my feet, when every knee shall bow, when none shall tempt another person any more.

Lord, we await Thy day!

> But when the fruit is ripe, straightway he putteth
> forth the sickle, because the harvest is come.
>
> —MARK 4:29

ONE of the secrets of all growth is that its ultimate objective is the ripening of the fruit. Indeed, from life's first beginnings, *everything* is directed toward the maturing of the fruit.

This solves many of life's riddles. We all have experiences that we cannot begin to understand. And none of our experiences are so difficult as those whose meaning we are not able to fathom.

But if we can see them in the light of the ripening and the harvest, then we can grasp their meaning. He who has all power in heaven and on earth, He who guides our little lives, He directs all things toward the ripening of the fruit.

He who is the Lord of the harvest *waits* for the harvest, when He can gather the fruit of the field into His barns. With this in mind He sends the things that are necessary to further the ripening. Do not become frightened, therefore, if the weather shifts and you have rain, sunshine, wind, warmth, lightning and thunder. It all hastens the ripening. You are no doubt acquainted with what is known as "corn weather." The air is laden with electricity; it is sultry and hot, making breathing difficult by night as well as by day. The corn, however, thrives in such weather.

Prosperity and adversity, sorrow and joy, illness and health, honor and dishonor, good repute and evil, temptation and despair, all serve as a means of ripening the inner person. Remember, we do not live in order to have an easy time of it, but to be made mature for eternity. This teaches us to rejoice in anticipation of the harvest.

The Lord is waiting: "When the fruit is ripe, *straightway* he putteth forth the sickle."

> "O joy that seekest me through pain,
> I cannot close my heart to Thee;
> I trace the rainbow through the rain,
> And feel the promise is not vain
> That morn shall tearless be."

And unto one he gave five talents, to another two, to another one; to each according to his several ability. —MATTHEW 25:15

IT was the man with the single talent who buried it. Small gifts tempt most readily to unfaithfulness. Our text today would therefore speak in particular to those of us who have received only one talent.

They who have received two or five talents in the kingdom are the exceptions. We who have received only one talent constitute the great majority of the servants of Jesus.

As a matter of fact, I am inclined to think that we shall be surprised on the great day to find that the most important work in the Lord's kingdom has been done by those who have received only one talent.

No disciple of Jesus has received less than one talent.

The day that all who have received the one talent make use of their lesser gifts in humility and faithfulness—that day will be a great one in the history of the kingdom of God.

The reason that the great kingdom-work of Jesus has made such slow progress is that most of His servants, those with the one talent, have been inclined to look too much to those with the many talents, and have gone away and hidden their talent, either in a well-managed farm, a successful business, or a good trade.

Yes, you say, but I cannot preach, not even give a testimony. It is difficult for me to pray aloud at a prayer meeting or to speak with even my nearest of kin about God.

But listen now: The kingdom of God does not consist of words, but of power.

If you cannot speak by word of mouth, by admonitions, then speak by your *silence* and by your *love*. Desist from sin and from the ways of the world, even though you cannot say a word. Let your light shine in such a way that darkness becomes black indeed.

And you will see that not many words or admonitions are needed.

Be faithful in little things!

Well done, good and faithful servant: thou hast been faithful over a few things, I will set thee over many things; enter thou into the joy of thy Lord.

—MATTHEW 25:21

THOU has been faithful over a few things," it says. That is just our difficulty. But you who think that you have received only a few things and that therefore it is difficult for you to say or do anything in the kingdom of God, have you not noticed how much of Jesus' precious time was occupied with doing favors for people, showing them *love?*

You have received the *love* of Jesus. It is a part of your talent. Make use of it and you will perform a service in the kingdom of God the value of which you can scarcely realize. What a service do you not render God and neighbor by being *friendly*, friendly in your home and friendly at your work, friendly when you are busy and friendly when you are at leisure. Be faithful in the little things!

You have received *joy* in the Holy Spirit, which is also a part of your one talent. Do you make others happy with it? Is it a part of your daily work to make glad the hearts of others, if not more than one single person?

You have received *peace*, also a part of your talent. Do you make peace wherever you go? Do you forgive those who offend you? Do you cover up the sins of others rather than broadcast them by slander?

Be faithful in little things!

You have received the *humble and patient mind of Christ*, again a part of your talent. You know that nothing draws others as effectively as a humble mind. Be a savor of a sweet smell unto Christ wherever you go.

You who think that you must have great speaking ability or much wealth in order to accomplish anything in the kingdom of God, do you not know that the greatest favor you can do a person can be done for that person in secret on your knees? And the day that all those with the one talent take up the holy work of intercession according to God's promise, on that day hell will tremble with fright and heaven resound with jubilation.

And when she had said this, she went away, and called Mary her sister secretly, saying, The Teacher is here, and calleth thee.

—JOHN 11:28

MARY sat and wept for her dead brother. Perhaps she wept fully as much because Jesus had not come, even though they had sent a message to Him that Lazarus was sick. Then Martha came and whispered to her: "The Master is here, and would speak with you." And when she heard this, she arose quickly and went to Him.

Yes, we can understand this.

Suppose that you, in an hour of distress, received a message that Jesus had come and desired to speak with you.

It is my privilege today to come with this very message to you: The Master is here and is calling for you.

He is here. Here with you. Now, at this very moment. He has received the message that you sent Him. Moreover, He has all power. He can help you, no matter what your trouble may be.

If these words could move you to do what Mary did! Rise up quickly and go to Jesus! And tell Him, as Mary did, your greatest sorrow, the thing that causes you most distress.

Jesus is waiting for you.

Perhaps He has waited a long time already. Why have you not confided in Him? Why do you keep your difficulties to yourself?

Speak to Him about the worldliness that is choking your hidden life with God. About the spiritual coldness which is freezing your heart to the very bottom. About the sinful habits against which you are putting up such a feeble struggle.

The Master is here and calleth thee!

52

Behold what manner of love the Father hath bestowed upon us, that we should be called children of God!

—1 JOHN 3:1

Yᴇꜱ, do the thing that the Word tells you to do today. Behold the great truth that God calls you His child.

Often your eyes grow moist at the thought of the defeated life you are living. And your heart shrinks within you when you feel the sin that is in your members and how impotent you are both to love God and to die from self.

But behold now the love of God: it is for Jesus' sake that you are a child of God. He accepts you as His child, not because you are holy, and pure, and spiritual, but because your heart condemns you and, knowing not what else to do, you hide yourself in the wounds and stripes of Jesus.

God's kindly Father-smile shines upon you in your daily life every time He looks at you, you who would know nothing else unto salvation save Jesus Christ and Him crucified.

Thank Him both for His love and for His smile!

And honor Him and make glad His heart by being cheerful and happy as you live your daily life.

Yours shall be the privilege, for Jesus' sake, of being a child of God in whom He will glorify His Father-love, in time and in eternity, by forgiving you your sins, by wooing you away from worldliness, by hearing you when you pray, by sending you difficulties, both inner and outward, in order that both you and the world may know what the power of Christ can accomplish.

And at last you shall honor Him by passing unharmed through the hands of your last great enemy into the eternal glory of God.

Not until then shall we know in all its fulness what it means to be a child of God.

For we are God's fellow-workers: ye are God's husbandry, God's building.

—1 CORINTHIANS 3:9

GOD'S fellow workers! To be a fellow worker is to enjoy even greater confidence than to be a child. Much time must elapse before our children become our fellow workers. We should thank God for the confidence and honor He shows us by making us His co-workers.

The first and most important of these cooperative tasks to which God calls us concerns our own goal. "Work out your own salvation," are His first working orders. "For it is God who worketh in you both to will and to work," we are told in the same breath. Here we note *cooperation!*

Next after our own *heart* He assigns us our *home* as a field of labor. We are all to begin at Jerusalem and from thence proceed to Samaria and Galilee and to the uttermost parts of the earth.

God works in your *home.* And He has appointed you His co-worker. In the first place, then, be careful that you do not by your thoughtlessness and egotism destroy some of the things which the Lord has done already in your home. In the next place, live your daily life in such a way that it will be easier for your dear ones to be good Christians, and in such a way that those who have not yet become Christians may be drawn to God by your life rather than that Christianity should be made distasteful to them because of you.

From your home proceed to your *neighbors,* friends, ac-quaintances, and associates. God is working on all of them. And He has chosen you to be His fellow worker here also. In the first place, be kind, be willing to work, and be ready to make sacrifices. By so doing you will be doing the work of God. And in the next place, pray for eyes that see the needs of people wherever you are, both the spiritual and the physical needs of others.

And make use of your time! "Night cometh when no one can work."

But now abideth faith, hope, love, these three; and
the greatest of these is love.

—1 CORINTHIANS 13:13

I<small>F</small> faith is the power to live right, love is the right way
to live.

Yes, love is, without a doubt, life itself.

God is love, as we know. And God is life. Of us it is said
that we are dead until this life of love has been planted
within us.

Love is as much a mystery as life itself is. No one can tell
what love is.

But it can be *experienced.* God be praised!

And this is the joy of life. Yes, eternal bliss itself consists
in this that in heaven we shall love perfectly, that is, live
exclusively in love.

Love expresses itself first, and in its most essential aspect,
in our *wills.* To love is a definite way of willing. As soon as
the will begins to function in this manner, then the feeling of
happiness is also awakened within us.

Love would live for others. Perfect love knows no other joy
than to make others happy.

Only one has lived His life in this way, namely, Jesus.

All the rest of us think instinctively that the meaning of
life is to live for oneself, for one's own happiness, enjoyment,
advantage, and comfort. Only after we have experienced the
miracle, the miracle of the new birth, does it dawn on us that
the meaning of life is to live for others.

And a whole long life lived after this miracle takes place
cannot remove the vestiges of our old selfish life. Not until we
reach heaven will our old life be completely obliterated. There
we too shall say: "My meat is to do the will of God."

And he shall wipe away every tear from their eyes;
and death shall be no more; neither shall there be
mourning, nor crying, nor pain, any more: the first
things are passed away.

—REVELATION 21:4

OH, what a day, when all that has defiled *this* world shall
be no more!

Sin shall be no more.

Think of it: we shall never grieve our Savior any more!

The one and only real sorrow of the Christian is his sorrow
because of sin. That sorrow never leaves him.

The Christian is permitted to believe in a full forgiveness
for all sin for Jesus' sake. Yes, all that she has thought, and
said, and done is blotted out and cast into the sea of oblivion.

Nevertheless, sorrow because of sin never subsides. On the
contrary, it becomes ever deeper and more painful. The closer
we live to the cross of Christ, the harder it becomes for us to
endure the fact that we grieve our precious Savior.

"One radiant morn when sinless souls assemble,
Where each desire is born in purity,
No more the thought of wrong shall make us tremble,
But, ransomed, I shall live forever free."

On that morn sin will be no more in the lives of others
either. Never another wicked person to meet. It is difficult to
conceive of such a thing. But imagine if everybody about us
were like Jesus. Yes, you say, if all people were like Jesus, heaven
itself would be in our own very midst. And I agree.

All whom we shall meet on that day will be good, both
people and angels. For that reason temptation will be no more.
Danger will be no more. Forever within the portals which open
in but never out.

All the consequences of sin will be forever gone. No tears,
no weariness, no sickness, no sorrow, no longing.

In brief: no disharmony any more. Our whole being, soul
and body, will finally be in its rightful element—in God!

The sower went forth to sow his seed: and as he sowed, some fell by the wayside; and it was trodden under foot, and the birds of the heaven devoured it.

—LUKE 8:5

AN exceedingly timely word to us who sit here together. For this parable tells us what takes place in people's hearts as they hear the Word of God. There are four kinds of hearers, Jesus says.

He mentions in the first instance those who hear to no avail whatsoever. They are *robbed.* They hear the Word, it is true; but before it has an opportunity to do its work in their hearts it is plucked from them.

There are, as we know, always some who sit thinking of other things and do not remember a word of what is being said. You know, do you not, that God has no other means of saving you than by His Word?

It is not strange, therefore, that Jesus adds this word of warning: "He that hath ears to hear, let him hear!"

Then there are some who hear, and who hear well, too; but they sit and criticize. Some are critical of the preacher and are annoyed at all his mistakes and shortcomings. Others criticize not only the speaker but also the biblical message which he proclaims.

Dear friend, the danger as far as you are concerned is that you may really have grounds for your criticism. We who preach the Word of God are very deficient. Moreover, there is something about the very Word of God itself which evokes criticism on your part: the word of the cross is a *stumbling-block* to the Jews and *foolishness* to the Greeks (1 Cor. 1:23).

You are no doubt acquainted with the deadly disease of the blood which causes the white blood corpuscles to destroy the red ones. The result is death. It makes no difference how much the afflicted person eats.

As long as you sit in a critical attitude during the preaching of the Word a similar process takes place within your soul. It makes no difference how much you hear.

Oh, pray the Lord to deliver you from this deadly disease of the soul!

And other fell on the rocky ground, where it had not much earth; and straightway it sprang up, because it had no deepness of earth: and when the sun was risen, it was scorched; and because it had no root, it withered away. —MARK 4:5-6

HERE we read about those hearers who enjoy the Word but unto whom the Word does not become salvation.

They are easily touched by the Word. As a rule theirs are emotional and sensitive natures. They are quickly affected by the things which they hear, both in sermon and in song, and especially by the stories that are told.

Before long their eyes grow moist and their tears begin to flow. They also enjoy being moved in this way. They yield to the feelings which surge through their souls. They follow along with others who are laid hold of by the Word of God. With them they pray, sing, and testify.

But no fruits of repentance ever develop. The whole thing stops at the *flower* of repentance. The roots never really do begin to function properly. Under such circumstances it does not matter how many emotional thrills have been derived from meetings. Nothing helps.

There was no *accounting* made with God, no break with sin. Every time the Word struck deeply into their consciences, they edged away carefully and comforted themselves with their own inner sentiments.

Some elderly Christians are in a similar situation.

They were once right with God. But they lost their life in Him. And they did not, as so many backsliders do, go out into a worldly or openly ungodly life. On the contrary, they still desire to be looked upon as children of God. They want to *believe*, at any price, that all is well.

And they base this faith of theirs upon the very fact that they enjoy the Word when they hear it. When their emotional life is set on fire again, they become fervent, pray and testify. Of course they are all burned out even before they get home from the meeting.

"Search me, O God, and see if there be any wicked way in me, and lead me in the way everlasting!"

> And that which fell among thorns, these are they
> that have heard, and as they go on their way they
> are choked with cares and riches and pleasures of this
> life, and bring no fruit to perfection.
>
> —LUKE 8:14

Here there is nothing wrong with the nature of the soil. These people have deep, introspective natures. Their spiritual awakening is oftentimes hard and full of struggles, with deep sorrow because of sin. We rejoice to see how these souls dig deeply and build their house upon a rock.

They continue in this manner for a long time. But then we notice that things begin to come to a halt. These hearers become shy and lose their candid and cheerful natures. The thorns have taken the upper hand.

Jesus speaks of the deceitfulness of riches. Indeed, it is natural that Jesus should mention this first. To become a slave of mammon is a danger that confronts us all, though the temptation is not equally great to all people. The deceitfulness of riches lies in the fact that it so often resembles thrift and therefore adorns itself with this name.

Do *you* desire to know whether you are greedy or thrifty? I think you will find that out most easily when you *give* of your means. Dare you take counsel with the Lord when you are to give, or do you determine that matter by yourself?

The *pleasures of this life,* Jesus mentions further.

Yes, these thorns have choked the Christian life out of many believers. What promising fruit have not worldliness, vanity, and carnal-mindedness destroyed!

As a result a pampered, muddled type of Christianity, without sacrifice, develops, affording the soul neither joy nor sorrow, only that lukewarmness which the Lord spews out of His mouth.

> "Thy light to every heart impart,
> And shed Thy light in every heart;
> The weakness of our mortal state
> With deathless might invigorate."

> And that in the good ground, these are such as in
> an honest and good heart, having heard the word,
> hold it fast, and bring forth fruit with patience.
>
> —LUKE 8:15

HERE at last we hear about those who hear the Word in such a way that they are saved by it.

The first thing we hear is that they received the Word. Yes, that is the beginning. The Word of God comes to a soul; God speaks. That is the beginning, what we know as the *awakening.* They have been awakened who have been spoken to, called, by God.

Those who heed God when He speaks, they are *converted.* To be converted really consists in this: to *accept* the Word of God; to continue to pray each day, "Lord, speak; Thy servant heareth. Tell me all that I must hear about my sins! And speak in such a way that I shall hear Thee!"

The Word begins to *bear fruit* at once in such as receive the Word in this way.

First they begin to *suffer* under the burden of their sins and to be *sorry* for them. Then they begin to *confess* their sins, old and new, great and small, secret and open sins. Next they begin to be *afraid* of themselves.

Everything goes to pieces. They feel that they cannot be as sorry for sin as they should, cannot hate sin, cannot love God, cannot believe. But still they cannot live without Christ. However, souls such as these have reached a state in which grace can be imparted to them. The cross has become their only refuge.

And all this fruit they bear with *patience,* Jesus says.

Yes, indeed, it is not always easy. For they themselves do not always see the fruit.

The seed grows without their knowing it.

> But when he saw the multitudes, he was moved with compassion for them.
>
> —MATTHEW 9:36

SUCH a person is Jesus.

When He saw the multitudes, He saw their needs.

He is like that now also.

He is here today. We cannot see Him, but He sees us. And now also He sees human needs. Yours, too, you who often know not what else to do but weep.

You have become old, worn out, and lonely. A few years ago your nest was full and you were the center of a home that was rich in happy associations. Every one asked for you. But now the nest is empty. You feel so lonely.

Yes, you are old now, and forgetful. But, my dear, do not forget that there is One in heaven who sees you and follows you.

> "His eye is on the sparrow,
> And I know He watches me."

You who are sick, who have lost your health—Jesus is near and suffers with you. He was tried in all things in order that He might be able to help us.

You who grieve so bitterly because you have lost your loved one—you remember, do you not, that Jesus stood at the grave and wept with the sorrowing sisters?

Jesus sees all of us here today.

How do you feel as Jesus looks at you?

Many become fearful when Jesus looks at them. Indeed, there is scarcely anything they fear as much as that. Therefore they flee from Him. And hide.

There are some on whom Jesus has special compassion. Their need is so great. Not so great that He could not easily help them. But when He comes to help they turn away from Him.

But His greatest compassion is on those who are in need and desire help but *dare* not ask for it because of fear of others.

Oh, flee as a bird to the mountain, thou who art weary of sin!

But when he saw the multitudes, he was moved with compassion for them. . . . Then saith he unto his disciples, The harvest indeed is plenteous, but the laborers are few. Pray ye therefore the Lord of the harvest, that he send forth laborers into his harvest.

—MATTHEW 9:36-38

W HEN Jesus saw the multitudes and their needs, He began at once to speak with His friends about that which met His eye.

There is something touching in the fact that Jesus communicated His thoughts and feelings to His lowly and imperfect earthly friends. As soon as Jesus saw something that cried out to His heart of compassion, He turned at once to one of His friends nearby to speak about that which He had seen.

But not all of the friends of Jesus are desirous of having such conversations with the Lord. They prefer very much to be edified, to hear something good about God, as they say. Both in secret and in fellowship with others.

But if Jesus comes and says: "Have you heard that he is ill? Have you heard that she is in poor circumstances now? Have you heard that I have not secured any of my friends to perform a certain task that I have in mind? Have you heard that they are in need of funds for the work that I bade them start?"— When Jesus begins to speak thus to them, many say that they do not have time to listen.

Others, however, rejoice when Jesus begins to speak to them about need and about the things for which He needs them. They are truly happy to have such quiet hours as these. For they feel how easy it is for them to be preoccupied with their own needs and to forget those of others.

When Jesus has spoken to them and they have once more gained a vision of the needs of others as seen by Jesus, they enter gladly into the work of the Lord again.

And as they go about their tasks they hum their favorite stanza:

> "Thus in Thy service, Lord,
> Till eventide
> Closes the day of life,
> May we abide . . ."

62

Sir, we would see Jesus.

—JOHN 12:21

EVER since early times the church of Christ has fasted during the seven weeks before Easter. The fast has consisted in partial abstinence from food and drink and in complete abstinence from all festivities and amusements.

The purpose of this fast has been that Christians might disentangle themselves as much as possible from earthly things of all kinds in order that they might follow Jesus in His passion with singleness of mind.

It is true that in the course of time much that is unspiritual and un-Biblical has become associated with this fast. But, nevertheless, there is a deep evangelical thought underlying it.

May it not be that many of us evangelical Christians need such a period of fasting? Because of our work, whether it be spiritual or temporal, it is easy for us to become occupied with outward things. No doubt many of us need to dedicate some portion of this year to a deepened appreciation of the meaning of our Savior's passion.

It would certainly be of value, not only to our own spiritual life, but also to our home, to the communion of saints, yea, also to the unconverted.

Many of us live a weak Christian life. I am not now thinking only of those who bring dishonor to the name of God by dishonesty and deceitfulness. They are, after all, not so numerous.

No, I am now thinking of the many among us who live a very weak and lean Christian life. Here it is not a question of dishonesty. It is a lack of the *Holy Spirit*. Their inner life has become threadbare and worn.

We who are that way, let us now during these weeks agree to pray for one another. Especially will we pray for this one thing: that we might see Jesus.

My soul longeth, yea, even fainteth for the courts of
Jehovah.

—PSALM 84:2

THE ancient poet has in some way or other been cut off from
access to the temple where God in the Old Covenant met His
people. He sings in this beautiful and impressive psalm about
his longing for the holy place.

He sees before his inner eye the little sparrow building its
nest under the roofing stone and the swallow whose nest is
under the eaves. He almost envies these happy creatures. They
are in the courts of the Lord every day!

There are many such longing souls.

Here sits a child of God, old and gray, trembling and frail.
It is a long time now since you last trod "the beaten paths" up
to the house of God together with the others. You long for
fellowship with the saints, for the hymns and the prayers, for
the preaching of the Word and the sacred moments at the
communion table, for the unspeakable things which so often
filled your soul when you were gathered with the believers.

There lies a child of God upon her bed of pain, year after
year. You struggle not only with your pains, but also with your
loneliness.

You have no doubt become better acquainted with the place
of secret prayer since your illness. But you have also learned
to appreciate the fellowship of believers more now than you
did when you lived in the midst of it.

And you are no doubt often tempted to envy those who
now enjoy Christian fellowship. Yes, now and then you even
entertain bitter thoughts toward those who would visit with
you when you were well but who now cannot spare even ten
minutes to see you.

You are not a poet and cannot give expression to your
longings as the ancient psalmist did. But, together with your
groanings which cannot be uttered, they ascend to Him who
sees every longing in the depths of our souls.

> He who began a good work in you will perfect it until
> the day of Jesus Christ.
>
> —PHILIPPIANS 1:6

THIS is a good passage for all seeking souls.

They seek but they do not find. They knock, but God will not open unto them. They ask but never receive the one thing for which they make supplication night and day, namely, assurance.

They read the Word of God, but find no permanent help, even though now and then an occasional gleam of light finds its way into their souls.

They hear the Word of God. How they do listen! It is as though they drink in every word that is spoken. But things remain as dark to them as ever.

They confer with preachers and other believers. And for a little while they experience release and joy in their souls. But then it becomes as dark as ever—or darker.

They strive against their sins. As a rule go down to defeat. Suffer the mortifying pangs of discouragement.

What can really be the reason for their not gaining the peace and assurance which others have received?

Sometimes they seek in their despair to acquire a forced assurance. They seat themselves, as it were, in a chair before God's door and tell Him that now He *must* give them assurance. Others also encourage them to pursue this course. But God does not answer. And as a result they are only one disappointment richer than they were before.

My seeking friend! Listen now to the Word today: He who began a good work in you, *He* will perfect it. He will continue to do His good work in you. Every day.

Yes, but nothing happens to me, you reply.

Yes it does; more takes place than you can see and understand. Only do not oppose Him. That is to say, in the first place, do not conceal anything from Him. And, in the second place, make use of the means of grace: the Word, the Lord's Supper, prayer, and the communion of saints.

Then He will *perfect* the work. You shall receive *assurance*. When *His* time comes.

O faithless generation, how long shall I be with you?
how long shall I bear with you?

—MARK 9:19

WHAT can it be that presses these bitter words of distress
from the gentle lips of Jesus?

It was not the worldliness of the Sadducees, nor the enmity
of the Pharisees, nor the indifference of the multitudes, nor
the ungodliness of the publicans.

Nay, it was the unbelief of the disciples.

When Jesus came down from the mount of transfiguration,
the disciples were trying to heal a boy possessed with demons.
But they did not succeed. And that notwithstanding the fact
that Jesus had given them authority to drive out demons.

It was then that these woeful words were pressed forth from
the heart of Jesus: "O faithless generation!"

The unbelief of His disciples grieves Jesus more than the
hatred of His enemies, someone has said.

Now, we are disciples of Jesus.

We, too, have received His authorization, one which reads
as follows: "Ask, and ye shall receive!"

Jesus places His own omnipotence in our hands and says:
Make use of prayer, and you will move both heaven and earth.

No doubt there are few words that are harder for Jesus to
speak to His disciples than these: "Ye have not, because ye
ask not."

Unlimited power has been placed at our disposal, enabling
us to feel our own helplessness and the guilt of sin, to rest in
the finished work of Christ, rejoice in God, and loathe all
disobedience; enabling us to deny ourselves and to serve others,
to praise God, to pray and to make intercession, to work and
to rest, to rejoice and to suffer, to live and to die.

All this we have in Christ.

And He says: Ask, and ye shall receive! Thereby is my
Father glorified and your joy made full.

> In nothing be anxious; but in everything by prayer
> and supplication with thanksgiving let your requests
> be made known unto God.
>
> —PHILIPPIANS 4:6

OLD Mary had been at the country store. She had a long distance to go and therefore bought as much as she could carry. Now she had it in a sack on her back and was making her way home with great care.

Along came her neighbor. He had a horse and was driving. "You have a great deal to carry, Mary; get in and I'll give you a ride," said the friendly man.

Mary accepted the invitation, thanked him very much, and climbed into the back seat of the wagon. Her neighbor sat in the seat in front of her and drove. During the course of their conversation the man turned around to see if Mary was sitting comfortably. "But my dear Mary, are you sitting there with the sack on your back?" he inquired. "Oh," she replied, "it is enough that you are giving me a ride; I can at least carry the sack myself."

Well, old Mary was not particularly keen mentally. And we sort of smile at her. But, after all, we do exactly the same as she did.

God comes along one day with His great wagon of salvation. He stops to pick us up, and promises to take us all the way home. But we sit there day after day, the sacks on our backs filled to the brim with anxieties. And we answer as did Mary: "It is enough that Thou hast taken me and all my sins; my anxiety and cares I will carry myself."

The Lord has cared for you up to this time, and He will continue to do so. When anxieties come, mention them to Him. He will say to you: Be not anxious. I have already thought of all these things for you. But you will not receive my help until you need it.

What a release to be permitted to lay aside our cares! The most difficult tasks, the worst disappointments, the most grievous sufferings can all be borne with patience when our souls rest by faith day by day in the gracious providence of God.

> And Jesus stood, and commanded him to be brought
> unto him: and when he was come near, he asked
> him, What wilt thou that I should do unto thee?
>
> —LUKE 18:40-41

I AM particularly fond of this story about the blind man. It gives me a picture of my Savior which does me so much good.

I see Him here in His royal greatness and goodness.

Think of it! He is so great that He can move along the highways of earth and say to those whom He meets: "What wilt thou that I should do unto thee?" And when we poor suppliants have presented our petitions, He can fulfill them, no matter what we may have asked of Him.

And His royal goodness is such that He does not turn aside from anyone who turns unto Him in need.

The falsest hypocrite, the greatest scoundrel, the most licentious adulterer, the most painted street-woman, the basest perjurer, the boldest murderer—as soon as He hears a sincere prayer from any of them, He bows down and asks: "What wilt thou that I should do unto thee?"

Jesus turned first to those places where there was need. His eye sought out the suffering. He proffered Himself first to the suppliants of earth.

Perhaps you have become such a beggar. Life has become so hard that you do not know how to carry its burdens any longer.

I have good tidings for you.

Jesus stands before you and asks: "What wilt thou that I should do unto thee?"

As long as you have not gone to Jesus with your needs, you must not say that you do not know what to do.

Why then do you not go to your mighty Friend?

Can it be that you are afraid of His help?

Perhaps you are afraid that you might receive your *sight?*

And the seventy returned with joy, saying, Lord, even
the Demons are subject unto us in thy name.

—LUKE 10:17

HERE we meet some happy people.

The seventy have just returned from their first missionary
journey. They are now seated around Jesus telling Him all about
it.

They are as happy as children. All of them dwell on the
things which have made the greatest impression upon them.
The mighty acts which they had before with wonder and trembling seen Jesus perform they had now been permitted to perform themselves. And Jesus rejoiced with them.

And when they had related their experiences, He told them
of a vision which He had had during their absence. He had
seen Satan fall.

Now that Jesus had won His first followers, whom He could
send out in the supernatural armor of God against the kingdom
of Satan, "the beginning of the end" had come for Satan.

We hear the rejoicing in the words of Jesus as He tells His
simple-hearted and weak friends that He has equipped them
with an invisible armor against which the weapons of the enemy
are vain. How happy Jesus was in that moment we see most
clearly from the words which follow immediately after our text.
There we read: "I thank thee, O Father, Lord of heaven and
earth!"

Verily, Christianity and joy are inseparable, our passage tells
us today.

Does that hold true of my Christianity, you inquire. How
can I be happy when I see how disobedient and unfaithful and
useless I am?

No; but Jesus knows that, too. Therefore He said: "In this
rejoice not, . . . but rejoice that your names are written in
heaven."

"Oh, if I only knew that!" you say.

Well, you learn that from the Word of God. The names of
those who have washed their robes and made them white in
the blood of the Lamb are written in heaven.

69

> Simon, Simon, behold, Satan asked to have you, that he might sift you as wheat: but I made supplication for thee, that thy faith fail not.
>
> —LUKE 22:31-32

TEMPTATION is the danger-element in life, the temporal, yes, eternal risk inherent in human existence.

Temptation is part and parcel of personal life.

There can be no human life without temptation. Both the first and the Second Adam were sinless, but both had to be subject to temptation. Character cannot be formed except it be tested in the purging fires of temptation.

The hour of temptation is life's fateful hour. It is in such hours that the course of our life is determined.

Between such hours life flows along in comparative quietude and safety. But in the hour of trial something *takes place* within us. Something decisive.

Something decisive with respect to our own life.

The seasons of temptation are brief, but they are fraught with eternal decisions and consequences.

The course of our lives, not only for time, but also for eternity, is determined during these brief moments.

That is why the citizens of the *invisible* world are so active during the hour of temptation. They know how fraught with consequences these moments are; therefore they follow us in our temptations with great unseen activity.

That is what Jesus tells us in our passage today.

Let us note the *strong* words He uses: "Satan *asked* to have you, that he might *sift* you as *wheat.*"

It is the devilishly active, the aggressive, the purposive character of temptation that Jesus would emphasize here. The invisible, eternal aspect of temptation. This imparts a seriousness to it which transcends the fleeting moments of time, yea, even the bounds of time itself.

Nevertheless in this rejoice not, that the spirits are subject unto you; but rejoice that your names are written in heaven.

—LUKE 10:20

HERE we hear about the Christian's joy in doing the work of the Lord.

All Christian work is a fruit of joy, of the joy in God which is the precious possession of souls that are saved.

Jesus rejoiced with the seventy when they returned, filled with the joy of accomplishment. Jesus desires happy co-laborers.

Now, we are His co-workers. And we have reason to be happy. We rejoice when we think of the men and women whom the Lord sent out to the mission fields, to whom He gave authority to bring the message of God to those who sit in darkness and the shadow of death. We rejoice to think of the many here at home who work, sacrifice, pray, and endure hardship in order that the great cause of missions may go forward among our people.

And we rejoice because of all the work that is being done for the salvation of our own beloved people, the self-sacrificing, many-sided, and purposive work which is being done from day to day.

We dare believe also that Jesus rejoices with us.

But it is His desire to give us, as He did His disciples that day, a gentle but earnest admonition: Let not Christian work nor the fruits thereof overshadow the life, the life in God.

For there is a danger that this may take place.

With all of us. Great danger, too. In all Christian work.

Our Word for today also raises two important questions for us to answer:

Are we joyful workers?

Are we happy because we are successful in our work, or do we work because we are happy? If the latter is true, we work with rejoicing whether we succeed in our work or apparently fail. Then we appreciate what Jesus meant when He said: "Freely ye have received; freely give."

Honor thy father and thy mother . . . that it may be well with thee, and thou mayest *live* long on the earth.

—EPHESIANS 6:2-3

MANY have thought, in their younger years, that they could grieve their father and mother and go unpunished; but, as the years have passed by, they have found that life becomes a burden to those who willingly grieve their father's and mother's hearts and thus put them into an early grave.

You dear children who hear these words today, be kind and obedient toward father and mother while you have them with you. Then you will not need to shed tears of *remorse* when they are no more. Let father and mother see that you appreciate the care they have taken of you, as well as their labors and sacrifices on your behalf. They think of you constantly.

Make father and mother happy while they live. It is too late when they are dead.

You dear young people who have ceased to pray the prayers that mother and father taught you, you who despise the God who is the consolation of your parents in life and will be their comfort in death, you who follow pathways that bring tears to your father and mother, do think of what you are doing to their tender hearts.

You know how they love you and pray for you. You know how they weep over you. Every step that you take upon the broad way is like thrusting a dagger into their hearts.

How can you endure to do this? How can you play with those sins which quietly and slowly are torturing the life out of your father and mother?

And you young people who have been won to God by father's and mother's prayers, let me tell you what they look for in you from day to day. They look to see whether your Christianity manifests itself in your home, toward your father and mother, your sisters and brothers, toward the servants. They yearn fervently to see their children practice real *everyday Christianity.*

> But this is your hour, and the power of darkness.
>
> —LUKE 22:53

J ESUS uttered this deep and dark saying in Gethsemane just as His enemies came to arrest Him.

The devil had been after Him before, too. First in the wilderness, and many times after that. But His Father always intervened. In the wilderness Satan had to leave, and angels came and ministered to Jesus. In Gethsemane likewise. The temptation was no doubt an exceedingly terrible one; but His Father had a hand in it: "An angel from heaven came and ministered unto him."

But now Jesus felt that the Father's hand had been withdrawn. He was in the power of people and devils *without protection.* No doubt it was this that filled His heart with such fear and horror.

Now Satan and his human agents were to be permitted to do what they would with the Holy One. They blasphemed Him, they struck Him, they spat in His face, they scourged Him, they pressed a crown of thorns upon His sacred head, and they took His life in the most shameful manner that they knew.

All this was terrible. But Jesus' real sufferings were other than these. They were of an inner and spiritual nature. First and foremost this, that the Father withdrew Himself. Next, that Jesus had to look upon sin. At last the wicked nature of humanity stood revealed in its true light, in its hatred of, and enmity toward, God. And this was the last Jesus saw of humanity before His death.

The gospels indicate that Jesus was remarkably quiet during His last sufferings. There was not so much to *say* now: there was more to *see.* He saw people in their most miserable state of degradation, now that they had been given freedom by the Father to do exactly as *they had a mind to.* He saw the raging multitudes, crying themselves hoarse that he should be crucified. Finally He saw them beneath the cross. They felt safe, now that He had been crucified.

This provides us with material for many a Lenten meditation.

He who began a good work in you will perfect it until the day of Jesus Christ.

—PHILIPPIANS 1:6

HE began. He began in Baptism. With all of us. But, unfortunately, most of us *broke off* His good work. We left the Father's house and went out into the far country.

But though we forsook Him, He did not give us up. He followed us in all our ways. He called to us, no matter where we went. Even in the midst of our most wicked hours of sin we heard His gentle and earnest voice.

In our childhood years, during the time we were preparing for confirmation, in the years of our youth, He *showered His grace* upon us. Finally we paused, and He *convicted us* so thoroughly that there was no doubt in our souls but that we had to be converted.

Then He put us to death, spiritually speaking. He spoke to us about our sinful life and our sinful heart until every avenue of escape was closed and we did not think it was possible that we could be saved.

But then, too, He intervened. The grace of Baptism from which we had shut ourselves off by our deliberate sins now streamed in upon our souls again. We had been baptized into the death of Christ, and now through the Word we saw the Lamb of God again.

And we? What did we do during all this? We added difficulty to difficulty. *Before* our conversion we fled every time we heard His gentle voice. We practiced deceit. We lied to ourselves and to God in order to gain peace in sin. It was He who subdued our obstinate wills. It was He who worked in us both to will and to do. He *gave* us conversion.

And *after* conversion? Well, have we done anything but make things difficult for Him? How have we not grieved and disappointed Him day after day by our wilfulness, our selfishness, our rebelliousness, our indifference, our lack of trust!

But He *continues* the good work which He has *begun.* And puts our feet back on the right pathway again. By His unspeakable faithfulness!

74

And behold, a woman who was in the city, a sinner; and when she knew that he was sitting at meat in the Pharisee's house, she brought an alabaster cruse of ointment, and standing behind at his feet, weeping, she began to wet his feet with her tears.

—LUKE 7:37-38

SIMON was one of the few Pharisees who felt drawn to Jesus. He had become personally acquainted with Him, and now he was giving a banquet in honor of Jesus and the apostles. He had also invited his own friends.

Simon was still in doubt about Jesus. He was no doubt hoping now that he and his skeptical friends would be able to have their doubts cleared up.

Then all at once Simon's whole party was disturbed.

A woman of the street came in. That lookers-on came to such gatherings was not strange in the Orient. Therefore Simon did nothing to have her removed. But she touched Jesus, thereby making Him unclean. It was this that was so annoying to Simon. And he said to himself: Were this man a prophet, He would understand at once what kind of person she is.

But this was not the worst.

Jesus began to defend the woman. And even worse: His defense of her became an attack upon Simon. He said: You gave me no water for my feet, no kiss, no ointment. You gave me politeness, but not love.

The woman, on the other hand, had wet His feet with her tears and wiped them with the hair of her own head. She had kissed and anointed, not His cheek and His head; she had kissed and anointed His feet.

How blessed it is to be numbered among those who have begun to weep over their sins and break their way through all hindrances to the feet of Jesus! What difference does it make, dear friends, if people blaspheme and criticize, as long as Jesus defends us?

Thou gavest me no water for my feet: but she hath wetted my feet with her tears, and wiped them with her hair.

—LUKE 7:44

THE Lord looked upon the heart, both of the woman and of Simon.

He also looks at your heart.

What does He see? Would you like to know what Jesus thinks about your innermost attitude of heart?

We all have some *friends* and *acquaintances.*

We meet some people on the street, greet them, stop and talk. And think it very congenial. Then we say good-bye. And think no more about them until we chance to meet again on some other street corner. Thus it is with our acquaintances.

But our friends—well, it is not certain that we meet them much oftener. But we do call them by telephone and write to them. And think of them every day.

God has many acquaintances. They appreciate the opportunity of visiting with Him on Sunday mornings in church and occasionally also in their homes, when they have time. But as soon as the visit is over they think no more of Him until they meet Him again the next Sunday in church.

With God's *friends* it is entirely different.

It is true that they are never wealthy. As a rule they are in poor and humble circumstances. Oftentimes they can only do what the woman in the house of Simon did: Weep. They weep because of their sins. They as she. But that they are friends of Jesus becomes clearly evident to God and to others. They cannot live without Jesus. And they creep to His feet with all their sins and all their needs.

Moreover, Jesus helped Simon also. He helped him to see himself in his true light. And to see *Jesus.*

This put him where he had to choose. Would he acknowledge that he was only an acquaintance of Jesus, and not His friend?

Cast not away therefore your boldness, which hath great recompense of reward.

—HEBREWS 10:35

MANY of God's children have cast away their boldness. Perhaps you are one of them?

You have only some fond memories of the days when holy boldness made your soul strong, enabling you to bear the burdens of life, the great as well as the small, not only calmly and with self-control, but with serenity of soul.

How did you lose your boldness?

It is written of Jehoshaphat: "His heart was lifted up in the ways of Jehovah." In truth, only in the ways of the Lord can we keep our boldness.

But we stray from the ways of the Lord every day, more or less. How then can any of us keep our boldness?

Well, it is not *sin* that causes us to lose our boldness, but what we do after we have sinned. If we condone and cover up our sins, we lose our boldness. For then we have slipped into a secret covenant with sin. And dare not look God in the face.

There are many believers today whose eyes are cast down because they have compromised with their carnal desires and no longer oppose them in earnest. Others have yielded to vanity, comfort, or fear of others, or have begun to fashion themselves according to the world. Others have lost their boldness through love of mammon.

And when boldness goes out, worry and anxiety enter in.

You dare not look to the cross, because there your eye meets the Savior's sad and searching glance. Then you try to console yourself and hope for the best. Especially do you hope that things will become better later.

You know, do you not, that it is only by a complete reconciliation that you can be saved?

But whoso shall cause one of these little ones that
believe on me to stumble, it is profitable for him that
a great millstone shall be hanged about his neck, and
that he should be sunk in the depth of the sea.
—MATTHEW 18:6

I DOUBT that Jesus at any other time ever spoke such sharp
words as those we read just now.

It is our responsibility toward children that Jesus would
impress upon us. He says that it would be better for a person
to be put to death than to cause a child to stumble.

These words apply to all of us. Not only to fathers and
mothers, but to sisters and brothers, companions and servants.
Oh, that they might pierce us all to the very marrow and make
us all feel our responsibility to the little folk!

Be careful lest you entice little ones into sin! Be careful lest
your life entice little ones into sin!

But our passage today applies especially to fathers and
mothers.

No one can help a child as can its father and mother. But
neither can any one lead it astray as can they.

We think of the many parents who never tell their children
about Jesus, never teach them to fold their little hands in
prayer; who never send them to Sunday school, but instead
perhaps withhold permission even when the children themselves desire to go.

From the time some children are small they hear father and
mother curse and take the name of the Lord in vain. Yes, they
even hear them lie and use foul language.

And if the children are awakened by the grace of God from
the life in sin into which they have been led by their parents,
they often encounter opposition and persecution in their
own home.

You father and mother, you who are living without God,
hear the earnest words which Jesus speaks to you this day!

You are ruining not only your own soul, but also the souls
of the children whom you love, are you not? Remember the
words of Jesus about the millstone. And be saved today!

This kind can come out by nothing, save by prayer
and fasting.

—MARK 9:29

THE disciples had tried to cast out an evil spirit, but had not
succeeded, although Jesus had given them complete authority.

Most of us have not driven out the evil spirit either, although
Jesus has given us the power to do so.

Notice how selfishness not only defiles our daily lives, but
how it follows us also into our Christian work.

Notice the love of honor, the love of display, the striving
for effect which steal the power from our preaching and render
our Christian contacts valueless, yes, oftentimes outright
destructive.

Notice the attention we give to outward things—for which
the excuse is generally offered that we live in such a busy world
or that there are so many Christian enterprises requiring attention. We can converse for hours and be very much interested
in Christian activity of some kind, especially in the more or
less inefficient work that others are doing. At times the conversation may be about the inner life in God, but often only
because the subject *should* be talked about.

We speak often of the spirit of the times: the spirit of unbelief, of skepticism, and of atheism.

However, none of these evil spirits can furnish such opposition to the gospel and can so grievously wound the heart
of Jesus as the spirit of powerlessness in His disciples.

This kind can come out by nothing save by prayer and
fasting.

Why fasting?

Fasting is intended as a means of making prayer real. It is
intended to help us lay hold of the omnipotence of Jesus
in prayer.

Now, more than ever before, the Lord needs disciples who
will withdraw regularly from the tumult of the world and become still before the face of the Lord, strengthening themselves
for their task by prayer and fasting.

> Straightway the father of the child cried out, and
> said, I believe; help thou mine unbelief.
>
> —MARK 9:24

THUS did this believing father cry out in his distress. And
thus cries faith in every time of need.

The Scriptures speak of the mystery of faith. And faith is
indeed a mysterious thing. Among other things, we find this
mystery in connection with faith: Faith can never arise except
where the old self dies. The death of self and the birth of faith
are inseparable.

Since death is always painful, so is also the death of the
old self. There will always be an aspect of faith which is painful.
Sinners cannot come to faith in Christ without at the same
time losing faith in themselves.

Faith, therefore, is to begin with, always a sorrowing, sighing, weeping, doubting faith. For sinners do not see their faith;
they see only their unbelief. And therefore they pray incessantly, as did the unhappy father in our text: "Help thou mine
unbelief!"

But that faith *is* present the rest of us can see without
difficulty. We see it in a number of things. First and foremost
in this that sinners suffer as a result of their unbelief and pray
for faith.

At such a time faith is already fully active within them. For
to believe is to come to Christ with your sins, as the Haug-
eans said.

Those who keep near the cross of Christ with all their sins
believe, even though they as yet cannot see their faith, only
their unbelief.

Faith lives only as long as it struggles, says Luther.

Hear that, dear child of God, you who are restless so much
of the time and never can get your faith to be as good as you
desire it.

Say as the man in our text did: "I believe; help thou mine
unbelief!"

> For the word of the cross is to them that perish
> foolishness; but unto us who are saved it is the power
> of God.
>
> —1 CORINTHIANS 1:18

G OD has spoken many times and in many ways to us in the prophets. "At the end of these days," He has spoken to us in His Son. And a mighty speech it is, both in word and in deed.

However, the cross is beyond all comparison His mightiest speech.

The cross of Calvary is the center of history and of the world.

It is the most terrible and the most glorious place on earth.

There God unveils the two mightiest and most mysterious realities in the universe: *sin* and *grace*.

No one knows what sin is until that person has stood at the cross of Christ.

And because most people will not pause at the cross, they have such a thoughtless and frivolous view of sin.

What does the cross tell us about human sinfulness?

It tells us that humanity is at *enmity* with God. It tells us that humanity is not merely *evil*, but that people are *so* evil that they will not tolerate the good. Our race put to death the Only Good One that ever lived. Not by accident, but deliberately, by a well-planned judicial murder.

And the *most* religious people of that generation did it.

The cross of Christ tells us further that sin is so terrible that not even our almighty and all-loving God can forgive it *without atonement*.

However, He does not require this satisfaction of others. He becomes man Himself, to suffer and to die for His enemies.

Dear children of God, let us take note of the appalling seriousness of sin! Let the pleas of Jesus and His cries of distress pierce us to the very bone and marrow, that the sufferings of Jesus may impart to us that fear and trembling with respect to sin which will preserve us from *misusing* the grace of God.

What is this word? for with authority and power he commandeth the unclean spirits, and they come out.

—LUKE 4:36

WHEREVER Jesus went He was the strongest. Calm and gentle, but firm and possessed with authority, He walked among both His friends and His enemies.

In the synagog that day He had spoken with such authority that His words penetrated into the very depths of the souls of His hearers. They were not accustomed to that.

During the service Jesus was interrupted by a possessed man who began to cry aloud in the midst of the assembly. But Jesus remained as calm and authoritative as ever. He simply spoke these words: "Hold thy peace, and come out of him!" And the evil spirit came out. When the service was over, Jesus accompanied Peter to the latter's home. Here Peter's wife's mother lay ill. But Jesus touched her hand and healed her, and she arose and ministered to them.

When the sun had set and it had become cool and pleasant, they brought to Him all the sick people of the community. And He laid His hands on every one of them and healed them.

It had been an eventful day indeed. But the most remarkable thing in all that day, as otherwise, was, nevertheless, the power which Jesus had over the unclean spirits.

Verily, that was the greatest.

Jesus is great in His power over nature, walking on the water and rebuking the winds. He is great in His power to heal our bodies, yes, in His power over death. But He is even greater in His power over our *spirits*, our *unclean* spirits. Not all people know that they have an unclean spirit. Many, however, do know it. And suffer. More than others suspect.

Jesus can help you. He has, moreover, already helped you. He has *shown* you your uncleanness and made of it a thing which causes you *suffering*.

But the really effective agent against your unclean spirit is this: The blood of Jesus Christ, the Son of God, *cleanseth* from *all* sin.

82

My son, give me thy heart!

—PROVERBS 23:26

Most people seek God.

They pray, even though they do not do so regularly and diligently. They hear and read the Word of God, at least occasionally. They strive against their sins also. They deny themselves many a pleasure in which they feel they cannot take part if they are to seek God.

But they do not *experience* God in any way.

They find no peace, no joy, no power. They receive, on the whole, no response from God. Their religion is a continuous monolog, a soliloquy only. God does not speak.

Why not?

These people will do nearly everything possible except the one thing that God asks of them: Son, daughter, give me thy *heart!*

They carry on negotiations for peace, as it were, and haggle all they can in order to get away as cheaply as possible.

Their whole Christianity is one continuous attempt to keep God outside of their *hearts.* They try to gain peace without an accounting with God.

Listen now to what God says: "Give me thy heart!"

Admit your Savior into the realm of your heart, and do it now. It is there He desires to be. Let Him speak to you about the secret thoughts and desires of your heart. Then consent to a complete *reconciliation* with Him. Admit Him into your will. Cease your self-rule and let Him decide for you what is sin and must therefore be eliminated from your life.

Then you, too, will experience the life which is hidden with God in Christ Jesus.

He will receive you unto Himself and speak with you in His quiet, impressive way. About sin, in such a way that your soul will be filled with fear and trembling. Moreover, do not become discouraged if He takes a great deal of time to talk to you about your sins. You can be certain that He will also speak to you about His grace.

Only see to it that He is given entrance to your *heart* each day.

Wherefore receive ye one another, even as Christ also received you, to the glory of God!

—ROMANS 15:7

THE Bible speaks of saved people as the children of God.

They constitute a holy generation. They are the family of God on earth.

Ties of blood are strong; kinship of spirit is stronger.

This holy family is made up of sinners only. Sinners who have received grace, to be true. But "in many things we all stumble," and "if we say that we have no sin, we deceive ourselves."

But even sinners such as these are bound together in neighborly love. Children of God love one another notwithstanding their many failings, errors, sharp corners, and weaknesses. We are loved by God's children, not because we are lovable or sympathetic but because we are born of God.

Neighborly love is, after all, a mighty miracle in this egotistical and loveless world of ours.

And now we have the admonition of the apostle: "Receive ye one another!"

Verily, we need this admonition. For we forget so easily that a child of God is oftentimes an ailing and suffering child. Many a time he does not fare so well in this wicked world. The children of God encounter opposition constantly; they are oftentimes also despised and blasphemed.

But no one treats a true Christian more severely than she does herself. She accuses and judges herself oftener and more severely than others suspect. And therefore she is often tired and sick and sore of heart.

Receive the true Christian when you meet him. Do not wait until he pours out his heart to you. That, too, is often difficult for him to do. On the contrary, say something kind to him, give him a little comfort, a little encouragement. Mention some passages of Scripture which have been helpful to you.

I love none of the children of God more than those who *help* me when I meet them. Help me with the most difficult thing in life: to be a Christian, a true Christian.

One died for all, therefore all died.

—2 CORINTHIANS 5:15

IN all religions we come in contact with the notion of the human race that sinners cannot approach God *without atonement.*

In His revelation of salvation God confirms this apprehension. God gave His chosen people a *means of atonement* in order that they might abide God's holy wrath and not be consumed by it. They were given a *substitute*, the sacrificial animal, which gave its life in the sinner's stead.

But the sacrifices of the Old Testament were only a shadow. Christ is the perfect sacrifice. While the high priest went into the holy of holies with *strange* blood, in Christ the race's *own blood* was sacrificed.

Our progenitor, Adam, was our first substitute. He acted on behalf of the whole race. Therefore his sin became the sin of the whole race.

Christ is the Second Adam. It was His task to *suffer* on behalf of all humankind, to atone for the sin of the whole race.

Wherein did His atonement consist?

In the first place, He took upon Himself our *punishment.* "The chastisement . . . was upon him." None but a *God-Man* could take upon Himself this punishment, the fearful temptations and anguish of soul, even to being forsaken by God.

In the second place, He suffered our penalty *voluntarily.*

He became obedient unto *death*, even the death of the cross. A single moment's impatience and unwillingness in the mind of Jesus would have nullified the whole atonement and all humanity would have been plunged into eternal perdition.

How much did Jesus have to suffer? He had to suffer as long as people and devils had a single suffering left by which they might torture Him. When He had suffered through the experience of being forsaken by God, Satan had no worse suffering with which to afflict Him. *Then* Jesus could cry out His mighty: *"It is finished!"*

> Now I rejoice in my sufferings for your sake, and fill
> up on my part that which is lacking of the afflictions
> of Christ in my flesh for his body's sake, which is the
> church. —COLOSSIANS 1:24

THIS is a mighty verse of Scripture. Brimful of great thoughts and deep mysteries. The clearest thing here is the wonderful saying of the apostle: "Now I rejoice in my sufferings." We have far to go before we can make his statement our own. We rather shrink from suffering.

The apostle says that there is something lacking in the sufferings of Christ and that he is filling up this lack by his own sufferings.

Obviously the apostle does not mean by this that there is anything lacking in the *atonement* sufferings of Christ. By the sufferings of Christ he means here the sufferings which Christians bear for the sake of Christ.

He says, further, that God has appointed to each individual Christian his measure of this suffering. The apostle knows that he must suffer a certain measure of tribulation in *his flesh*. By that he means that it is the will of God that he should endure *bodily suffering* for the sake of Christ.

The apostle had conquered suffering. As far as we can see from his statements there are two discoveries which have solved the problem of suffering for him. ,

First, that also in his sufferings he is united with Christ; in fact, he cannot know Him and the power of His resurrection without having fellowship with His sufferings.

In this way suffering becomes a holy thing to the apostle, not only the outward proof of his fellowship with Christ. As, for instance, when he says that he bears the marks of the Lord Jesus in his body. But, above all, through his sufferings he himself gains inner strength and assurance. So he *glories* in his tribulations and *rejoices* in them.

Secondly, the fact that his sufferings have benefitted the whole church of God has shed light upon the problem of suffering.

O Lord, help us in our sufferings! Help us to *will* to suffer! Amen.

86

Even so let your light shine before men; that they may see your good works, and glorify your Father who is in heaven.

—MATTHEW 5:16

HERE Jesus speaks to us about a Christian task which we all have in common, old and young, children and adults. No matter who we are or where we are. A task which more than any other is made up of little things, little and obvious things, which, however, are great and significant. Both to us and to God.

The most essential part of this task we perform at *home,* where we spend the greater part of our daily lives.

To live our daily lives at home as they should be lived is our first and most important task as Christians. But, unfortunately, this task is accorded very little attention and is not evaluated very highly. Either by individual Christians themselves or by public opinion.

Though a believing mother gives of her time, her energy, her life to win and keep her children for Christ, few Christians seem even to notice it. It is not included in what is known as "Christian work." But if she teaches in the Sunday school or is active in other organizations, committees, or meetings, her work and her readiness to sacrifice herself are noted. If she will only continue a few years her picture will no doubt appear in Christian periodicals together with many a lofty word of praise.

Now what is expected of us in a Christian home?

First and foremost that we be good natured. By that we mean that we are to be straightforward and agreeable, willing to sacrifice ourselves and to serve, contented and conscientious. We expect a Christian to be the kindest person in the house. And if there is more than one, that they should vie with one another in kindliness.

We are not expected to be sinless, but we are expected to do battle earnestly against our besetting sins. And to be willing to beg pardon when we have erred in the home.

God grant that the Christian homes of our country may be filled with life and joy of this kind!

I am the living bread which came down out of heaven:
if any man eat of this bread, he shall live forever.

—JOHN 6:51

HUMANITY was created with body and soul.

Both had to have food in order to live. The body received
its food from the earth from whence it came. And the soul
received its food from heaven, whence it had come.

And God provided abundantly for their sustenance.

The body received the pure air of earth and the soul the
pure air of heaven in which to breathe. At that time heaven
was still down on earth. For God was here. He went in and
out as the Great Good Father of His two happy children. At
every breath of the soul they inhaled God. They lived by every
word that came to them out of the mouth of God.

But we are familiar with the account of the darkest day in
the history of our race, when humanity broke away from God.

The soul had now no heavenly air to breathe, no word from
the mouth of God by which to sustain itself. Now it inhaled
the *world*.

But the world is poison to the soul. And this poison produces
an insufferable pain.

Poisoned and without food, that is the situation in which
the human soul has found itself since the fall. The wages of
sin is death, says Scripture. Yes, and not only death by star-
vation, but painful death by poisoning.

Death is mighty, but love is mightier. In order to save people
who were doomed to die, Christ entered into the race that
had been poisoned and permitted the virus of sin to concentrate
all its death-dealing venom upon His own soul and body.

But the wounds and the stripes He received contain the
only effective means by which this poison can be driven out
of our souls.

> Except ye eat the flesh of the Son of man and drink
> his blood, ye have not life in yourselves.

> —JOHN 6:53

Y OU who do not go to Communion must listen to this.

Jesus tells you that if you do not eat the flesh of the Son of Man and drink His blood you do not have life in God.

But *I* go to Communion, you say.

Very well. But the Bible says that it is possible to eat and drink *judgment* unto oneself.

Yes, you say, but my confidence is in the sufferings and death of Jesus.

That is well. But you remember, do you not, that the Bible speaks of two kinds of faith, living and dead!

Have you never been afraid lest your faith might be *dead?*

Jesus speaks today about the heart which has life, which has a living faith. To such a heart Jesus is as indispensable as food is to the body. You know the process: you become hungry, eat, are satisfied; become hungry again and eat. And so on day after day.

Does this apply to your relationship to Jesus Christ?

Now be honest!

Is Christ indispensable to you? Or does the whole day pass, perhaps the week also, without your thinking about Jesus?

A corpse does not need food, you know. Suppose you are a spiritual corpse.

This is a hard saying, you reply. Indeed, they said so that day in Capernaum, too. And turned their backs upon Jesus.

But I read the Bible and pray every day, you say.

Very well, but how does it affect you? Does it work the same way as food does when you are hungry? Or are you happy when you have finished reading? Has it not been a source of surprise to you that you have no *desire* to read and pray?

He that eateth my flesh and drinketh my blood abideth in me, and I in him.

—JOHN 6:56

W E spoke yesterday of the heart which is in living fellowship with its Savior. As we did so, no doubt many a child of God sat sighing: "This does not apply to me. I am undoubtedly one of those spiritual corpses that does not need food."

Therefore I would very much like to comfort you today with this word of God: "They that eat my flesh and drink my blood abide in me."

But is not this comfort dangerous, you say. There would be no difference, then, between a living and a dead faith. Unbelievers would read and pray with a slothful and unwilling heart, and believers likewise.

Indeed, my friend, there is a difference, a difference, moreover, which is very clear and distinct.

Unbelievers read and pray with an unwilling spirit, but will not acknowledge this fact either before themselves or God. Believers experience also the unwillingness of their old nature toward God and His Word. But they suffer under it, are fearful of it, and acknowledge it before God.

And in the instant that they do this they receive forgiveness for it; for the blood of Jesus Christ, the Son of God, cleanses from all sin which is confessed unto Him.

Permit me to indicate what is meant by *hungering* and *thirsting*.

We think, as a rule, that to thirst after God is something unpleasant. But we are mistaken. When we experience this thirst, we feel how empty and distant from God we are, how unworthy we are of reading and praying and having fellowship with God in our daily life.

This is, of course, *painful*; but, at the same time, it is conducive to our spiritual health. It is thus that we learn to know that we have need of God and His mercy.

To all such souls the Gospel says: "Ho, every one that thirsteth, come ye to the waters, and if ye have no money come ye, buy and eat; yea, come, buy wine and milk without money and without price."

We were reconciled to God through the death of his
son.   —ROMANS 5:10

W AS God irreconcilable then, since an atonement was
necessary, people ask.

No. God has never been unconciliatory toward His enemies.
He loved them from the day of the fall, loved them so much
that He gave them His only begotten Son.

But if God was never unconciliatory, then no atonement
was necessary, people reply.

God says that He *loves* sinners even without atonement.

But He cannot forgive sinners without atonement. Therefore
He gave His Son to suffer and die on behalf of our sinful race.

By the atoning death of His Son God has removed that
which hindered Him from forgiving His enemies. Now God
can, unhindered and unbound, overwhelm His enemies with
His boundless love.

Yes, now God can establish the New Covenant, whereby
He pledges Himself to bring to every member of the race
everything that our Substitute has won for each and for all of
us by His atoning death.

So real, so mighty is the substitutionary atonement wrought
by Christ that every member of the race, child and adult,
ungodly and pious, is entitled to have a part in the fulness of
salvation wrought for us by our Substitute.

This is a gracious prerogative to death-doomed criminals,
is it not!

And the most gracious thing about all this mercy is that
God Himself brings salvation to all of us, overwhelms us with
His gracious love, melts away our enmity and opposition, transforms us from any enemy into friends, and woos us away from
sin.

Then we are permitted to enjoy the real fruit of the atonement: to be *in Christ*. Now we meet God in Christ and are in
the same relationship to God as Christ is. Wherefore we hear
the triumphant refrain through the saved church of God:
"There is therefore now no condemnation to them that are in
Christ Jesus."

I have compassion on the multitude, because they
continue with me now three days, and have nothing
to eat.

—MARK 8:2

ALL the accounts of the miracles of the loaves bring out
Jesus' practical realization of the needs of humanity.

This spiritual man had a clear vision of the natural requirements of daily life.

As He stood speaking to these great multitudes, He noticed
that they had brought nothing with them to eat. At once He
sympathized with them. Of course He also saw that these people
were in greater danger than that occasioned by their lack
of food.

But this did not prevent Him from seeing the *lesser* need
and relieving it.

He called to His disciples and apprised them of the situation.
The account does not really make it clear whether they had
seen the need of the people or not. But as they now began to
think about it, it seemed hopeless to them. Bread for so many!
Out here in the wilderness! They had enough for themselves,
seven loaves. But what was that to feed a multitude of four
thousand people?

Then they hear Jesus inviting the people to come and eat.
What is He thinking of? He has only seven loaves!

But He takes them calmly and lifts His eyes toward His
Father in heaven in thanksgiving and prayer. Then He bids
the disciples distribute the bread among the people.

And the miracle takes place, as quietly and simply as everything else God does.

In common with the first disciples of Jesus, we have the
idea that Jesus thinks only of our spiritual needs and offers to
help us only in that connection. As a rule we think that our
physical and temporal needs lie beneath the horizon of Jesus'
thinking.

Today Jesus would tell us that He provides for all our needs.

Before they call I will answer; and while they are yet
speaking I will hear.

—ISAIAH 65:24

JESUS' miracle of the loaves in the wilderness shows us how
literally this passage is to be understood.

The people had not as yet begun to think of the difficult
situation in which they would find themselves, how impossible
it would be to secure food out in the wilderness. Nor had the
disciples given any thought to the matter.

But Jesus was aware of the difficulty of the situation. And
before any one had asked Him for help, He had planned the
help He would extend and had made ready to intervene at the
right moment.

It is comforting to us to know that He hears our feeble
supplications and comes to our aid when we cry to Him. But
it is much more comforting to know that He answers before
we call. Even before we have discovered the danger and the
difficulty in which we may find ourselves, His loving eyes have
seen it. And without our knowing it in the least, He has
prepared help for us.

As a mother's eye follows her little child and notices any
spot on its little body which might indicate that something is
wrong, so Jesus watches over His children. No difficulty is so
little and insignificant that He cannot see it and find the best
way of solving it.

By His ceaseless care Jesus would help us to lay aside our
anxieties and trust in Him who rejoices each day in surprising
His friends with His help.

It is thus that he brings happiness and security to His friends
and binds them to Him in everlasting gratitude.

"What blessed joy overflows my spirit,
Because Thy wondrous grace was granted me."

93

> He who began a good work in you will perfect it until
> the day of Jesus Christ.
>
> —PHILIPPIANS 1:6

THIS passage tells me something about my Christian life which makes me so happy. It tells me something about its *beginning* and something about its *perfecting*. In fact, about what it is *all the way*: a work *of the Lord* in my heart.

This passage becomes significant to me when I strive and become weary and things will not go as they should.

"He who began a good work," it says.

It is so good to think only of this: *He* began, not I.

And He began early. In Baptism.

Many years of my Christian life passed before I began to thank God for Baptism. Now I thank Him often for the wondrous grace that was conferred upon me in that I was baptized as a child.

It was then that God *began* His good work. It was then that He took the wild branch and grafted it into the True Vine. Think of having one's life's deepest roots planted in God Himself, of having life together with God!

Through all the subconscious channels that are known to God but not to us, He worked in our little souls.

Yes, but I do not remember any of this, you say.

No, you do not. But think if God had not done any more for you than you can remember! You do not remember today all the things that God did for you yesterday. But God in His mercy did it nevertheless. So good beyond all thought is God.

As we grew older and were able to understand, mother told us about Jesus. We became acquainted with Him and learned to love Him. We felt so secure when we went to bed at night, after we had folded our hands and prayed to the Lord Jesus. And if we had disobeyed Him during the day and thus grieved Him, we felt so happy when we had asked Him for forgiveness.

Verily, he who began continues His good work in us.

They that are whole have no need of a physician,
but they that are sick.

—MATTHEW 9:12

A FEW years ago I visited America and saw many of the
things that have been accomplished by our compatriots over
there. Among other things I saw a large, modern hospital.
Everything that modern medical skill and equipment can do
for the sick was being done there. When I had seen it all, the
thought struck me: Here all that is necessary is to be sick.
Everything that the sick need has been provided before they
arrive as patients: room, bed, doctor, nurse, operating room,
and surgical instruments. Everything is in readiness. The patient does not need to think of any of these things.

Then another thought came to me: Everything is ready also
at our Lord's great hospital. There, too, one need only be sick
and permit oneself to be put to bed.

You soul-sick friend, you who cannot understand how you
can be saved, everything is ready and waiting for you.

Will you permit yourself to be entered as a patient? Will
you submit to the painful operation?

The Great Physician of souls is waiting for you. He is ready.
It cost Him His blood to provide the means of healing which
your soul, sick unto death, requires. And He rejoices over every
suffering soul that He can save from death.

You are fearful. I know it. You are afraid of the many and
great sins which cry out against you in smothering accusation.
But listen to what the Physician has done: "He was wounded
for our transgressions, he was bruised for our iniquities; the
chastisement of our peace was upon him."

Yes, you say, but my *heart!*

My heart is worse than all my sins! But He knew that too.
That is why *His* heart broke in death. He had made full satisfaction for everything in you that is sinful.

My Spirit hath rejoiced in God my Saviour.

—LUKE 1:47

THESE words are the beginning of Mary's song of praise.

Here we meet a happy soul. We do not meet such spirits very often.

We meet jovial, laughing, boisterous people frequently. Also frivolous ones. But happy people? No, they really are not easy to find.

Mary's joy was in God.

Such people are even more exceptional. Many think that it is impossible to be happy in the Lord. They think that God and joy are related to each other about like fire and water. They look at it in this way: they must choose one of two, either God or happiness.

But Mary says: "My spirit hath *rejoiced* in God." Her whole song is exultant with rejoicing.

Some believers are happy very little of the time, some scarcely ever. Which indicates that something is wrong. It is not that they are experiencing *sorrow*. A true Christian *always* has sorrow. Nor that their sorrow now and then overwhelms them.

That was also Mary's lot. It happens during our seasons of doubt and despair. And cannot be otherwise.

No, the mistake is that they do not see the *great things* which the Lord has done for them. Mary did. Therefore she rejoiced. David says to his soul: "Forget not all his *benefits.*"

As soon as we *forget* His blessings, our joy and thanksgiving cease.

Indeed, it seems that many of God's children *never* see His benefits. They see only that which is contrary and out of harmony, everything that goes against them.

What a joy it is to *see* the blessings of the Lord. Happiest are they who can see the Lord's blessings also in adversity and tribulation. "As sorrowful, yet always rejoicing," says the apostle.

> Ye husbands, in like manner, dwell with your wives
> according to knowledge, giving honor unto woman,
> as unto the weaker vessel, . . . that your prayers be
> not hindered.
>
> —1 PETER 3:7

THE apostle gave husbands a special admonition to be kind and good. And it is needed. We husbands undoubtedly have more sins on our conscience in this respect than our wives.

The Word for today raises a pointed question in the very midst of our domestic and marital life: Do you respect and honor your wife? Or are you one of those who go about complaining, now about the food, now about the housekeeping, now about financial matters, in fact, about nearly everything with which she has anything to do?

Do you give her the money she needs for the household and for clothes for herself? Do you give it to her with a word of good cheer or do you complain of her lack of economy?

I know husbands who, when they are away from home, speak well and in glowing terms of their wives, but who never accord them a word of recognition or encouragement at home.

Do you know that your wife is hungering for even the least evidence of the fact that you are grateful for her love, for all that she sacrifices and does for you and for your home?

I know husbands who are polite and respectful toward their wives among strangers, but at home are neither the one nor the other. There they show her neither respect nor honor, scarcely even any interest.

"That your prayers be not hindered," says the apostle.

There are many Christian husbands whose prayers are hindered, whose life in God is weakened, yes, suffers extinction because of the fact that they sin against their wives day after day without being willing to listen to the reproof and admonition of the Spirit.

Perhaps this is the leak through which all the grace that you have received continuously flows out of your life.

> Martha, Martha, thou art anxious and troubled about many things: but one thing is needful: for Mary hath chosen the good part, which shall not be taken from her.
>
> —LUKE 10:41-42

THERE are many Martha-souls. In every age. And they are oftentimes judged severely. As a rule Martha fares very badly whenever we preach on this text.

But let us not forget that Martha was a *believing* soul. And let us not forget either that what she was anxious and troubled about was to honor her Savior and make things pleasant for Him.

Martha-souls are motivated by a holy zeal. Nor should we forget what they accomplish. They are practical people who know how to do things. They are, moreover, capable people who get things done and do not merely wax enthusiastic, talk, and make plans. They aim to make glad the heart of the Savior, but in this they do not succeed as well as the Mary-souls do.

For we must remember that Mary was not a dreamer, one who shirked work. She could *act* also. We see this a few weeks later when she anoints the feet of Jesus.

That incident shows us too that she also knew how to choose the right time to act, as well as how to choose the right time to sit quietly at the feet of Jesus. On that occasion she was praised just as highly for her *action* as she had been previously for her quietude.

The great danger confronting Martha-souls is that they may become restless and outward. They are impelled by a desire to serve; they are always active, continually occupied with something or other in the kingdom of God. But their many interests result in a divided and distracted mind. The one thing needful is inadvertently pushed aside.

They are, after all, occupied with Christian problems. And for this reason they do not seem to think that it is very dangerous to be somewhat neglectful of the quiet hours at the feet of Jesus.

And Jesus stood, and . . . asked him, What wilt thou
that I should do unto thee? And he said, Lord, that
I may receive my sight.

—LUKE 18:40-41

PERHAPS some of us too would pray that we might receive
our sight.

You have perhaps noticed for some time that there is something wrong with your inner vision.

You could see better before.

When you read the Bible, for instance. Just think of the
things that you saw with your childlike eyes of faith when you
read the Scriptures in those days! Even the most insignificant
things took on a large meaning and became a source of edification to you. You saw God in them.

Do you see things in a similar way now when you read your
Bible? Or do you not see anything any more? Do you read a
portion merely for the sake of having read it?

You could see better before also in matters pertaining to
your daily life.

Do you remember how strict you were with yourself in your
home life? Do you remember how severely it pained you when
you had been unkind to one of your dear ones and had grieved
your Savior?

Do you see as well now? Are you as strict with yourself now
as you were before?

You could also see better before when you looked at other
people. A new convert begins at once to look at other people
in a new light.

You spoke to your dear ones. To begin with they were perhaps
kind and courteous and listened to you. Later they became
impatient and said to you: "No, now you must keep still a
while! You make life impossible for us with all your preaching!"

But do you remember how you walked among them and
held your peace until the tears rolled down your cheeks?

Then you *saw* well. Do you see anything like that now when
you look upon your neighbor?

Perhaps no prayer is more necessary for you and me to pray
than this one: "Lord, that I may receive my *sight!*"

Cast not away therefore your boldness, which hath great recompense of reward.

—HEBREWS 10:35

THIS is the word of the Lord to all His co-workers. And so are we all, if we are His.

He needs workers who have boldness. If any one should be bold, it should be the co-worker of the *Lord*.

He says to us now: Cast not away your boldness, even though you come upon difficulties and hindrances in the work.

The work of the Lord always receives its baptism of difficulty. But the Lord is in the midst of our difficulties and says: I shall supply all your needs.

You, dear parents, lose your boldness very easily in your homes and in the rearing of your children. You are often fearful lest your weaknesses and failures might become a hindrance to your children's tender life in God.

But go to God with the things in which you have erred toward your children. As long as you walk in the light, God will make right again the wrong that you have done also toward them. He does *wonders*. Do not forget that.

And then you become fearful when you remember that your dear children must go out into a world that is both large and dangerous. Oh, how such thoughts can bring pain to the heart of a father and mother both by day and by night!

But cast not away your boldness! Remember that the salvation of God has been ordained precisely for those who live in this wicked and dangerous world.

Many parents see their children go out into worldliness, yea, into open sin. They pray, but see no fruit. And they ask: Will not God hear our prayers? But remember that none of you loves your children as exceedingly much as the Lord Himself loves them.

Continue to pray and to weep for your erring children. All people must be prayed into the kingdom of heaven. Some must also be wept in.

That I may know him, and the power of his resurrection, and the fellowship of his sufferings, becoming conformed unto his death.

—PHILIPPIANS 3:10

HERE we meet one who has understood Jesus' words about suffering, one who has grasped the secret of suffering.

He is not only resigned to suffering, he not only thanks God for the suffering assigned to him, but he *desires* suffering. He has no greater desire than, through the power of Christ's resurrection, to have fellowship with His sufferings. He considers his friends in Philippi fortunate to have had granted to them not only to believe on Christ but also to suffer in His behalf.

As suffering was the secret of the life of Jesus, so suffering is the secret also of the believer's life.

Many of us ask ourselves and others why we do not grow and develop more as Christians. The answer, as far as most of us are concerned, would in all likelihood be this: "You take unto yourself the unmerited grace of God in order to make things easy for yourself, instead of using it as a power to enable you to suffer with Christ."

Are there times when you are burdened? What do you expect at such times? That they should pass as quickly as possible? That is not why they have been given to you, but to bring you new glory.

What do you see back of the cup of suffering, back of the cross? Do you see the glory back of it?

To go out of the way of suffering which God places along our pathway always means to miss some of His glory.

Suffering brings a renewal of life to the new person within us; it brings death to the old.

"To the old rugged cross I will ever be true,
Its shame and reproach gladly bear."

If therefore the Son shall make you free, ye shall be free indeed.

—JOHN 8:36

To begin with we all look upon sin as pleasant, harmless frolic. But it soon manifests itself as a most bitter reality.

To be whipped by one's own desires into doing things which one's conscience condemns becomes so unendurably painful that we do not know what to do with ourselves.

In such moments we resolve with all the energies of our soul that this shall be the last time, that the chains of sin shall now be broken.

But all we achieve is to make clear to ourselves how helplessly we are bound by the chains which we once put on with a smile in order to frolic with sin.

Then do we feel the truth of Jesus' words: "Every one that committeth sin is the *bondservant* of sin."

But listen now to the rest of the truth which Jesus speaks in this connection. It reads like this: "If therefore the Son shall make you free, ye shall be free indeed."

He has overcome your tyrannical master. And therefore He has power to free you from his bonds. You shall be *free!*

First He will set your conscience free by proclaiming to you the Gospel that He has suffered for all your self-imposed slavery to sin. You shall never more be required to account for it. You have been acquitted, really set free.

Yes, but when temptations come again? I have not the power to resist, you say.

He knows that. Therefore He Himself will go with you. And every time you feel that you do not have strength to withstand, you shall be permitted to behold Jesus in such a way that you cannot sin against Him.

> "God is faithful, no temptation
> Shall o'ertake you on the way.
> God is love, His consolation
> Turns the darkness into day."

102

Except a grain of wheat fall into the earth and die, it abideth by itself alone; but if it die, it beareth much fruit.

—JOHN 12:24

THESE are some of the words that Jesus spoke when the Greeks came and asked that they might see Him.

Apparently it made a tremendous impression upon Jesus, this coming of the Greeks.

He no doubt saw a great deal in that hour.

He saw the dawn of the new day which was about to come upon the earth. He was conscious of the fact that he had been called to be King of all the nations of earth. Now the Gentiles were coming to Him. And at the very moment when His own people were planning His execution.

He saw the fields that were white unto the harvest. He saw the weary, sin-sick race waiting for its King and Deliverer.

But as He stood and contemplated the glorious work which now thrust itself upon Him, He saw also that the hour of suffering had come. The Gentiles were knocking at the portals of the kingdom of God. With this, the decisive hour, both to Him and to the race, had come.

He knew that he could not help the bleeding, suffering race until He Himself had passed through death. The grain of wheat must fall into the ground and die before it could bear fruit. To Himself and to the race the decisive hour was the dark hour of death.

But of this He could not think without anxiety of soul. However, He went to the right One also with this anxiety— to His Father. But He did not know for what He should pray. And therefore broke out first in the anxious cry: "Father, save me from this hour!"

But then He went on to victory with these glorious words: "But for this cause came I unto this hour. Father, glorify thy name."

"Thine, O Jesus, now and ever,
My desire and my endeavor."

If any man serve me, let him follow me.

—JOHN 12:26

JESUS has many adherents but few followers.

For no one can be a follower of Jesus without going the same way as His Master: *through death*.

We love *our* life, our old self-life. We love it, hedge about it, and defend it. We would improve upon it and dress it up, making it look like new. If we could only escape *death*.

But *life*, life in God, never becomes ours until our old self-life dies.

And this death is a fearful thing.

Therefore a long period of time often elapses before a seeking soul will deliver itself and all *its* life up to God.

But whosoever will lose their life shall find it, Jesus says.

Indeed, when we finally accept the judgment of death upon ourselves, we really learn what it means to pray for mercy. And when we have seen the firm basis upon which mercy is granted in the voluntary death and glorious resurrection of Jesus Christ, then we feel within ourselves the life which never passes away. The life which cannot be attacked or weakened by death, but is most vital, most sound, and strongest in the very midst of death.

This is the innermost and most enigmatic secret of life in God: we live by dying. Our life depends upon whether we are willing to become nothing before God, before ourselves, and before our neighbor.

But this involves a death-struggle. Every day. With fear of suffering and a dread of being completely undone. With a dread of acknowledging before God every day our miserable relationship to Him and of accepting His mercy as lost souls. With a dread of denying ourselves and serving others.

Dear child of God! Do not be dismayed when you experience these sufferings in your daily life. It is the death-struggle. And that *must* take place.

Eternal life is won and can be lived only *by dying*.

Now I rejoice in my sufferings for your sake.
—COLOSSIANS 1:24

LOVE brings new joys, but also new sorrows. A compassionate sympathy, yes, a suffering with all who are in distress. Most of all with the unsaved.

We are to suffer with Christ.

Here is the most important aspect of the suffering which we are to share with Him. This suffering is a part of love. Self-love will not and cannot bear this suffering. It must be sought voluntarily.

It was this new anguish in which Jesus put His confidence. This was the fire He had come to send upon earth.

And to the extent that the first of *this* anguish burns within the hearts of believers, so rapidly does the spread of the Gospel go forward.

This sympathetic mind also suffers with the church of God in its inner, as well as its outward, distress. It would experience the deep pain of the hurt of Joseph. This very suffering constitutes the beginning of the healing of this hurt.

The criticism and the struggles which arise during such inner anguish will never rend asunder the body of Christ. Healing, rather, will be the result.

That there are so many open wounds, wounds that will not heal, in the fellowship of saints in our country is due to the fact that there is so much criticism and so much striving without this inner sympathy.

There is an optimism blinded by culture which does not see the guilt nor the power of sin. And there is a pessimism which grumbles and complains about the times and about the young people, yes, about everything under the sun.

Let us take the middle road here. We know the power of sin, and we know that the world is hopelessly lost in itself. But we also know the power of Christ. And that it is our place to love unto salvation all those whom Christ has redeemed. And if we will do that in the spirit of Christ, we will not find time for complaining.

Create in me a clean heart, O God;
And renew a right spirit within me.

—PSALM 51:10

THE psalmist speaks here of renewal. And in so doing touches upon an important thing in our lives.

All life has this in common: it continues only as long as it is renewed and dies as soon as renewal ceases. Daily renewal is vital to our Christian life in more ways than one.

In the first place, our life would cease growing if it were not renewed.

In the second place, we should be rendered incapable of doing Christian work.

We see this very clearly in the case of sick people. As their power of physical renewal diminishes, because of illness, their strength wanes until they at last can do no work at all. They must sit down. Finally they must go to bed.

There are many Christians who, because their spiritual selves have not been renewed, have become so weak that they cannot do anything for the Lord.

This shows, in the third place, how important daily renewal is in connection with our eternal salvation. Life that is not renewed dies. It is no doubt a question whether most of the people who have fallen away from the Lord have not died from lack of nutrition. Their falling away may have manifested itself in various ways *outwardly*, but fundamentally their backsliding was due to neglect of daily renewal. By that we mean a neglect of the means of grace: the Word, prayer, the Lord's Supper, and the communion of saints.

There is no little difficulty connected with daily renewal. Everything pertaining to our daily life is on the whole difficult. Repetition has a dulling effect.

Therefore it is necessary for us to pray as the psalmist did: "Renew a right spirit within me." We must receive new and fresh grace and not live on old experiences of God's mercy. There is nothing the Lord would rather do for us. He says: "I came that they might have life, and might have it *abundantly.*"

106

Jesus himself drew near, and went with them.

—LUKE 24:15

THE two did not know Jesus when He came and began to walk with them on the way to Emmaus. But He succeeded in telling them what He wanted to, nevertheless.

Jesus walks upon all the ways of the world. And joins the company of us all.

We did not ask Him to come with us. We did not even know Him when He did come. But He began to speak with us, to engage us in conversation.

I do not know how far He has come in His conversation with you. Perhaps He has not come so far that you have recognized Him. But He has nevertheless spoken to you a great deal.

He has spoken to you of the emptiness of the life you are now living. You are having fun and pleasure. But now and then you see straight through your noisy amusements and the loud people who are participating in them. As you do, you look down into something which not only makes you weary and bored but unspeakably anxious.

At other times you have felt the uncertainty of life. Death has been tangent to that circle. You felt as though you were paralyzed when death took from you the most precious thing you had on this earth.

And your conscience has spoken its authoritative language. Not equally strong at all times, but now and then you have felt something exceedingly sensitive in your soul. You could not say exactly what it was nor what it came from. You felt more like weeping than anything else.

Your soul is drawn to God with a longing that cannot be uttered.

You desire to be on good terms with God. You wish that you might draw close to His heart and weep out upon His bosom all the distress and anxiety of your soul.

My friend, it is Jesus who has done this good work in your soul, without your knowing Him. Open your heart to Him now, that He may enter in and give you that for which you are longing so earnestly.

And their eyes were opened, and they knew him.

—LUKE 24:31

JESUS has many friends who are just as discouraged and bewildered as these two on the way to Emmaus were.

A short time before they had been happy Christians. But then everything went wrong. It was as though Jesus had been lost to them completely.

These discouraged ones cannot pray right, nor can they get anything out of the Bible. They cannot believe as they ought, nor love Him as they should. They cannot live as they should, either at home or away from home.

Life has become so burdensome and so bitter. Oftentimes they feel a desire to get away from it entirely. Yes, they feel so weary at times that they would welcome death.

Now listen, dear friend! Jesus is walking with you on your way through life. You fail to recognize Him, just as did the two who were journeying to Emmaus long ago.

He is in your adversity. He is present in your doubts. He is furthering His work in you.

Furthering it, you ask. Everything is going the other way. Everything is dead and gone!

No, there is no danger of that. He knows what He is doing and what you can endure.

It is the poor in spirit whom He calls blessed. That is why He is permitting you to feel your impotence, your lack of spirituality, and your worldliness.

"He made as though he would go further," it says.

He does so with you, too, to see what you will do.

The two on the way to Emmaus constrained Him to abide with them. Is it not that which you are also asking Him to do?

Thereupon He prepared a table for them. Today He would do so for you. He who was delivered up for our trespasses and was raised again for our justification.

Praise be to His holy name!

108

Jehovah is merciful and gracious.

—PSALM 103:8

No, say many, God is not gracious.

If He were gracious, He could not permit all the suffering and need that there is in this world. Look at what a drunkard's wife must suffer day and night! Or think of the children who grow up in the homes of drunkards and criminals! Or the children who fall into the hands of sexual perverts! Or think of the unmentionable horrors of the World Wars!

If God is almighty, then He is unmerciful if He can look at all this and permit it to take place.

Yes, indeed, it does not take a world war to create doubt with regard to the mercy of God.

He took your health. He took your money. He took your wife or child. He took your happiness and crushed it before your very eyes.

Was not that unmerciful?

And then some people say that God is merciful and gracious. How do they know that?

Yes, how do we know it? It is well that we have an opportunity to give an answer to this question, both for our own benefit and for the benefit of others.

We know it because *Jesus* was merciful. Can you think of any one more merciful? No father, no mother is as merciful as Jesus. No one has cared more tenderly for ailing human souls than Jesus.

Jesus shows us that God is merciful. When He saw our distress, heaven became too strait for Him. He stepped down into our needs, was born in a manger and put to death on a cross. He permitted Himself to be crucified by His enemies because He could not save us in any other way.

O Thou merciful God! We praise Thee now and through eternity!

109

But Simon Peter, when he saw it, fell down at Jesus'
knees, saying, Depart from me; for I am a sinful man,
O Lord.

—LUKE 5:8

BEFORE the Lord can dwell in a human heart He must first
crush it.

Nor does He crush any heart so thoroughly as those He is
to *use* in His service.

Peter is not the only one who has been made to feel *fear*
in his heart. If the Lord is to make us useful, we must see sin
in such a way that it becomes *the* thing of which we are afraid.
We must be given to see our own heart, our own fear of God,
our Christian work in such a way that it becomes our despair.

If we are to receive "that sufficiency which is from God,"
then we must first realize our own insufficiency, our own in-
capability.

Be not dismayed therefore, my dear fellow worker, when
you experience these crushing blows at the hands of the Lord.
To you everything seems impossible and nothing quite so impossible as that you should be able to do anything in the
kingdom of God.

You feel that you are unworthy. Indeed, but who is worthy?
No one. It is only through God's mercy that we are permitted
to have a part in the work of the Lord. As long as you feel
that such is the case your work will prosper.

You feel that you are incapable. Indeed, that is as it should
be. As long as you feel that way the Lord can use you. For
there is nothing else that can make you qualified for this work
but that which you *receive* from God. He gives grace to the
humble.

No one is as well qualified to win souls as the humble person
is. Such a person is never too prominent in a group of believers.
She never causes division or strife within the flock of God.

Moreover, she gains access to the hearts and consciences
of the unconverted as no one else does.

The disciples therefore were glad, when they saw the
Lord.

—JOHN 20:20

THESE had been terrible days for the disciples.

On Thursday evening Jesus was arrested. On Friday morning
judgment was passed, and before noon He was crucified. Before
sundown He lay in the tomb.

To belong to His most intimate circle of disciples was now
a serious matter. It does not surprise us that "the doors were
shut for fear of the Jews."

Through these closed doors the wildest rumors reached
them.

These were terrible days and nights.

Sunday evening had come. Suddenly Jesus stood in their
midst, verily alive. He had come through the closed doors.

He spoke with them as He had done before. To make them
fully certain He showed them His wounds. "The disciples therefore were glad." Jesus was back again. When He was with them,
whatever would, might come.

It is always thus with the disciples of Jesus. If Jesus disappears
from their sight, they become as unhappy and frightened as a
driven hart.

Jesus has many such frightened disciples who have hidden
themselves behind closed doors.

But He knows about them.

He knows about you and your inner distress, you who formerly were so happy in the Lord but are now so miserable.

And today He stands before you in the midst of all your
needs. He extends to you His pierced hands and points to His
open side. He would make you a *glad* disciple.

And he saith unto them, Come ye yourselves apart into a desert place, and rest a while.

—MARK 6:31

AGAIN Jesus took the apostles with Him, away from their fatiguing labors, away from the multitude and the commotion to a lonely place on the other side of Lake Gennesaret.

This was one of the *quiet hours* which Jesus arranged for His disciples.

Most disciples want to be where there is commotion, where there are people. They have so many good reasons for declining when Jesus would take them aside.

You who formerly were active in Christian work but have now been put aside as it were, either by illness or by something else, you feel, no doubt, as though you were in a desert place.

That was what Jesus wanted.

If He cannot get us aside voluntarily, He must use force. Oftentimes He must send us urgent messages in order to get us away from the multitude and the commotion.

And the place to which He takes us may oftentimes be an exceedingly unpleasant desert place. How unspeakably lonely cannot a death in the family make one! Economic ruination also makes for loneliness. And those who have been sick abed for a long time can also tell about desert places of loneliness.

What is it that Jesus seeks to accomplish by this?

Even the prophet saw it: "I will . . . bring her into the wilderness, and speak comfortably unto her."

Before He could not really get to speak with us. Therefore He had to lead into the desert place. Not to torture us, but to speak *comfortably* unto us.

"Rest a while," said Jesus to His disciples.

Indeed, our souls find rest when we permit Jesus to speak to us.

"I'll go where you want me to go, dear Lord!"

And as they spake these things, he himself stood in the midst of them, and saith unto them, Peace be unto you.

—LUKE 24:36

JESUS understood the human race.

There is nothing it needs as sorely as peace. We live in a world of strife, a world of war.

Human history is essentially one long history of wars. And things are not getting any better in this respect, but worse. The last war was the greatest the world has ever seen. A war in which the whole world participated, in one way or another.

It is not strange that there is war in this world of ours; for nothing is as warlike as the human heart.

Think of the "wars" in our homes. Between husband and wife. Many live under an armed truce, others fight each other mercilessly.

Think of the "wars" between brothers and sisters. It is not for nothing that people have formulated the old proverb that "love between brothers and sisters reaches as far as the probate courts."

Or think of the "wars" between neighbors. To begin with, the bone of contention is some insignificant little thing: a chicken, a sheep, or a fence. Whereupon we have unfriendliness, enmity, bickering, and, finally, the supreme court.

Most people are carrying on warfare of one kind of another. It depends chiefly upon their temperament and training.

But even the most peaceful promote strife, even though it is only an *inner* "war," one of thought and imagination. How much of a person's time is not devoted to *attacking* others in their thoughts. With thoughts as sharp as awls, filled with the poison of envy, we wound others, without mercy.

Yes indeed, we all need Him who can impart peace to our hearts!

113

My peace I give unto you.

—JOHN 14:27

W E spoke yesterday of outer and inner wars in this world of ours.

But there is one war which is worse: the war against our own conscience.

Conscience says that you are not telling the truth now. But you will not listen, and you compel your conscience to be still. This war is often carried on in bloody gruesomeness.

It hurts so much; people suffer so terribly under the authoritative judgments of conscience. But they will not yield.

The war against conscience is often carried on in an even worse, more dangerous, manner: *insincerity* is resorted to, and people call their sins by different names in order to pacify their consciences. Vanity is called esthetic sense and greediness is called thrift.

To make war against one's conscience is exceedingly painful. It is terrible to have one's conscience against him. The fact that many people are melancholy, moody, uncontrolled, and nervous in their homes can in most instances be accounted for by the fact that they have been vanquished in their "wars" with their conscience.

Even worse is the fact that people carry on warfare also against *God.*

They live in permanent disagreement with God. If He sends them adversity, that is wrong. If He sends them prosperity, even then they are dissatisfied. Others have received more.

And as they look forward into the future their disagreement comes to light even more clearly: they become anxious and fearful. Why? Because God will deal with them as *He* wills.

Is there a greater miracle than this, that God can create peace in the warlike human heart? Let us thank God each day, we who have experienced the miracle and have been lifted up into that which the Bible speaks of as peace with God.

I dwell in the high and holy place, with him also
that is of a contrite and humble spirit.

—ISAIAH 57:15

THE hard and warlike human heart must be made *contrite.*
There is no one else but God who can accomplish this.

It is a fearful process, both to Him and to us. But there is
no other way of salvation.

How God does it, I do not know. That is the mystery
connected with *spiritual awakening.* But I do know that He must
often use harsh means. To us it often means terrible struggles
because we are so hard and rebellious.

But behold what a miracle when the heart has been made
contrite!

The soul which only recently was making war against God
comes forward and confesses all. He is now in *agreement* with
God about his sinfulness. He makes no excuses; he has no
objections to offer to that which God tells him.

Now this soul does not haggle any longer with a view toward
smuggling some sin with her into her relationship with God.
She is fearful now lest there be guile in her spirit. Now she
has acquired a holy suspicion of herself. She would willingly
turn her heart inside out, if it were possible, in order that she
might be fully assured that nothing unaccounted for remained
there any longer.

Now this soul does not argue himself away from the reproach
of Christ. He takes his place in the midst of the fusillade. Now
people may smile and laugh at him, yea, sneer and blaspheme
as they will. He is *determined* to share reproach with his Savior.

Now he *surrenders to God.*

Without stating any conditions or making any demands.
The thing that is hard for this soul to believe now is that God
will and can accept her. By a mighty miracle of God she has
become a helpless sinner, who never feels so secure as when
she is at the foot of the cross.

> Well done, good and faithful servant: thou hast been
> faithful over a few things, I will set thee over many
> things.
>
> —MATTHEW 25:21

WITHOUT a doubt more work is being done in the church of God in our day than has ever been done before.

Never has so much work been done, never has the work been so many-sided, never so purposive and well planned. Never have the gifts of grace been made use of and organized as now.

No child of God can note this without being filled with hope and joy.

Praise be to God for those Christian men and women who no longer can endure to bury their talents in the ground, but put themselves and all they have at the disposal of the kingdom of God, according to the Word and the will of God.

But, together with this joy, a secret sorrow makes its presence felt now and then. Especially when one sees how easy it is for organized Christian work, particularly that which is carried out in meetings and through organizations, to steal the interest and the power from *that* work to which Jesus gives the highest rating and of which He expects the most, namely, the *personal* work of each individual disciple. Her daily endeavor in word and in deed to let her light shine amidst her surroundings. That his neighbors might gain a glimpse of the Savior they need.

The servant in our parable had received a return of one hundred percent on his talent.

He had achieved this, Jesus says, be being faithful in little things.

That our talent produces such slight returns is due, is it not, to the fact that we strive to be faithful in the *great* tasks, in the work connected with our societies and meetings, before we have learned to be faithful in our daily, little duties at home, in our associations, among our fellow workers? In the personal, unobtrusive but purposive, work of winning souls for the Lord?

I know mine own, and mine own know me.

—JOHN 10:14

Do you not hear the rejoicing of Jesus in these words: "Mine own know me!" He goes before them, and the sheep follow Him because they know His voice, He says in the verses immediately preceding.

The Good Shepherd does not *drive* His sheep; He goes before them and *appeals* to them to follow Him. They hear His voice and recognize it. Indeed, among all the voices of earth they can distinguish His voice.

They hear His voice in the Word. Throughout the whole Bible they hear the melody of heaven. Now and then they go with Him up to Mount Tabor, where they see and hear things so unspeakable in their import that their hearts exult with an exultation for which they cannot find utterance.

At other times He speaks to them with such severity and strictness that their souls tremble and their tears flow. But they listen; and they want to listen. They do not permit themselves to be frightened by what they hear, but pray unceasingly: "Lord, speak, Thy servant heareth."

Now and then they do not hear His voice at all, either in the Word or in prayer! He hides His face from them. According to His own word: "A little while, and ye behold me no more; and again a little while, and ye shall see me."

But at such a time, too, it becomes apparent how attached they are to Him. They become sad, dismayed, and bewildered, and do not know what to do with themselves. Now it becomes manifest that they are giving utterance to the full, personal truth when they sing:

"Jesus, Thou are mine forever,
Dearer far than earth to me."

They know of no greater joy than to live their daily life in His holy presence and thus, at work and at rest, in joy and in sorrow, in prosperity and in adversity, to hear His voice; and throughout every hour of the day to be admonished against sin, to be rebuked for disobedience, to be taught to fear that which is evil, and to be led by the Good Shepherd.

117

Go ye into all the world, and preach the gospel to
the whole creation.

—MARK 16:15

"To the whole creation!"—thus His orders read.

And all He had was eleven men. And He gave these orders
at a time when He was about to leave them.

Strange!

Of course, He did *not* leave either His friends or His work.
Did He not say: "And lo, I am with you always, even unto the
end of the world"? On the very first page of mission history is
written: ". . . the Lord working with them, and confirming
the word by the signs that followed."

He has not gone; He has only become invisible. He is
working with His friends. Indeed, now as never before, for He
has been given all power in heaven and on earth.

To these first friends of Jesus His last orders were not a
burdensome command but a joyful proclamation of the Lord's
will. The great commission was to them a divine promise, and
they obeyed it in childlike confidence. Never had they seen
their great Lord as great and glorious as now when they were
doing His work.

How does it affect us when our missionary obligations are
called to our attention?

To many people the word "mission" conveys the idea of a
multitude of demands, issuing, as a rule, in one thing above
all else: *money.*

When this is true of the friends of Jesus, it is an occasion
of poignant grief to Him. I am certain that Jesus would desire
to sit down among His working friends and speak with them
about the glorious *gift* which His missionary enterprise is, in
order that they might *rejoice* in the missionary cause, the cause
for which He died and for which He now lives.

> "Most wondrous is of all on earth
> The kingdom Jesus founded.
> Its glory, peace and precious worth
> No tongue has fully sounded."

Enter ye in by the narrow gate!

—MATTHEW 7:13

Many walk around outside the gate.

They have seen it. They have seen how narrow it is, and therefore they cannot get *through* it. Its very narrowness makes them restless. They cannot forget its exacting requirements. They have seen the heavenly splendor of the great ideal, through the narrow gate.

And it touches secret chords in their hearts and once more puts a hidden longing into their worldly and pampered lives.

Upon the easy, indolent life without sacrifice which they are living falls a ray of light from the narrow gate, revealing to them that their own lives are not only empty and void but mean and degraded.

My longing friend! You are rich, you who have this longing. You have received it from God. You know that, do you not? This is the best that He has been able to give you up to this time.

Your longing is no doubt a variable one. Now and then it is down at zero. At other times it strives for full realization. At such times your soul thirsts after God as the hart pants after the water brook. You bend your knee, you fold your hands, you cry out to your Creator.

It may be that you feel somewhat ashamed of your "sentimentality" the day after. And you are glad that no one heard or saw you in your distress. But in your innermost being there is a voice which says that you are never yourself more than during such sacred hours as these.

Many never get any farther than to long for God. They content themselves with their longings. They continue to walk around *outside* the gate, and never pass *through* it.

It is not enough to *seek* God. You must *find* Him.

Enter in by the narrow gate, says Jesus.

> So when they had broken their fast, Jesus saith to
> Simon Peter, Simon, son of John, lovest thou me?
>
> —JOHN 21:15

LAST week we heard about the seven disciples who went fishing. We heard about the long, disappointing night. They caught nothing.

But to Peter it had been night since Good Friday morning. But now after the long dark, a resplendent day was dawning.

It is true that the three questions had been very humiliating to him. He knew very well that there was a connection between them and his threefold denial. He no doubt felt also that the thrice-repeated questions were intended to remind him of his self-assurance and his ignorance of his own failings.

But it was nevertheless a glorious moment to Peter. Now he knew not only himself but also his risen *Savior.* He sank humbly down at His feet and said: Lord, Thou knowest all things. Thou knowest my terrible denial of Thee, and Thou knowest my self-righteous heart. But Thou who knowest all things, Thou knowest also that I cannot live without Thee.

Today He asks you and me: "Lovest thou me?"

This is an exceedingly painful question to all true children of God. Every time they proceed to examine themselves to see if they love Christ their love disappears between their fingers and they find virtually none.

They are slothful in prayer. The Word of God seems dry. Their hearts are cold. And even worse: their hearts are full of worldliness, evil thoughts and desires. When the question is put to them, they have only this to say:

> "My hope is built on nothing less
> Than Jesus' blood and righteousness;
> I dare not trust the sweetest frame,
> But wholly lean on Jesus' name."

Feed my lambs!

—JOHN 21:15

EVEN before the denial Jesus had said to Peter: "And do thou, when once thou has turned again, establish thy brethren!"

Now after he has turned, after he has answered Jesus' question: "Lovest thou me?" with such touching humility, Jesus assigns him his task anew: "Feed my lambs!"

Here Jesus tells us how our love of Him should *show* itself in our daily life. He had said it once before: "Inasmuch as ye did it unto one of these my brethren, even these least, ye did it unto me."

All that we do for our brothers and sisters, for whom Jesus died, He looks upon as having been done for Him.

My *lambs*, He says.

You fathers and mothers, Jesus expects above all else that you should tell your children about Jesus. Let not the day's struggle for a living, and not the various Christian activities, hinder you from performing your most important task, that of feeding His lambs.

Especially you mothers, to whom the children belong in a peculiarly God-given way—you are sacrificing time, and strength, and effort in order to bind your children's hearts to Jesus, are you not? Never assume any task which will hinder you from feeding the little lambs which Jesus has entrusted to *your* care!

And you who have no children, do you *see* the children along your pathway in life? Or are you among those who overlook them? If we looked to our children a little more carefully, not so many young people would be going out into the far country.

> And when he was entered into a boat, his disciples
> followed him. And behold, there arose a great
> tempest in the sea, insomuch that the boat was
> covered with the waves.
>
> —MATTHEW 8:23-24

IT was not only on the Sea of Galilee that the disciples had been out in a storm with Jesus. Never had they experienced so many and such a variety of storms as since they had forsaken their nets and followed Jesus. They could be frightened at times, as on this day out there in the boat. But no tempests, no adversity could frighten them *away from* Jesus.

If we could have asked them which they preferred—to live in fellowship with Jesus *without* all these dangers or *with* them— do you not think they would all have answered with one accord: With Jesus without the difficulties—that too would have been glorious. But the storms and the difficulties were the very things that made Him so *great* to us. When we were at our wits' end and did not know what to do, we turned to Him. And He never failed. So calm was He, so confident.

And they would no doubt have added: now we know that the joy of life does not consist in avoiding adversity and tribulation, but in knowing Him who is stronger than the strongest tempest, in being aboard ship with Him who rebukes every storm and gives us strength to bear every suffering.

Those who would have fellowship with Jesus can never avoid the storms of life. It has ever been thus.

How are things in your little boat today? Perhaps there is a frightened disciple who sits staring at the waves as they mount higher and higher. Cry to the Lord Jesus, and remember that he helped His disciples yon night on the Sea of Galilee, even though they grieved Him by their unbelief and fear. Oftentimes He waits a long time before He intervenes. We think He waits too long. We seek to avoid all hardship, both temporal and spiritual. But He does not intervene until our distress has made us dependent upon Him. Then His help becomes real help, renewing our childlike confidence in Him.

> That the creation itself also shall be delivered from
> the bondage of corruption into the liberty of the glory
> of the children of God.
>
> —ROMANS 8:21

NATURE, too, lies at our feet, bathed in the golden splendor of hope.

Because of sin it was subjected to corruption. As we look at nature now, we can, therefore, gain only an intimation of what God intended it to be.

But it, too, shall some day become what God intended. We have the beautiful words of the Bible about the new heaven and the new earth. This also tells us that nature shall share in the restoration of all things.

This is told us even more clearly in our Word today. It says that creation groans and longs to be delivered from the bondage of corruption.

Many think that this means that creation is groaning to be annihilated, thus to be delivered from the tyranny, misuse, and oppression of humanity.

And for that, no doubt it does groan.

But its groaning involves more than this, the apostle tells us here. Creation shall be delivered, not by annihilation, but by sharing in the liberty of the glory of the children of God.

It shall no doubt be consumed at the end of the world. But not annihilated. As we shall receive our bodies again in a glorified form, so shall nature also arise unto life incorruptible.

Then shall all creation bask in the splendor radiating from the new heaven. Then there will be nothing missing in all that God has created.

But sin shall be no more.

> "Then shall the kingdom bright appear
> With glory true and vernal,
> And bring His saved a golden year
> Of peace and joy eternal."

123

And this is life eternal, that they should know thee the only true God, and him whom thou didst send, even Jesus Christ.

—JOHN 17:3

Here we are informed, in the first place, that eternal life does not begin when time ends. Eternal life does not necessarily succeed temporal life.

Nay, from this temporal life one can enter into eternal death just as well as into eternal life.

Eternal life is therefore a certain way of living life both in time and in eternity. The difference between eternal life here and eternal life in the beyond is only a difference of degree. Here everything is, in part, also eternal life; there all shall be perfect and glorious.

Eternal life is to know God, Jesus says.

Here we are told the meaning of life in one brief sentence. That which people have speculated about in every age.

The true meaning of human life is to know God.

To this we should devote our life. This is the only reason for our existence. And that in a literal sense. Therefore they must die who will not devote their lives to learning to know God.

No one can know God without knowing Christ. He Himself says: "Neither doth any know the Father, save the Son, and he to whomsoever the Son willeth to reveal him."

Eternal life, accordingly, dates from the moment of the new birth, when God reveals His Son to us. And the Spirit makes use of the rest of our days for this one purpose: to teach us to know Christ.

Yea, we shall be occupied with this throughout all eternity. For this is eternal life, both here and hereafter, to know Thee the only true God, and Him whom Thou didst send, Jesus Christ.

And this is life eternal, that they should know thee
the only true God, and him whom thou didst send,
even Jesus Christ.

—JOHN 17:3

To know Christ is the salvation and life of the soul from
first to last.

To behold Jesus, that is the beginning of our salvation. A
soul has not been awakened spiritually in a Christian sense
until the Spirit has brought it face to face with Christ.

Then sin becomes bitter and distasteful; then we begin to
see the selfishness and spiritual coldness of the human heart.
Then a *reckless* sinner is transformed into a *despairing* sinner.

And this despairing sinner never becomes a free and peace-
filled Christian until the Spirit draws aside the veil and enables
him to see Christ as his Savior in the Word. Then slavish fear
of God is banished; likewise fear of other people.

A believer strives daily against her old sinful habits and the
wickedness of her old heart. Oftentimes she strives and loses,
makes good resolutions and fails again.

What is it that can bring victory in this unequal struggle?

A glimpse of the Savior is enough to make sin loathsome.
Then temptation loses its enticing power, and the sinner feels
that it is blessed to say no to sin.

We live in a world of suffering. We all suffer. Children of
God should suffer willingly, in fact, thank God for suffering
and rejoice in tribulation. But as a rule we are afraid of suffering,
even long before it comes. And when it does come, we sigh
and complain.

But a glimpse of the suffering, bleeding Savior is enough to
set our impatient minds at rest. We become ashamed of our
impatience and our complaining.

Verily, this is eternal life: to know Him whom Thou didst
send, Jesus Christ. O God be praised!

The heavens declare the glory of God;
And the firmament showeth his handiwork.

—PSALM 19:2

GOD has put something of Himself in all His creation, that we might see Him also in nature.

But many do not "see" nature, not to speak of seeing God in nature. Many believers also are blind in this respect.

Either they live such a hyper-emotional spiritual life that nature is beneath their dignity or their plane of interest. Or they bury themselves so deeply in their striving for daily bread that they have a mind for nothing else but fear of God, food, and clothing.

On the other hand there are many who have a fine appreciation of nature. They hear the song of the sea and the sighing of the wood; they listen to the thousand-throated choirs of the birds, the sounds made by the various animals, the buzz of insects; they pause often for the happy babbling of the brook and for the gentle quivering of the leaves. They know every leaf and flower which delights the eye by its form and color.

But many of these noble and fine lovers of nature are unable to see God in nature.

If, however, ours are "the opened eyes of the heart," then the rich and beautiful life of nature, saturated with sentiment and filled with eternity, will bring us face to face with the Creator. Also in this way would He encircle us with His divine presence, overwhelming not only our spirit but also our soul and body with His majestic goodness.

Godly people of old understood God as He spoke through nature, and they made reply in beautiful and exalted songs of praise. If we had only Psalms 8, 19, 104, and 148, these poems alone would be enough to show us how the seers of Israel saw God also in nature.

> He made of one every nation of men to dwell on the
> face of the earth, having determined their appointed
> seasons, and the bounds of their habitation.
>
> —ACTS 17:26

God meets us also in *history*. Even more mightily than in *nature*.

The Scriptures tells us that God *makes* history.

He did not shape it all at once at the dawn of time, like a clock which is wound up and makes its regular rounds until it stops. Nay, God creates it piece by piece, day by day.

How God makes history we see best in the Old Testament as we follow the history of the chosen people.

We see how God intervenes, not only in the history of the chosen people, but also in the affairs of the world powers. He employs the latter as a scourge upon His own disobedient and rebellious people. And when He has thus made use of a nation, He turns and sends another nation to chastise the nation which He has used as a "scourge."

God meets us, then, in history. And He would have us see and recognize Him here also. The events that take place in time become of eternal import when we look through their temporal shell into the eternal content and thus note the footprints of God.

This is what Jesus had in mind when He charged us to "discern the signs of the times."

Let us first discern the signs of the times in our own country. If we are not blind, we shall see forces of disintegration at work undermining our nation and imminent danger threatening our beloved people.

This will drive us to humble and fervent prayer. For there are powers at work which cannot be overcome save by the power of *God*. That is why we are praying for a nation-wide spiritual awakening. We are crying to God that it may come before the powers of disintegration have made our nation ripe for catastrophe.

Be of good cheer; it is I; be not afraid!
—MATTHEW 14:27

GOD meets us, not only in world history and in the history of our people, but also in our own little history, in our daily life. He personally leads and orders our lives from day to day. Prosperity and adversity, health and illness, sorrow and joy— He ordains them even unto the minutest detail. Not a hair of our heads shall fall without the Father's will, Jesus tells us.

If the eyes of our heart have been opened by the Spirit, we shall recognize God when He meets us in our daily life. We shall be able to see through the lesser as well as the greater events of our daily life into God's loving purpose in all that comes to us each day.

However, this is not equally easy for us every day.

When Jesus came walking on the tempest-tossed sea that night, the disciples did not recognize Him. They thought it was a ghost. And they cried out in fear. But Jesus called to them: "It is I; be not afraid!"

This occurs again and again in the lives of the disciples of Jesus.

When the billows of life roll high, when adversity, suffering, and death break in upon us, we often fail to recognize Jesus. We stare at these ghosts until our hearts tremble with anxiety.

But then, too, Jesus cries out to His frightened friends: "It is I who am permitting these tribulations and sufferings to be laid upon you; be not afraid!"

Old King David had lived through many tribulations. His heaviest one came toward the close of his life when his dear son, Absalom, revolted against his father. David had to flee hurriedly in order not to be taken captive in his own capital. And as he made the steep ascent up Mount Olivet, a man of Saul's family came and cursed the king. This was, of course, *lese-majesty*, a crime against the king, and the king's men were about to strike the man down. But David said: "Let him alone, and let him curse; for Jehovah hath bidden him."

David recognized God, even in the most bitter hour of his life.

128

> But we are not of them that shrink back unto
> perdition; but of them that have faith unto the
> salvation of the soul.
>
> —HEBREWS 10:39

ACCORDING to the Scriptures, faith is the right and normal relationship of a soul toward God.

What is it to believe?

It is not to speculate wildly about God or to form a mental picture of Him according to our own ideas. Not to think about God or to define God. Not to desire or long for God.

To have faith is to permit oneself to be convinced of God.

This we see from the expressions which are used about faith in the Scriptures. Both the Greek "pistis" and the Hebrew "aemuna" really mean "to be convinced" and are used in connection with the origin of faith.

Faith is not *action* but *reaction* in the soul. A result of our meeting with God. Faith is our right *answer* to God. We cannot give this answer until God has spoken to us. It is God who *creates* faith. This He does simply by meeting us. God is like that. It is His nature. Because God is God He needs only to make Himself known to us and conviction results.

God does not need any one to *introduce* Him, nor does He need any one to *recommend* Him. He needs but confront us, and we all recognize that it is *God* we are experiencing. And we are not only convinced *that* God is, but also *who* He is. The Absolute, the Holy, the Pure.

And at the same time we are convinced of who *we* are: the unclean, the guilty. We see our own lives as one continuous offense against God.

Thus does God's speaking to us take effect.

Moreover, when He speaks, we must make *reply*. Yes, we *must* answer Him. We may answer as we ourselves will. But there are only two replies to choose from: either to *have faith* or to *shrink back*. Those who do not shrink back are convinced by the quiet words of Jesus and are drawn to the foot of the cross of Christ, which is God's most convincing message to sinners.

129

And if he shrink back, my soul hath no pleasure in
him.

—HEBREWS 10:38

We spoke yesterday about the two replies which we can
make to God's gracious invitation: acceptance or recoil.

Those who shrink back from God's convincing message do
it in somewhat varying ways.

Some break off completely, immediately.

They feel deeply impressed when God shows them how
selfish and unclean their life is. And they are afforded a glimpse
into a bright and happy life of forgiveness, lived in a good
conscience. A life of love and purity, of willingness to sacrifice.

But they see what it will cost them each day in the way of
sacrifice and self-denial. This seems too burdensome. And as
a consequence they shrink back, breaking off brutally the contact with God which they have had.

Others shrink back in a finer way.

They would be religious. They would *enjoy* the richness of
life to which the soul is given access by experiencing the eternal,
the invisible. Their sensitive souls have discovered that the
melody of heaven is earth's finest music. And they seek it
wherever possible. Out in God's free out of doors or within the
stillness and impressiveness of a church. They are deeply impressed by the music of the church and by the mystery of the
sacrament of the Lord's Supper.

But they will go no farther. They have provided themselves
with a religion for their senses, but not for their consciences.

Every time God touches their consciences, they shrink back
at once. With arguments that are more or less valid, as the
case may be.

It is of serious consequence to shrink back when spoken to
by the living God.

Therefore the Scriptures speak of those who shrink back
unto perdition. Those who are spoken to by God, but shrink
back, betray their most sacred convictions. They practice that
guile by which they injure their own souls.

> And he, when he is come, will convict the world in
> respect of sin, and of righteousness, and of judgment.
>
> —JOHN 16:8

IT was *the* great disappointment in the life of the disciples that the multitudes would not recognize Jesus as the Messiah. On the contrary, they took His life.

Now Jesus comforts them with the thought that He will send the Spirit to conduct the case against all His opponents. The Spirit will convince the world that Jesus is the Christ.

All disciples of Jesus need this consolation.

It is also the sorrow of your life that people will not believe in Jesus Christ. You behold doubt, blasphemy, and denial all about you. You see the great, threatening indifference to church and Christianity everywhere. In the city and in the country. Even in your own community. Among your own neighbors, who are otherwise kind and good.

It becomes even worse when you observe it among your own dear ones. You note their unconcern with respect to things holy. Indeed, at times you note outright animosity toward such things. And you become very anxious. Jesus would comfort you today, as He points to the one great task of the Spirit: to convict the world of sin.

He is working uninterruptedly, unceasingly, at this matter of convicting. He convicts children, in a simple, childlike way enabling them to understand Him and feel the sting of sin of *their* consciences.

He convicts youth. Oftentimes quietly and unnoticed by others. But how He can speak to young people about their sins! Oftentimes they may *appear* indifferent, yes, they may even give expression to animosity both toward Christian people and toward Christianity. But still they are *convicted* within. Their broken-hearted souls long for God, and oftentimes they sigh: Oh, that I had peace with God!

Now let us, both you and I, pray the Spirit to perfect the good work which He has begun in these young hearts.

131

And he, when he is come, will convict the world in respect of sin, and of righteousness, and of judgment.

—JOHN 16:8

W E noted yesterday the quiet comfort contained in these words of Jesus.

But you will perhaps say: the comfort is only half-way. Of what good is it that people are convicted if they are not *saved?* Why are not more of those who come under conviction saved?

Indeed, you have touched upon a painful question.

Christ has not come into the world to *compel* us to accept salvation. Therefore the prophet said at His very birth: "Behold, this child is set for the falling and rising of many in Israel; and for a sign which is spoken against."

And the apostle Paul, who saw this fulfilled among his own people, says that the gospel is to some a savor of death unto death, but to others a savor of life unto life.

It is the work of the Spirit to *convict.*

He does not *fool* any one into following Jesus. Nor does He *frighten* any one into the kingdom of God. Still less does He seek to *force* any one in.

He simply convicts. But He does do that. Not a soul slips down into eternal perdition without first having been convicted of sin and grace by the Spirit.

Do you hear that, you who are convicted?

You think, and talk, and wait, and hope, and long for that to happen of which you have already been convicted. Yes, there are some who are waiting for something *besides* this. They expect God virtually to strike them down and in a way compel them to be converted.

My friend, God has only one means of saving you, namely, by *convicting* you. If you will not follow the conviction which the Spirit of God has worked in you, not even God can save you.

See that ye despise not one of these little ones: for I say unto you, that in heaven their angels do always behold the face of my Father who is in heaven.

—MATTHEW 18:10

DEAR children! Listen now! Jesus says that each one of you has been given a guardian angel who follows you wherever you go. You cannot see him, for an angel, you know, is invisible, just as God Himself is. But your angel can see you. That is the important thing. He can see you both when it is dark and when it is light.

Remember this when you are alone and become frightened. Your angel is with you. You are safe, even though it is dark and you are alone.

Then you must thank God every day for this guardian angel. Think of it, God has so many angels that we can each have one of them!

This angel will help you, not only when you meet ugly dogs and wicked people, but also when you are tempted to do things that are bad and wicked.

You are tempted to become angry or to pout, to say something bad, to cheat at school, to lie or do something else that you know your parents do not want you to do, to think impure thoughts. You know also that Satan whispers into your ears that it is not dangerous to do these things.

Then your angel helps you. He whispers to you at once: There is only one thing that is dangerous, and that is to sin. Do not do it, your guardian angel says.

If you nevertheless do that which is wrong, the angel becomes sad. When he returns to heaven again, Jesus will see this at once. And He will ask the angel why he is sad. Then the angel will have to tell Jesus about the wicked thing which you did. And Jesus will be sad, too.

Then what will the angel do? Well, he will come directly down to you again and will whisper into your heart: Jesus is sad. Hurry and ask Him to forgive you, and He will wipe out all the wrong you have done. And then both you and Jesus will be happy once more.

133

Come unto me, all ye that labor and are heavy laden,
and I will give you rest!

—MATTHEW 11:28

Many of God's children have grown weary.

Their Christianity has become a burden and a drudgery;
they have become restless and anxious.

They strive with their worldly minds, their hard and un-
emotional hearts. They dishonor God by their daily lives. Instead of growth and progress there is retrogression on every
hand. Oftentimes they feel weary unto death. Tired of themselves and their self-seeking hearts. Listen now as Jesus calls
to you: "Come unto me, all ye that labor and are heavy laden,
and I will give you rest."

Why do not the children of God come to Jesus and
find rest?

Our worst hindrance is that which the Scriptures speak of
as "the sorrow of the world." What is that? It is that sorrow
for sin which is vexed at itself and its own weakness and
foolishness. That is, it is a *rebellious* sorrow.

We have a great deal of this kind of sorrow in our daily
lives. It arises from our old *pride*. The right kind of sorrow for
sin yields and humbles itself instead of becoming vexed.

It submits to the humiliating fact which I myself and my
daily life constitute. It concedes that the Spirit of God is in
the right when He points out all my wretchedness. And, instead
of becoming surprised, or vexed, or dismayed, prostrates itself
quietly and *gives thanks* to the God of grace for conviction.

And thereupon it gives thanks for the fact that salvation
is for the lost, that the physician is for the sick and not for
the well.

Thus my weary soul finds *rest* again.

It has now humbled itself beneath the mighty hand of God;
now it agrees with God that in me there is nothing that can
stand before God. Now it rests again upon the firm foundation
of grace. And beholds the wounds and stripes of my Substitute,
praising and thanking God for them.

> And other sheep I have, which are not of this fold:
> them also must I bring, and they shall hear my voice;
> and they shall become one flock, one shepherd.
>
> —JOHN 10:16

IT is the *Gentiles* of whom Jesus is here speaking.

During His humiliation He was limited in His work to the lost sheep of the house of Israel, He says. But He spoke often of the Gentiles and looked forward with rejoicing to the day when His humiliation would be ended and He could come to the aid of all His lost sheep.

In our text today we hear of the joy which Jesus experienced at the thought of the salvation of the Gentiles. "When I am lifted up from the earth, I will draw all people unto me," He said, as the Gentiles came and knocked at the portals of the kingdom of God a few days before His death.

When he had risen, He said to His co-workers: Go out and make disciples of all the nations!

It is true that a number of years passed before the full meaning of this really dawned upon them. To begin with, they worked only among the Jews. But with the coming of Paul this was changed.

The gospel was brought by Jews to Rome. The Romans brought it to others. Eventually it reached America also.

The voice of Jesus is being heard here in our own country. God be praised that the gospel is being proclaimed in all its fulness and clarity also across the length and breadth of our beloved land.

And, God be praised, American Christians have heeded the voice of the Lord as He bids them bring the gospel out to those who sit in darkness and the shadow of death. It is our turn now, we who are the Christians of today.

Do you know, friends, that there are still so many heathen that it will take three hundred years until all hear the gospel unless we sacrifice more for missions than we do today!

135

But I say unto you, Resist not him that is evil.

—MATTHEW 5:39

J ESUS would speak to us today about a very difficult matter. None but Jesus' true friends will follow the counsel He gives us here.

Here in our home, too, it no doubt happens that some one becomes angry, angry also with you. Perhaps the cause of it all is something very insignificant, but you have to listen to some harsh and cross words.

What do you do then?

Jesus knows how you and I act. And now He asks us: "Resist not him that is evil." Hold your peace and pray to God when you are met with harsh and unjust remarks. And remember: as you do so you are doing something for Jesus which is worth more than your most fervent testimonies or your greatest financial contributions.

Oftentimes there is trouble between neighbors. Now it is the children, now the chickens, the sheep, the road, the fence, or the line that are involved. It begins with disagreement, develops into quarreling, leads to slander, and finally ends in enmity.

If you are a friend of Jesus and are on such terms with your neighbor, Jesus would say to you today: "Give place unto wrath! Not in your own life, of course, but in the life of the other. Resist not him that is evil."

Hold your peace and pray God for patience!

Put your trust in Him who says: "Vengeance belongeth unto me; I will recompense, saith the Lord."

God will avenge His elect.

O God, teach us to look upon our adversaries with Thine own eyes. Help us to look upon the losses they inflict upon us as inconsequential, and let us see the salvation of their souls as the great thing, the thing that matters.

Amen.

He that believeth on me, as the scripture hath said,
from within him shall flow rivers of living water.

—JOHN 7:38

Is this descriptive of you, dear child of God?

Alas, no, you say. My soul is withered and dry. There is no
spring within me and therefore no rivers of living water.

Now listen to what Jesus says: "Let all those who thirst come
unto me and drink."

Yes, but I do not thirst either, some will say. My heart is
worldly and earth-bent. And the worst is that I do not know
what to do about it.

Yes indeed! And that is the way the Christians of past
generations felt about it, too. They oftentimes bemoaned the
fact that they were spiritually cold and dead.

It is difficult for you and me to learn that thirst for God
expresses itself also in this way. But we should really know that
such is the case. The food we ate for breakfast this morning
will not *continue* to satisfy us until evening. All life declines
and must be renewed constantly. This is the normal way. Go,
therefore, to Him in all confidence with your empty and worldly
heart—to Him who is all in all.

And the rivers of living water will begin to flow from within
your life and out to all your surroundings.

Alas, I can do nothing either for God or my neighbor, you
say.

In this you are mistaken. You can do far more than you
think. Think of what you can do by *living* Christ, living as a
humble, sincere, grateful, and happy Christian in your daily
life. Such lives are living streams in the deserts of the world!
The greatest thing that you can do is to *pray!* Go your way
through this world praying, and things will grow behind you
all the way. Yes, long after you have passed away.

But thou, when thou prayest, enter into thine inner chamber, and having shut the door, pray to thy Father who is in secret. —MATTHEW 6:6

M ANY believers leave the nurture of their souls to chance. They read the Bible and pray if they "get time." Satan sees to it that they do not "get" time.

In the morning they lie a-bed a little too long, and the many duties of the day begin to press for attention; they decide to do their praying a little later in the day.

At noon their minds are full of the many things they have to do. Then, perhaps, they do not even think of feeding their souls.

In the evening they are so deathly tired that, as a rule, they go to sleep before they have prayed at all.

No, we do not *get* time to read and pray. We must *take* time for that. We must arrange our daily program in such a way that we have time. We must arise early enough in the morning to have the time and peace of mind to be still before the Lord before daring to go out into the labors, temptations, struggles, and sufferings of the day. Those who begin the day with a quiet season before the face of the Lord receive something that will stand them in good stead throughout the whole day, something which will help them to maintain a holy poise.

We all recognize the necessity of bodily nurture. For that we make provision thoroughly and regularly. Three or four meals a day.

Brother and sister! Care just as regularly for your soul. No one will be more surprised at the results than you. You will see that there is nothing magical about living a rich and vital life in God.

The simple and regular use of the means of grace will impart to the sincere soul exactly the thing which the Lord has promised: life, yea, *life abundant.*

Let us lay aside all slothfulness and subject ourselves to holy restraint and discipline so that there will be definite provisions for our spiritual nurture.

"God is not a God of confusion," says the apostle.

> I dwell in the high and holy place, with him also
> that is of a contrite heart and humble spirit.
>
> —ISAIAH 57:15

THE Lord dwells with those who are of a humble and contrite heart.

He *dwells* there.

We call the place where we dwell our *home*. The Lord tells us then that He feels at home in our contrite and humble hearts.

It is no doubt hearts such as these of which the Lord Jesus was thinking when He said: "Blessed are the poor in spirit!" "Blessed are they that hunger and thirst after righteousness!" "Blessed are they that mourn!"

Many of God's children read these beautiful words with a deep sigh. To them they have become words which breathe judgment. Since their hearts do not hunger and thirst after righteousness, since their hearts do not mourn, but are cold and indifferent, of what avail, then, is all God's mercy and goodness?

At such times it is not easy to be a child of God.

But listen now! You have misunderstood what is meant by a contrite heart; you do not understand what it is like on the inside.

If you take a glass tumbler and dash it to the floor with all your might, you will see what a broken tumbler is like. It lies there in a thousand pieces. And no glass-maker can put it together again.

Just so with the heart which God has crushed into contrition. Your faith and love, regret and sorrow, praying and reading, sacrifice and self-denial—everything has been dashed to pieces. You sit looking at the remains. And to you the whole thing looks hopeless.

You forget that it is God who has crushed your heart—in order that He might dwell there.

My contrite friend! We can honor God in no better way than by believing His *grace*. That is precisely the reason why He crushes our hearts. Over and over again!

And whatsoever ye shall ask in my name, that will
I do, that the Father may be glorified in the Son.

—JOHN 14:13

HERE we are told what the real purpose of prayer is, namely,
to glorify the name of God.

We are quick to make use of prayer for the purpose of praying
ourselves away from suffering and difficulty and of gaining some
advantage for ourselves and our dear ones. That is why we
have so many *disappointments* in our prayer life. That is the
reason for the many *unfulfilled* petitions of the past.

We have misused prayer. We have used it contrary to the
purpose for which it was given to us. "Ye ask, and receive not,
because ye ask amiss, that ye may spend it in your pleasures,"
says Scripture.

But if we will make use of prayer for the purpose of asking,
for ourselves and for others, for those things which will glorify
the name of God, we shall see the strong and bold words of
the Bible with reference to prayer fulfilled also in our feeble
little prayer life.

"Yes," you say, "that is just the trouble. Think of me: I have
taken everything to God, great and small; in fact, I have prayed
to Him about the most insignificant things in my daily life.
That is to misuse prayer, is it not?"

No, my friend; on the contrary, you should pray God for
even greater simplicity of heart in your daily fellowship with
Him. It is written, as you know: "In *everything* by prayer and
supplication with thanksgiving let your requests be made known
unto God." Nothing in your daily life is so unimportant and
inconsequential that the Lord will not help you by hearing
your prayers with reference to it.

But let us remember that the purpose of prayer is to glorify
the name of God. Whether we pray for things large or small,
let us always add: If it will glorify Thy name, then perform this
miracle and help us. But if it will not glorify Thy name, then
let us remain in our extremity. However, give us power to
glorify Thee through it.

He hath done all things well; he maketh even the
deaf to hear, and the dumb to speak.

—MARK 7:37

Yes, that is exactly the way our Savior does things!

First He makes the deaf hear. I wonder if in our whole
personal salvation we have ever experienced a greater miracle
than this. When I look back upon all the remarkable things
that I have experienced, this seems to me to be the most
remarkable of all: that God made me hear, hear in such a way
that my frivolous soul began to tremble at the Word of God.

Almost as remarkable was the miracle by which He opened
our deaf ears and enabled us to hear the Gospel of unmerited
grace, causing our hearts to sing jubilantly with other ransomed
souls: "He hath done all things well."

Is it not this miracle which He has wrought in us continuously since then? We become deaf again, and hear neither
His law nor His gospel, live an empty and unhappy life in the
accustomed forms of godliness. Then He takes us aside, as He
did the deaf of long ago, and speaks His mighty "Ephphatha!"
We hear once more, and our souls both tremble and rejoice.

He maketh the deaf to hear *and the dumb to speak.*

As long as we were deaf, we were dumb. We did not have
a word to say about our Savior. But as soon as we heard the
Word of the Lord, the dumb began to speak. We could not
keep silent.

It is the way the Lord raises up *witnesses* unto Himself.

Not only preachers who speak because they believe and
cannot remain silent. But also all others who seldom or never
speak in public because they have not been given the gift to
do so, but who speak privately, in daily life, because they cannot
refrain.

There are many children of God who have become dumb
again. Why? They can no longer see that the Lord does all
things well. Pray that you again may *see* the blessed works of
the Lord. Then you will not be able to remain silent.

> And behold, a woman that had a spirit of infirmity
> eighteen years; and she was bowed together, and
> could in no wise lift herself up.
>
> —LUKE 13:11

THIS daughter of Abraham, bowed together with a spirit of infirmity, gives me much to think about.

I look out upon the flock of disciples belonging to Jesus and see the *spirit of infirmity* which rests upon most of them.

I am not among the number of those who believe that living Christianity is on the decline among our people. As far as I am able to judge the situation, there have never been as many personal Christians in our country as there are today. Never has there been as much Christian work done, never such well planned work for the cause of Christ as at the present time.

And still I see that the spirit of infirmity, with its paralyzing effect, is upon us.

For our Christian strength cannot be measured by what we *do,* but by what we *are.*

It is not the Christian work that we set in motion, nor our concern about having meetings, nor our willingness to give of our time and of our means for the Lord's cause, no, not even our zeal for the salvation of souls, that gives true expression to our Christian strength.

We ourselves are to be the touchstones of our spiritual strength.

And here the spirit of infirmity shows itself in glaring colors.

You may find in a person great zeal and willingness to sacrifice for God's cause, but a personality so keen in its desire for power that it cannot stand either admonition or opposition. It is possible to find people whose souls are aflame for the salvation of souls in a large audience, but who lose their zeal entirely when the audience is small.

> "Behold the vineyard Thou hast tilled
> With thorns and thistles filled."

For godly sorrow worketh repentance unto salvation,
a repentance which bringeth no regret: but the sorrow
of the world worketh death.

—2 CORINTHIANS 7:10

W E are impelled by a variety of motives in our striving
against sin, motives which we oftentimes cannot distinguish
ourselves.

At times we do battle against sin because we are fearful of
its unfortunate and dangerous consequences in our lives, both
here and in the beyond. At other times our struggle against
sin is prompted by our own wise calculations: we see that some
advantage will accrue to us if we overcome it.

But we win real victory over sin only when we can say
deliberately: "How can I do this great wickedness and sin
against God?"

Here we are afforded a glimpse into the mystery of sanctification. God has no means of sanctifying us except that of
wooing us away from sin. By that we mean: He loves us until
we feel that it becomes more and more unendurable to do
anything contrary to such love.

Such distress as this is therefore the surest indication that
the love of God is being permitted to do its work in our hearts.
The deeper sorrow of this kind becomes, the more spiritual our
abstaining from sin will be.

This deep sorrow, this deep groaning because of sin, will
also help us to lift our eyes toward the *day of our redemption.*

No doubt not a little of the longing for heaven among us
is of a kind which those who are in heaven do not prize very
highly. When our earthly plans are crossed, when adversity
and tribulation set in and everything goes wrong, we begin
to long for heaven. But such longing is nothing but veiled
selfishness.

True longing for heaven is, on the other hand, a quiet
longing for the day when we shall never again defile our souls
by sin of any kind, never again offend any one by our love of
self, never again grieve God by disobedience.

143

Bear ye also witness.

—JOHN 15:27; MARGINAL READING

In our country a person's life is not endangered by being a witness for Jesus Christ. Nor do we suffer any loss of goods or property. We can on the whole, not speak of persecution. There are peace times and there are war times also for the church of God on earth.

Does it cost nothing, then, to be a witness of Christ today?

Yes, it costs something at all times and in every place to put oneself wholly on the side of Christ. There is something known as the offense of the *cross* and the *reproach* of Christ. And these will follow the true friends of Jesus all the way to the very dawn of the millennium.

The natural person has an inner, inborn antipathy toward vital Christianity. This opposition expressed itself in various ways: as contempt, scorn, blasphemy, frigid sneers, slight, slander, and enmity.

Then, too, religious but unregenerate people will meet true Christians with antipathy and enmity in one form or another. They look upon living Christianity as an exaggeration, as fanaticism. In their opinion believing Christians try to make themselves appear better than others.

They cannot look upon an absolute distinction between converted and unconverted as anything but intolerance and bigotry. And when Christians refuse to compromise about the Word of God, advancing it in opposition to all the opinions of others, the world looks upon it as contentiousness or imperiousness.

Yes, it costs something without question, to be a witness for Christ!

And Jesus tells us today that He has appointed us to be His witnesses in the midst of a world which is opposed both to Him and to us.

As truly as we are willing to bear His reproach, so truly does He promise us His spirit, who will impart divine power to our testimony.

144

Bear ye also witness.

—JOHN 15:27; MARGINAL READING

Do you bear witness?

Many will feel themselves crushed completely by this question, and will answer in their distress: "Alas, no; it is impossible for me to say anything at testimony meetings, although our leaders both coax and threaten us."

Do not be discouraged, my friend. Not all have been given the gift of grace to testify *in public*. The Lord has called you, then, to bear witness privately, as individual to individual in daily life. The Lord has appointed you as a witness to the people that you meet in that way.

Note well, too, that private witnessing of this kind is much more important than that which is done at public meetings. No testimony costs more to give than this. And no testimony reaches into people's consciences more readily.

But I have so little courage also when speaking with individuals, you say. True. Just tell it to the Lord, praying for new power, and you will experience to your own surprise that the Spirit will bear witness with you. He will make use of both your speaking and your silence.

You complain that you lack wisdom. That is not dangerous. Do as the Scriptures teach you: "Let any of you who lack wisdom ask of God!"

And you will be given wisdom to judge people and situations, to speak and to remain silent at the right time.

But do not forget that your most important testimony is that which you give by your life. "Even so let your light shine before others; that they may see your good works, and glorify your Father who is in heaven!" Peter comforts some wives with the fact that they may gain their own husbands *without words* by their chaste behavior coupled with fear, by a meek and quiet spirit which is in the sight of both God and humanity of great price.

"O Master, let me walk with Thee
In lowly paths of service free;
Tell me Thy secret; help me bear
The strain of toil, the fret of care."

Lord, teach us to pray!

—LUKE 11:1

THERE is probably not a praying soul who has not prayed thus.

But most of us do not really know what we are praying for when we ask the Lord to teach us to pray. We are completely surprised, therefore, when the Lord fulfills our petition.

He sends us *distress*. For that is the simplest way to teach us to pray.

He leads us into *spiritual* distress, hiding Himself from us for a season, thus making plain to us how much our own piety is worth. Our whole spiritual life dries up and withers away: prayer, reading of the Bible, faith, love, repentance, the self-denying attitude of heart, and the willing spirit.

Perhaps He leads us at the same time into *temporal* distress. And when spiritual and temporal tribulations have overwhelmed us, we feel that our cup is filled to overflowing.

At such a time every sincere soul becomes acquainted with one of the aspects of prayer with which he has not been particularly well acquainted before. He learns that prayer is for the *helpless*. She learns to prostrate herself quietly before God, often without saying a word. He learns that prayer is to open the heart to Jesus, that He may enter into our every need.

If you are praying the Lord to teach you to pray, you must make it clear to yourself that you are praying for distress and tribulation.

Dare you *then* pray: "Lord, teach me to pray"?

Well, let us be honest and admit that we are afraid of tribulation and suffering, in fact, that we are afraid even of God.

But neither you nor I will be happy until we have committed ourselves into the pierced hands of the Lord Jesus. And in so doing we will enter voluntarily into the school of prayer which the Spirit has established for people who cannot pray as they ought.

And behold, there came a leper and worshipped him, saying, Lord, if thou wilt, thou canst make me clean. And he stretched forth his hand, and touched him, saying, I will; be thou made clean.

—MATTHEW 8:2-3

I will," replied Jesus.

These two words give us a picture of Jesus which is very edifying to meditate upon.

He stands, not only before the leper but before every one, saying gently and tenderly, lovingly and quietly: "I will."

It is not possible for any one of us to turn our eyes toward the eyes of Jesus in prayer without His answering at once: "I will."

Jesus *wills* that you should be saved.

And when He wills something, he *does* all that it is possible to do in order to bring it to pass. Note this: Jesus has done everything possible to save you.

He came from heaven to earth, to make it possible for you to go with Him from earth to heaven. He lived the life here on earth which you should have lived, and made right again all the wrong that you had done. In His soul and in His body He endured all the sufferings which you should have borne because of your sins. He died that you might live.

Then He arose from the dead and now lives in this world of ours as the Savior with all power. Now He *draws* all people unto Himself. That He might succeed in so doing, He was given all power in heaven and on earth.

You, too, have felt the drawing power of the love of Jesus. To such an extent that your whole life thus far has been one of continuous resistance to it.

Think of devoting your brief span of life to resisting and opposing the Lord Jesus! Think of wearing yourself out in hindering Jesus from drawing you unto Himself and up to heaven!

Oh, cast yourself down at the feet of Jesus today!

But he answered her not a word.

—MATTHEW 15:23

IT is as though we do not recognize Jesus in this account. The unhappy mother stands there and prays so humbly for her child. But he does not answer a word. Then the disciples begin to help her. And not until then does He reply that He has nothing to do with the Gentiles.

Still, He had made exceptions to this rule. The centurion of Capernaum, for instance, received help. Why did He not make an exception also of this unhappy mother?

She does not yield, however, but falls down at His feet and says despairingly: "Lord, help me!" Then He meets her with the harsh words about the dogs. The Jews looked upon the Gentiles as dogs. And He does not help her until she takes Him at His own word and tells Him that it is not necessary for Him to take the bread away from the children; for the little dogs can get along with the crumbs that fall from the table. All she asks for is such a crumb.

We, too, experience similar silence on the part of Jesus.

Distress drove you, also, to Jesus. You pleaded very humbly. Perhaps you, too, like the woman, prayed for a sick child. But you received no help. All He had to do was to move a finger and your child would have been well. But He did not. It was that which was so hard. Perhaps you began to murmur against God.

Our passage today tells us that Jesus saw your distress and suffered with you.

"But why did He not help me, then?" you ask.

What is hardest for Him also is that He does not dare to help you out of your temporal need. You would forget Him again. He has brought you to a point where you will listen to Him, and there is something He must tell you. He must get an opportunity to speak to you about the needs of your *soul,* which are greater than the temporal distress from which you are asking Him to save you.

> And he answered and said, It is not meet to take the
> children's bread and cast it to the dogs.
>
> —MATTHEW 15:26

W<small>E</small> considered briefly yesterday the *harsh silence* of Jesus.
Let us today consider for a little while His *harsh words*.

Jesus was determined to answer the woman's prayer. But
first He had to let her know who she was. That necessitated
a hard saying. But she did not take offense. She yielded to the
Lord and humbly sank down at His feet.

Perhaps you have experienced something similar. After you
have been confronted with unfathomable silence on the part
of Jesus, you have also had some hard sayings directed at you.

The woman listened and yielded. Will you do that?

If you will, your Savior will speak these earnest words to
you: When you are in temporal distress, you weep and plead
for help. But the distress of your soul does not move you. You
never think of God unless you need Him. It is selfishness that
impels you, even when you kneel in prayer. Moreover, you are
self-willed even in the presence of the Almighty. You *prescribe*
to Him what He should do. And if He does not do what you
want, you murmur against Him.

But is it not harsh to speak thus to you when you are in
distress? Yes, but love is hard when the loved one is in danger
of death and does not see it herself.

The woman yielded, was convicted by the truth of Jesus'
words and His manner of dealing with her, and committed
herself to His mercy. She was saved, not only from her temporal
distress, but also from her imperious and demanding spirit,
saved into a sinner's humble surrender to the grace of God.

Jesus would save you, too, from the greatest cause of your
distress, your lack of confidence in God, so that you calmly
and trustingly might leave the distress of both your soul and
your body in His pierced hands.

I am the vine, ye are the branches.

—JOHN 15:5

THE vine bears the branches, and the branches bear the fruit. This truth sheds a glorious light upon our task in life. We are to receive into our lives the living power of Christ, are to let it grow within us and mature into fresh fruit for Jesus.

The comforting thing in this is, then, that it is not a question of our talents, of our knowledge, of our powers, but of this one thing: Will we open our lives to that fulness of redemptive power which at all times waits to flow from the vine into the branches?

In the next place, it is comforting that it is not a question of whether I am a small or a large branch. The question of decisive importance is this: Am I a *living* branch?

At one time we were all living branches. In baptism we were grafted into Christ as little branches into the True Vine. But how are we today? Are we withered or are we living branches?

If we are living branches, we can bear fruit no matter where we are on the vine, either high up or low down. Only one thing matters: Are we in *our* place, the place where the Savior would have us?

When my travels had taken me so far into southern Europe that I could see vineyards, I noticed that the finest clusters of grapes were to be found on the branches lowest down. Do not be anxious, therefore, if your place is a humble one.

What do you think of first when you hear of fruit bearing? Perhaps we all think first of *work*. But God thinks first of other things: "The fruit of the Spirit is love, joy, peace, longsuffering, kindness, goodness, faithfulness, meekness, self-control."

God does not think first of the things we do, but of what we *are* and of the things we *suffer*. Now think of this today. And let the people with whom you associate enjoy some of the fruits, some of your love, joy, peace, longsuffering, and meekness. Then all of you will be happy today.

That the God of our Lord Jesus Christ, the Father of glory, may give unto you a spirit of wisdom and revelation in the knowledge of him, having the eyes of your heart enlightened.

—EPHESIANS 1:17-18

HERE we are told a little about the fulness of the Spirit. Spirit-filled persons are those who have had their eyes opened to see the realm of the invisible. The realm which surrounds us by day and by night but which few people know or have any consciousness of because most people lack the mind of the Spirit to see and to share in its rich, quiet life.

As soon as the Spirit is permitted to open the eyes of his heart, the sinner beholds Christ, His wounds and His blood, His suffering and death. More he does not need to behold in order to be blessedly assured that all his sins are blotted out.

The sinner sees in the Word the finished work of Christ and stands at the cross of Christ with all the sinfulness and uncleanness of her heart, secure and happy. She sees now that in herself she is completely lost, but she relies upon the glorious promise of God: "My grace is sufficient for thee." And the peace which passes all understanding descends upon her soul with its mighty bliss and divine protection.

With the eyes of his heart enlightened, the sinner looks at everything about him from a new point of view. He sees his dear ones in a different light, his friends and those who are opposed to him, his superiors and his subordinates, the prosperous and the needy.

But above all the sinner looks upon the unconverted in a different way. She sees straight through their outer shell and into the distress and anxiety of their souls. She sees their danger of being eternally lost.

But no one can "see" this without being filled with a great and holy passion, the passion of Christ for us.

> "Thine, O Jesus, now and ever,
> My desire and my endeavor,
> Thine to be in life, in death."

> And a certain man was there, who had been thirty
> and eight years in his infirmity. When Jesus saw him
> lying, . . . he saith unto him, Wouldest thou be made
> whole?
>
> —JOHN 5:5-6

SICK for thirty-eight years! And still Jesus asked the poor man if he wanted to become well?

Yes, because there was a direct connection between the man's sin and his illness. Therefore he had to choose. Jesus asked therefore: "Wouldest thou be made whole?"

Jesus stands every day before such sick people.

They have been ill for thirty-eight years, many twice as long. And their illness is worse than the infirmity from which this man was suffering. For their souls are sick. Sick unto death, eternal death.

They have suffered much, many unspeakable pains. For the soul is the most sensitive part of a person.

And in the whole wide world there is only one who can heal our soul's diseases.

That one is Jesus. With His own heart's blood He has won for us the only means by which the virus of sin can be driven out of the souls of those who are sick unto death.

Then, one day, He stands before the weary, suffering soul. Do we hear a heartrending cry to Him for help?

Nay. Now, as on that day at Bethesda, He must ask the sick one: "Wouldest thou be made whole?"

Most of those who are sick do *not* desire to be made whole. So they keep their sin—and their sufferings.

What do you choose?

If you knew the joy of having a soul made whole, a soul at peace with God and at war with sin, you would make the right decision this very day.

Every branch that beareth fruit, he cleanseth it, that
it may bear more fruit.

—JOHN 15:2

THE life of Jesus was full of love, joy, peace, longsuffering,
meekness. And it is His will that the world should benefit by
this through His disciples. They are the branches which receive
the life of Jesus in order to live this life out in the world.

It is this which is to *win* the world.

Therefore the *lives* of the disciples are more important than
their *work*.

The disciples of Jesus live only to bear fruit for Jesus. As
much fruit as possible. And Jesus, who has been given all power
in heaven and on earth, guides the history of our little lives
and directs everything in our daily walk with the one end in
view that we may bear as much fruit as possible.

That is what Jesus speaks of as cleansing or *pruning* the
branches. The pruning is intended to make the branches as
fruitful as possible.

If we reflected upon this a little, many of the things that
happen to us in life would be easier to bear. Many of the deepest
problems of our lives would be solved in a simple and edifying
way.

At some time or other we all meet with adversity or sufferings
so great that we cannot fathom or understand them at all. But
if we can look upon these things as the gardener's wise and
loving cleansing of the branches, we will be set free within,
even though outwardly the adversity and the suffering still
continue.

If a vine is not pruned, there will be no fruit, only foliage.
And if the Lord did not prune us, we would first become
spiritually barren, and thereafter die. We should thank the
Lord that He does not hear all of our many prayers to be spared
everything that is hard and heavy to bear.

We do not live in order to have a good time, but to bear
fruit. Unto the glory of the Lord. If we will remember this,
we will not be so surprised when the Gardener comes to us
also with His pruning knife.

153

Every branch that beareth fruit, he cleanseth it, that
it may bear more fruit.

—JOHN 15:2

To be cleansed, then, is necessary to the life of the branches.
All of us must be cleansed, as surely as we are branches.

When we think of this cleansing, we all tremble a bit. When
we look at our possessions—our dear ones, our health, our
work, our finances, our name and reputation—when we look
at all these things and think of the Gardener's coming to take
them one after the other, we all shudder.

But let us remember the following three things:

In the first place, the hand which holds the pruning knife
is pierced through for your sins. If you will remember this, you
will be more calm when He comes with the pruning knife.

In the next place, He never cuts away anything that would
benefit either you or His cause. He takes away only that which
would prove hurtful. And if you feel that what He takes is
indispensable to you, remember that He never takes more than
He gives in return.

In the third place, He prunes the branches at the right time.

The vine cannot stand to be pruned at any and all seasons
of the year. It would bleed to death.

Our Savior knows exactly when you can endure the cleansing. He has promised that with the temptation He will also
make a way of escape, that you may be able to endure.

When the vine-dresser has cleansed the vine, he covers the
incision, in order that the vine may not be destroyed. The
Gardener in the garden of God does likewise.

We all have memories of the wonderful tenderness which
He showed toward us during or after a particularly grievous
season of suffering. He poured a few drops of that remarkable
heavenly balm into our wound. And what we experienced
cannot be told in words.

The Holy Spirit, whom God hath given to them that
obey him.

—Acts 5:32

Our generation of Christians differs from preceding generations in many ways.

We are a hearing and speaking generation, a reading and
writing generation, a capable and industrious generation.

But I do not know if there are many in our midst who would
dare to say that we are a *Spirit-filled* generation of Christians.

The realm of the unseen is distant and unreal to us, notwithstanding all that we read and hear and know about it. It
impresses, captivates, and interests most of us only to a comparatively slight degree.

I gather this most clearly from the conversations I hear.

I am not now thinking only of the many empty and meaningless conversations which take place among Christian people.
I am thinking mostly of our conversations about *Christian*
themes. We speak of our *work* with fervor and enthusiasm. But
as soon as the conversation turns to *the hidden* life it grows dull.

How rare it is to meet believers who live such a rich inner
life with God that they need but open their mouths and let
quiet, fervent words come from their overflowing hearts.

In our day we know very little about walking in the Spirit
and overcoming the flesh. Wilfulness, craving for power, passionate love of honor, envy and slander are not only *unconquered*
but oftentimes *unacknowledged* sins in Christian circles.

God gives the Spirit only to those who obey Him. They
are not sinless folk, but they are such as permit themselves to
be *convicted* of their sins. And who have a *will* to overcome them.

" 'Tis true, Thy plants are there;
But, ah, how weak and rare!"

155

Except one be born anew, he cannot see the kingdom
of God. —JOHN 3:3

HERE we come in contact with Christianity's vital secret,
that which distinguishes Christian from all other religious life.

According to the Scriptures we are certain that our religious
longings are from God, and that the various religions of the
world represent the many attempts on the part of the human
race to satisfy its religious longings—attempts to think God,
to feel God, and to find God.

And, as far as they go, they have their significance as a
preparation for the "fulness of time," when God through His
revelation meets people and saves them.

The experience of God, fellowship with God, we find only
in Christianity. "No one cometh unto the Father, but by me,"
Jesus says.

This, then, is the vital secret of Christianity, that we in Christ
have that life in God which all the other religions have had
intimations of and have sought, but have never experienced.

The Christian's religion does not consist in the religious
self-exertion, of the reaching out toward a holy and distant
God. The religious secret consists in this, that God Himself
has come down and lifted the Christian up into most intimate
and blessed fellowship with Himself. This is the mighty miracle
of the new birth.

"How gladly I my place have taken
Among the flock of God's elect!
With them I have the world forsaken
And Jesus' coming now expect.
Redeemed by His unbounded love,
My home will be with Christ above."

Marvel not that I said unto thee, Ye must be born
anew.

—JOHN 3:7

THE new birth is undoubtedly Christianity's greatest *stumbling-block.* Even the noble and pious Nicodemus was startled
when Jesus told him in plain language that he could not enter
the kingdom of God without being born anew.

To the natural person there is scarcely any aspect of Christianity which is more unintelligible and more offensive than
that of the new birth. Irritated and angry, people say to themselves, and some also to others:

"Can God demand more of people than their best—that
they pray, and read, and listen to the Word of God, strive
against their sins and do good deeds as far as their time, ability,
and means will permit? Can God demand more? Is He not
just? Is it not even said that He is merciful?"

The new birth is the point at which Christianity differs most
radically from all other religions. They all say to humanity,
each in its own way: You shall become good. Do good, and
you will become good—perfectly good!

Over against these Christ stands alone and says: You are
wicked. And you cannot *do* that which is good until you have
become good. For it is the attitude of heart which makes a deed
either good or bad.

He tells Nicodemus, therefore, that he must be born anew
in order to acquire the good attitude of heart which alone can
perform deeds that are good.

The message concerning the new birth is thus the greatest
moral requirement, the highest moral ideal, which has been
raised in this world of ours.

But at the same time it is the most glorious Gospel which
can resound in any sinner's ears. If we have come to realize
that we do not love God and do not hate sin, then it is
good news that we can *receive* this attitude of heart. As a gift
from God.

157

> That which is born of the flesh is flesh; and that
> which is born of the Spirit is spirit.
>
> —JOHN 3:6

WHAT is the reason that people will not repent?

Oh, there are perhaps many and various reasons. But the real reason no doubt is that they think that Christianity will rob them of their joy and happiness.

If one is to become a Christian, they say, one must *cease* doing nearly everything that one desires to do—cease dancing, drinking, playing cards, attending the theater, and so forth. And one must *begin* to do things that one has no desire to do—begin to pray every day, in fact, many times a day, go to church every Sunday, associate with believers who, on the average, are good enough people, but who are too narrow-minded and boresome. Whenever they come together they feel that they must read and sing and pray!

Most people in our country think that the ideal way of living is to "enjoy life," as they say, as long as life lasts. And then, when one becomes sick or aged, to make one's peace with God, receive the sacrament of the Lord's Supper, die a beautiful death, and have the minister give an impressive eulogy.

Their lives show that this is the way they think.

Here is where the misunderstanding lies.

They think that Christianity consists in compelling people, with their old carnal and unwilling minds, to give up a number of things that they desire to do and to do a number of things that they do not wish to do.

But this has never been Christianity, only a weak *imitation* of real Christianity.

This is unregenerate humanity's attempt to serve God with its old, unwilling mind.

One becomes a Christian only by a divine miracle: the new birth.

Wherefore if any man is in Christ, he is a new creature.

—2 CORINTHIANS 5:17

To become a Christian is such a great and mighty thing that it cannot take place except the triune God intervene to perform a miracle: the new birth.

This miracle consists in God's bringing forth a new *creation*, our Word tells us today. He brings forth something that we do not have, the attitude of heart which loves God and hates sin.

There stands a sinner. By the miracle of the divine call he has begun to see that he does not love God and does not hate sin. He has tried to change this attitude of his, but knows that this is impossible. In his distress he now turns to the Lord and tells Him this desperate truth. Then the miracle takes place.

The Savior takes the sin-stained wretch up out of the mire and cleanses him in His blood. Then He lifts the trembling soul up to His knee, throws His eternal arms about him, whispers into his despairing soul: "Be of good cheer, thy sins are forgiven!"

As a rule, a period of time elapses before the sincere soul can apprehend that which is told her. But in God's appointed time the light dawns upon her. She sees that Jesus has died for her sins and that she is a child of God.

Then she feels as though her soul would burst with rejoicing. Now no one needs to ask her to love God. Her heart is full of grateful love to Her merciful Father.

The new thing has now come to pass in this person's heart. She *loves* God. That was what she did not do before. Then she was *afraid* of God when He was near and indifferent toward Him when He was far away.

"Any one who is in Christ is a new creature; the old things are passed away; behold, they are become new!"

> Wherefore if any man is in Christ, he is a new
> creature: the old things are passed away; behold, they
> are become new.
>
> —2 Corinthians 5:17

At the new birth God puts into our souls *a new power* with which to wage warfare against our sins.

Worldly people, too, struggle against their sins. But in a worldly way. They struggle against sin because of the unpleasant and dangerous consequences of sin. Sin itself they love; but they do not dare to commit it because by so doing they injure themselves.

At the new birth a change takes place in this regard. Sin itself becomes our enemy. To offend against God now becomes the worst feature of sin, because we love God.

Do not misunderstand me. Those who are born anew are not sinless. As long as we live here on earth "the flesh will lust against the Spirit and the Spirit against the flesh," as the apostle says.

We will therefore experience an unwillingness to pray and read the Bible also after the new birth; we will feel slothfulness and an unwillingness to do the will of God. Yes, we will even experience the desire to sin.

However, we know now that there is only one way in which we can overcome our sins, namely, by having the love of God shed abroad in our hearts again.

Now we will confess before Him that we fell because our love became lukewarm. And we will pray to Him that He will take us to His heart again and warm us thoroughly with His love.

This is the real secret of sanctification.

It does not take place by the will of the flesh, nor by the human will, but only by God. It is only an *experience* of Christ that can, after we have been defeated, give us the right inner attitude toward sin again. It is only love toward God that can make sin painful to us.

Behold what manner of love the Father hath bestowed upon us, that we should be called children of God.

—1 JOHN 3:1

Y ES, let us behold this a little while today!

Let us behold the grace of God by which we are saved into the *relationship of sonship*. He would not have us slaves who tremble at the voice of their master and are unwilling to do even the least that He commands.

Nay, He transforms His enemies into friends. He sets us free from the spirit of bondage and gives us the spirit of adoption by which we cry confidently, Abba, Father! And by which we rejoice to know and to follow the will of the Father.

What grace from God that He saves us in *this* way!

He woos us away from sin and from our former manner of life. Can you imagine anything more beautiful?

With the glow of His love He melts the chains which bind us to sin. In His unfathomable love He entreats us to cast ourselves into His open arms. With this same love He gives us courage to acknowledge the truth to Him and make full confession of everything.

From that moment He can begin to reveal to us the glory of the entire realm of the invisible.

By His love He draws us steadily farther and farther into this invisible realm. And the more we become acquainted in this realm of the divine, the easier it becomes for us to deny sin, the more circumspect we become with respect to everything sinful.

We experience a new wealth of life which enables us willingly and gladly to surrender the old.

Behold what manner of love the Father hath bestowed upon us!

"O Love that wilt not let me go,
I rest my weary soul in Thee;
I give Thee back the life I owe,
That in Thine ocean depths its flow
May richer, fuller be."

161

Nicodemus answered and said unto him, How can these things be?

I AM prepared to hear some one say: "I have begun to seek God; I tell Him everything and conceal or spare no sin from Him. But the things you have described during the past week as God's new creation, these things I have not experienced. Not the nearness of God, not the peace and rest, not the joy and bliss, not the aversion toward sin, and not the desire to do the will of God. What I have experienced so far has been principally fear and restlessness, even anxiety, with a few brief seasons of rest between.

"What then is my condition?"

In reply I would say first that every birth is painful. And the spiritual pains which you are experiencing in the form of restlessness, doubt, fear, and anxiety, are *birth* pains.

The Holy Spirit is in the full process of creating the new life within you. But this new life cannot be *born* unless the old at the same time *dies*.

That which you are now experiencing, the pain and restlessness of your soul, is *life's* beginning: *death*. You must be made aware of the sinful things in your life and in your heart, that these things must die. Only to see this is a terrifying experience which may well cause you despair.

But do not permit yourself to become frightened or bewildered. It is the work of God in your soul. It is painful, but necessary. Thank your merciful God who is now putting to death your old life and transforming you into a soul that hungers for His grace.

And remember this: you *experienced* the new birth the moment you turned in all sincerity to your Savior and confessed your sins. But that which you have felt so far is essentially only the *mortifying* aspect of this birth.

But it, too, is part and parcel of the vital secret of Christianity.

Thou foolish one, this night is thy soul required of thee.

—LUKE 12:20

As a little boy I thought there was something unmerciful about this story. Was not the man a good farmer? Did he not farm so well that his buildings were too small to take care of the crops?

Since that time I have begun to see how merciful Jesus is, also in this parable. It was not what the man did that brought him misfortune. It was what he did *not* do. The closing words of Jesus make this clear: "So is he that layeth up treasure for himself, and *is not rich toward God.*"

Every human being has the urge to *possess* something, therefore also the desire to *acquire* property. Many seek to attain this without work, by deceit, fraud, or force. But most people seek to acquire property by honest effort.

And such honest and capable effort is a vital factor in all human life, in the life of the individual, the home, and society at large. Let us thank God for all the diligent, capable, and conscientious effort that is put forth in our country, both by men and by women, both at home and away from home.

God's benediction and blessing is upon this work. God knows, however, that most people look at the wealth they are seeking to acquire for themselves in a wrong light. They are so occupied with laying up *earthly* treasures that they forget the *heavenly.*

It is this about which Jesus would speak with us today. He would tell us how *poor* that person is who is not rich toward God.

In this parable Jesus would illustrate this poverty by showing us that death takes all that we possess if we have naught but earthly treasures.

Are you rich toward God? Have you become poor in spirit, so that Christ has been able to make you the possessor of the whole kingdom of God?

Take heed, and keep yourselves from all covetousness!

—LUKE 12:15

THIS is a word to the friends of Jesus.

Both the Scriptures and experience prove to us that money is one of the very greatest temptations that come to God's people. Avarice is the hidden virus which quietly but surely destroys the life in God for many a child of the heavenly Father.

Jesus speaks not only of *avarice*, but also of *covetousness*. Are not these the same sins? Yes, essentially they are. But they manifest themselves in ways that differ to such a degree that many think they have been delivered from covetousness when they have only been set free from avarice.

The difference is this: the avaricious person desires money in order to *accumulate* it, while the covetous person desires money in order to *use* it. Common to both of them is *greed for money*, the *worship of mammon*.

To Jesus our *attitude* of heart is the important thing. It is for this reason that He would destroy our inner dependence on money.

"Take heed," Jesus says today.

Will you take heed to yourself? Will you look into your relationship to your money? Would you like to know whether you are covetous or not?

Here it is of vital importance that we search ourselves with uncompromising sincerity. Do not let yourself be fooled by the fact that you are poor. Poor persons can be slaves of mammon just as well as wealthy persons. Their hearts can beat in continuous worship of the money they do not have, but always hope to get.

Do not let yourself be fooled, either, into confusing *avarice* with *thrift*.

Stingy persons always excuse themselves by saying that they are practicing thrift.

It is your attitude of heart which determines whether you are avaricious or thrifty.

Will you investigate the motive for your thriftiness?

164

Take heed, and keep yourselves from all covetousness!

—LUKE 12:15

W<small>E</small> spoke yesterday about avarice and thrift.

This is a difficult subject, difficult in its relationship to living, and difficult to write about. It is easy to speak of avarice in such a way that we undermine the sense of thrift.

God wants us to be thrifty, contented, and careful in the use of the gifts He bestows upon us, that nothing may be lost, as Jesus said to His disciples after He had fed the multitude in the wilderness.

Never has it been more necessary to be thrifty than at the present time. Nothing but economy, thrift, and work can put the world back on its feet again.

We might well ask if any generation has been less accustomed to thrift than ours. The prosperous times that we have had during the past century have made us all extravagant and demanding.

Here we Christians should take the lead and live industrious, economical, and thrifty lives in the midst of the poverty and distress of our times.

But, says Jesus, we should take heed and keep ourselves from covetousness and avarice.

Avaricious people are thrifty. Their sin does not consist in the things they do, but in their attitude. It is their motive for being thrifty which is sinful.

Misers save in order to accumulate wealth for themselves and their nearest of kin, to brood over their wealth and to find elation in so doing.

The thrifty person saves, in the first place, in order not to become a burden to any one, and, in the second place, to have something with which to help others.

Would you know whether you are saving because of miserliness or not, then look into your giving. Or still better: Ask yourself if you dare to take counsel with God with regard to your financial affairs. Dare you ask Him how much of your income you should give away? He who does that is not avaricious.

> If any man would come after me, let him deny
> himself, and take up his cross, and follow me.
> —MATTHEW 16:24

Of those people who would be Christians there are two kinds. They are the happy and the unhappy.

The unhappy ones are no doubt in the majority.

They *want* to be Christians. They cannot live without God. They pray, they read and hear the Word of God. They seek the fellowship of believers. They strive against their sins. They do good deeds, take part in Christian work, and oftentimes contribute not a little to the work of the kingdom.

Spiritually they do not experience a great deal. However, now and then they do have some blessed moments in which they experience unspeakable things.

But in their daily lives they are not happy.

In reality, Christianity is a burden to them. A source of annoyance, an effort. A source of inner grief and restlessness. A bad conscience which often brings gloom into an otherwise bright and happy life.

Nevertheless they would not be without this burden.

For they want to be saved. And they can be saved only by clinging to Christ.

But they have no peace of soul, no joy in the Lord. They have no desire to pray. No need of the Word of God. They participate in Christian work, but without joy and inner willingness to do so. And they make their contributions because they feel that they cannot very well not do it.

When mention is made of the joy of the children of God, they feel that they have been cheated, or they subtract in the quiet of their own minds from that which is said and make it fit their own inner state.

To them Christianity is easily identified with *lofty phrases.*

These unhappy souls have tried the impossible: to follow Jesus with their old heart, with an unwilling spirit.

They would *save* their life. But Jesus says that only those who would *lose* their life shall *find* it.

Whosoever shall lose his life for my sake shall find it.

—MATTHEW 16:25

YESTERDAY we spoke of unhappy people. Today let us speak of happy ones.

Many of the latter do not have much temporal happiness. Oftentimes they are both poor and sick. Oftentimes, too, their homes are filled with adversity and trials.

Nor are people always kind to them. For which there may be good reasons. They are not faultless; they make mistakes, both in their own homes and elsewhere.

But they are happy.

Theirs is a remarkable happiness. It is not confined to festive occasions and meetings of various kinds, with music and exalted sentiment.

Nay, they are happy also in their daily lives.

The better we learn to know them, the more we see how happy they are. They are *experiencing* something, something which fills their lives and makes them rich, notwithstanding all their adversity, mistakes, and failures.

What do these people have? What do the joyless lack?

The joyless feel that the requirements of Christ are hard and unreasonable, and they rebel against the Spirit of God constantly.

The happy souls have felt this, too. But they have yielded; they have surrendered unconditionally and without haggling. And have been *saved* from their old selves and their old attitudes, saved into a new attitude which is *willing* to renounce sin and practice self-denial.

And when their old attitudes break through again and they find that they are not willing to deny themselves, they confess this to their Savior. And are saved anew.

This is why they are so happy and so rich. They experience continually the miracle-working grace of the Lord.

167

> For what shall a man be profited, if he shall gain the
> whole world, and forfeit his life?
>
> —MATTHEW 16:26

PEOPLE care well for their bodies. If they have injured them, they seek medical aid immediately.

But most people pay no attention to their souls. They live as though they did not have a soul. And the soul is, after all, the immortal part of us.

Jesus speaks to us today about forfeiting our lives, about injuring our souls.

What does He mean by this?

He does not only mean that our souls are sick. At the fall of humanity we all became infected with the virus of sin. And therefore the souls of all of us are sick unto death.

Jesus has more than this in mind when He speaks of injuring our souls or forfeiting our lives. He has provided a means of healing us from our deadly affliction, an absolutely unfailing remedy, namely, the atoning blood which cleanses from all sin.

The injury of soul of which Jesus here speaks takes place when we are offered this means of healing but refuse it. If we continue to refuse it, our souls will at last be damaged in such a manner that even the blood of Jesus cannot save it.

My thoughtless friend! Do not imperil your immortal soul any longer!

I know you are thinking of all that you will lose if you take up your cross and follow Jesus. You think of the pleasures you must give up, of the friends who will forsake you. You think of the many advantages you will miss when you can no longer resort to "white" lies.

Indeed, it is well that you count the cost. But why do you never think of what you will *win* when you take up your cross and follow Jesus? You will not win temporal benefits, but you will win a saved soul and hope, hope for the life which now is, hope in death, and hope for all the eternities to come.

And in his name shall the Gentiles hope.

—MATTHEW 12:21

For thousands of years the chosen people had lived in *hope*. God had promised to send His people a Deliverer.

When at last He was born in Bethlehem, He came as the hope of Israel. And throughout His earthly life He made it clear that He was sent to the lost sheep of the house of Israel. Among them He walked, all His days, among suffering souls and ailing bodies. And hope grew wherever He walked.

But He is not only the hope of Israel.

In Him the Gentiles also hope. Without knowing Him, without having heard of Him, all the Gentiles, too, have secret hopes of an emancipator. In Athens Paul found an altar to an *unknown* god.

At all events Christ is the fulfillment of our soul's deepest needs.

As soon as He had risen from the tomb, He gave His disciples the command to go out to *all nations* with the glad tidings of the Gospel of Him in whom they had all hoped and to whom they had all looked with longing.

The spiritual awakening in Sychar, John 4, and the desire of the Greeks, John 12, had shown Him that the Gentiles waited with earnest expectation. This has been confirmed in every place reached by the Christian missionary enterprise. The great apostle to the Gentiles had to witness the turning away of his own people from the Messiah while the Gentiles streamed to Him in multitudes.

But the world is large and the number of Gentiles great.

And the friends of Jesus have not been as zealous as their Lord in bringing the light to those who sit in the shadow of death. Today two-thirds of the people on earth have not as yet heard that God has become incarnate, that sin is expiated, and that they who will may be saved.

Let us all think about this today!

To do so will profit both ourselves and the cause of missions.

Leave the dead to bury their own dead; but go thou
and publish abroad the kingdom of God.

—LUKE 9:60

Many are of the opinion that Jesus was harsh in His dealings
with these three men. The one wanted to go home first and
bury his father. The other would first have bidden his parents
good-bye.

But Jesus did not accede to this. He uttered only this brief
and hard saying: "Leave the dead to bury their own dead!"

Was Jesus harsh?

Yes, love is harsh, irrevocably harsh when the loved one is
in mortal danger and is not willing to recognize it.

Jesus saw the danger which confronted these men. He saw
how near to the kingdom of God they were. But He also saw
their good-natured weakness, their persistent flight from decisive action.

In love and mercy He sought now to help them out of this.
He demanded an immediate decision. They had their liberty
and might decide as they chose. But He insisted that they
decide. They were always wanting to do something else first.
"No," says Jesus, "now or never!"

There are many people today to whom Jesus would say
exactly the same thing if they would only listen to Him. They
remain in a spiritually awakened state year after year, always
restless and often much affected. At times they almost do
violence to themselves in order not to cast themselves down
at the feet of Jesus and have their restless souls saved. Still
they never really become converted!

My unhappy friend! Tell me, what is it that binds you? Is
it some certain sin?

Then do tell Jesus the truth. He sets the sin-bound free.

> "He who alone can cheer you
> Is standing at the door;
> He brings His pity near you,
> And bids you weep no more."

170

A certain man made a great supper; and he bade many.

—Luke 14:16

God is making preparations for a great festival. It is to take place in heaven, and it is intended for the whole world. An eternal festival. So Jesus tells us today.

Yes, it is to be a festival indeed!

We get an intimation of this simply by looking about us these days. Have you not observed how God is again decking nature as unto a festival? The grass is growing in every meadow, in every crack and crevice. The grain is sprouting in the fields. And there are the flowers, odoriferous, bright and smiling. Birds are singing in every bush, praising their Creator. Bees buzz from flower to flower and gather their honey. Wherever one turns one sees the finest of forms and colors, and the air is filled with wondrous fragrance.

Think, then, of what it will be when God decks His *heaven* for a festival!

Everything that we read in the Bible about the preparations for this festival tells us that God is happy as He goes about His preparations. And the angels, too, for they have a part in the preparations also.

Our Word for today tells us that all things are now ready.

Then why does not the festival begin? We are told that, too. It all depends upon the *guests*. Those who were bidden have not come. He would have us all present. He is waiting for us.

We who are sitting here together today are all bidden. The invitation came to us as soon as we were born. In Baptism. There we all received an invitation written in God's own hand-writing. Let us join hands firmly and sing together:

> "Fair are the meadows,
> Fairer the woodlands,
> Robed in flow'rs of blooming spring;
> Jesus is fairer;
> Jesus is purer;
> He makes our sorrowing spirits sing."

171

And they all with one consent began to make excuse.

—LUKE 14:18

WHEN a beloved crown prince is married, people will travel long distances just to *see* it. The few who are invited speak of it with pride for a long time, both before and after the wedding. But when God invites people to a feast, they all begin to make excuses. The first one excuses herself for business reasons, the other on account of his farming interests, and a third because of marital relations.

What have you used for an excuse?

You cannot excuse yourself for business reasons as yet, perhaps, but you have another excuse. You are too young.

You have no farming interests to offer as an excuse, but you do have your friends.

As yet you cannot offer marriage as an excuse, but you might offer your pleasures.

You know, of course, that these are only pretexts.

The *real* reason for your declining the invitation to the heavenly feast is this: *You do not desire to go.* You despise the invitation. And that has a terrible implication: You despise Him who bids you come.

"Come; for all things are now ready," said the servants to those who were bidden.

Yes, all things are ready. But think of what it cost God to prepare a feast in heaven for sinners! He had to come down from His throne. He had to descend from heaven. He had to be born in a manger and die on a cross. He had to endure the anguish of hell and the torture of being forsaken by God.

But when He could cry out on the cross: "It is finished!"— then all things were ready for the feast. Now He could invite every sinner on earth.

Even today the good tidings go out: "Yet there is room."

> For out of the heart come forth evil thoughts,
> murders, adulteries, fornications, thefts, false
> witness, railings.
>
> —MATTHEW 15:19

HUMANITY fills the world with its sins. Sins of every kind and degree.

Conscious and unconscious sin. Individual and social sin. National and international sin.

Open sin and secret sin. Sin that is afraid, which hides itself in the darkness. And bold sin, committed on the wide open streets.

Oh, how people sin in this world! What must not God look upon, day and night! That He can endure us! He is indeed inscrutable, also when viewed from this aspect.

But the worst thing about humanity is not that it *does* that which is sinful.

The heart which people carry in their bosom is worse than all the sin which they commit.

From within, from out of the heart, come forth evil thoughts, Jesus says.

Behold, here Jesus has pointed out the low-lying and incessantly flowing spring from which sin inundates the earth and makes a floodgate to hell.

And still the worst thing about the heart is not that it is full of sin.

The worst thing about the heart is its hardness. Its antipathy and rebelliousness toward God. It is hard by nature. And it makes itself harder and harder toward God.

Most people live their lives far away from God. Think only of the large percentage of our people which, practically speaking, never hears the Word of God.

That is too bad. But even worse is the fact that they desire to be so far away from God. They would avoid God and His Word.

O God of grace, have mercy upon our beloved nation!

I am the voice of one crying in the wilderness, Make straight the way of the Lord.

—JOHN 1:23

A REMARKABLE expression! One crying in the *wilderness*. We would no doubt rather have suggested: one crying in the city, in the capital city.

But it says: in the wilderness. And that fits the situation. Has not the preaching of the gospel throughout all these centuries been a cry in the wilderness? There have always been only a few who have heard and heeded the divine call.

A cry in the wilderness! Is not this the case also with those who pause and give heed to the cry? Are not their hearts only a barren and unfruitful wilderness?

Only listen to what such persons say to themselves: What should I do? With my mind I realize that I ought to be converted. For the risk involved is great; it involves eternity. But I am worldly. And I dread the thought of having to pray to God and read the Bible every day.

Poor soul whose condition is such, this is terrible. But even worse is the fact that you once were moved to become a Christian, but would not turn to God. You postponed the whole matter indefinitely.

Now you are experiencing the consequences of this.

And the worst is that it will not end here. You will become still more indifferent. At last you will become so careless that you will not even go to hear the Word.

But what shall I do, you ask.

Well, there is not *much* that you can do. Only one thing. But if you *would* do that!

You can acknowledge before God what a wilderness your heart has become. And ask Him to cry out in the wilderness of your heart, cry out the mighty and divine Word that creates what it names.

Then you, too, will no doubt become earnestly concerned about your soul.

For the joy of Jehovah is your strength.

—NEHEMIAH 8:10

WE are created to be happy.

That is why joy has such a releasing effect upon us. Only to meet a person who is truly happy is to be made glad.

Never do we have such strength as when we are happy; never do we get so much accomplished. Never are we better able to endure the adversities of life. Never is it so easy to be forbearing with those who grieve and offend us.

Joy is undoubtedly one of the secret powers of life itself. The doctors tell us that the sick never become well so readily and quickly as when they are happy.

The imperfection of our joy comes to light most clearly by the fact that it is not enduring.

This is due to the nature of our joy. We gradually tire of some things which fill us with joy for a time. We feel empty. And the more of such happiness we have had, the more difficult it becomes for us to feel glad again. But at the same time we yearn ever more for joy.

Our Word for today tells us that there is a joy which does not lose its capacity for making us happy and does not cause us to lose our taste for happiness.

This joy is the joy of the Lord.

This joy no one knows save those who have dared to admit to themselves what an empty and joyless life they have been living, who have found peace for their insincere and guilt-laden hearts at the cross of Christ. And even these people lose their joy again the very moment they forget their sinfulness and no longer appreciate having their names written in heaven.

God, let me see that I myself am sinful and that Thou art gracious, so that I may have no greater joy than to behold the Lamb of God.

And make me a partaker in Thy joy, Thou who hast only one joy from eternity to eternity, that of making others happy! Amen.

And not many days after, the younger son gathered
all together and took his journey into a far country.

—LUKE 15:13

INTO a far country!

Jesus would show in his parable how far away from God
most people live their lives, without knowledge or thought of
the love of God.

Perhaps such a person is present in our circle today.

You have many interests. Good and noble interests, which
occupy your time and fill your soul. You have much joy, in
your work and otherwise. Clean and beautiful joy, which en-
riches your soul life and ennobles your character. You have
been spared, fortunately, the impure and debasing joys which
ruined the young man of the parable.

But you who are so keenly interested in everything in life,
what attitude do you take toward God and His love?

No doubt you never think of it. Now and then, of course,
you hear about it. What effect does it have upon you? Probably
it does not move you in the least. Rather, you perhaps smile
a little at the thought of these people who are always thinking
about God and His love.

Nevertheless, I would have you hear today the unbelievable,
the incomprehensible: God loves you, notwithstanding all your
sinfulness, all your indifference, all your ingratitude, all your
rebelliousness.

Moreover, mine is the privilege of proclaiming to you something even more unbelievable: This love which God has for
you will follow you wherever you go in life, no matter whither
you flee from the living God.

I would have you know also that there is a day coming when
you, too, will need this love. When the famine in the far
country will become so great that you will not know what to
do with your tortured soul.

God grant that you may awake in the time of grace! Before
it is eternally too late.

176

What man of you, having a hundred sheep, and having lost one of them, doth not leave the ninety and nine in the wilderness, and go after that which is lost, until he find it?

—LUKE 15:4

WE have spoken of those people who make use of the love of God as a means of wriggling away from religion, and who smile at the whole thing.

But there are others who do not smile.

They are never many in number. Jesus gives figurative expression to this in the parable when He speaks of the one and the ninety and nine.

Listen now, you lonely, fearful lost soul: Jesus loves you.

No, He does not love me, you say. He is angry with me. And rightfully so. I have never done anything but sin against Him.

Yes, you are right. If you were to receive according to what you have merited, you would have nothing to hope for. However, Jesus has taken upon Himself that which you should have suffered. "He was wounded for our transgressions, he was bruised for our iniquities; the chastisement of our peace was upon him; and with his stripes we are healed."

Such is *His* love toward you.

That is why He was so grieved when you went away from Him. He has sought you day and night. Have you not heard Him call?

Yes, you have. And it makes you restless. It is then that sin becomes such a burden to you. It is then that you begin to long for God, for reconciliation and forgiveness.

But how shall I find the way to God, you ask.

That you cannot do. Nor has God asked you to do that. It is He who seeks you. And now He has found you. Now the only question is: Will you yield and not run away from Him any more? If so, He will lay you on His shoulder and carry you home.

That is what it means to be converted.

177

And as Jesus passed by from thence, he saw a man, called Matthew, sitting at the place of toll: and he saith unto him, Follow me. And he arose, and followed him.

—MATTHEW 9:9

A SPIRITUAL awakening was in progress in Capernaum. Matthew, the tax collector, had also heard Jesus. And he had been deeply moved. It was all so strange. As he stood there in the crowd and listened, it seemed as though all the many and grievous sins he had committed passed in review before his inner eye. He had never before experienced anything like it.

And as he stood there he observed the happy people who had turned to Jesus. He knew most of them. They were fishermen from the city and vicinity.

Now Matthew sat at the place of toll again. He was supposed to work, but that was impossible. He could not keep from thinking about this remarkable prophet of God and His joyous disciples. Again and again it occurred to him how blessed it would be if *he*, too, could follow Jesus.

But *that* was impossible. He had fallen into exceedingly evil repute by accepting a position as a tax collector against the admonitions of his father and mother. As a result of this he, as well as all the other publicans of his day, was despised by all the Jews. Probably it was not possible for Jesus to accept a publican, either, he thought. Although Jesus was not like other people.

At this point Matthew was interrupted in his thinking. Some one was standing in the doorway. Matthew turned mechanically to expedite the business at hand.

But behold, there stood Jesus! At first Matthew was as though paralyzed with fear. What did Jesus want of him?

But Jesus looked at him in a friendly way and said, "Follow me."

At once Matthew became the happiest man in Capernaum.

They that are whole have no need of a physician,
but they that are sick.   —MATTHEW 9:12

WE noted yesterday how Matthew was converted.

Since that time many a publican and sinner has been converted. Also among us.

And He is calling more of them. That is why there are so many restless and brooding publicans and sinners also today.

And Jesus has come into your life.

Perhaps just as quietly as He entered the life of Matthew. Was it during a spiritual awakening, or in the quiet of some night, or at the deathbed of your child, or when your spouse, within the very portals of death, heard your solemn vow?

Since that time you have thought heavy thoughts and experienced fervent longings. I do not know what has caused you the most anxiety: your great sins, your difficult problems, or your cowardly and vacillating attitude.

You cannot understand your lack of will power at all. At times you are very much concerned about becoming converted. But then it all escapes you again. And your cowardice and fear of people! You cannot understand how God can help any one who is as cowardly and lacking in will power as you are.

Listen now to the words of Jesus: "They that are whole have no need of a physician, but they that are sick." He can successfully treat every ailment, including yours.

Lie down quietly at the feet of the Physician and tell Him all that ails your conscience. If you knew what Jesus offers you when He says, "Follow me," that He offers you fellowship with Him throughout all of life, you would stretch out both of your hands toward Him and say:

"Oh, take my hand, dear Father,
And lead Thou me,
Till at my journey's ending
I dwell with Thee.
Alone I dare not journey
One single day,
So do Thou guide my footsteps
On life's rough way."

And it came to pass, as he sat at meat in the house, behold many publicans and sinners came and sat down with Jesus and his disciples.

—MATTHEW 9:10

MATTHEW could not keep to himself the joy which he experienced when Jesus visited him at the place of toll. He had to share it with others. That was why he invited Jesus to his home, arranged a great banquet, and invited his colleagues and friends, all of whom were publicans and sinners. They, too, must see and hear Jesus and be saved into the same peace and joy which he had found.

Behold, how active the new mind has already become! Love is always full of solicitude. And love always finds a way. How beautiful and full of promise it is to see the zeal of new converts. As soon as they, by the grace of God, have become concerned about the salvation of their own souls, they are filled with solicitude for the salvation of their dear ones and their friends.

There are many who have been won by the fervent and active solicitude of their newly converted friends. One publican wins another. One fisherman, another fisherman. One youth wins another young person.

As I see it, Jesus planned that His kingdom should be extended in just this way. Was not that the way He Himself worked! He did not give very many addresses. During the two or three years that He worked in Palestine He was occupied mostly in private conversation with individual souls. No doubt that is the way the seventy were to have worked throughout the country also.

Jesus said once: "I came to cast fire upon the earth, and now would I that it were already kindled" (marginal reading).

This fire was to be spread by the setting on fire of one person by another.

Is anybody being set on fire by you?

> For we are his workmanship, created in Christ Jesus
> for good works, which God afore prepared that we
> should walk in them.
>
> —EPHESIANS 2:10

THE purpose of our being saved is here set before us. Most of us, no doubt, at some time or other in life, have thought that we were saved *to be made happy.* What else do awakened souls sigh for and seek after but to be made happy?

But nay, we are not saved in order to be made happy. That a saved person becomes happy is another matter. In fact, it is inescapable.

Nor are we saved in order to *find peace,* although in God's appointed time we find that also. For Jesus has also purchased and won this for us by His anguish. "The chastisement of our peace was upon him."

We are not even saved in order that we may *take up the fight against sin,* although none of us can refrain from doing battle against our sins as soon as we have been saved.

We are saved *to do good deeds,* our Word for today says.

Paul was afraid of legalistic works, but not of good works. These works are valuable, and not only because they are good. They are God's own works, worked in us by God's own Spirit. They are valuable also as weapons against sin.

My dear child of God, you who strive so hopelessly against your sins, listen: Do good deeds. Be gentle and kind to people and to beasts, yes, to plants also. You will discover that this is a very effective antidote to all sinful desire.

Good works, which God afore prepared.

They are near at hand. Do not therefore seek for something distant, something out of the ordinary. Seek first the good works which wait for you in your *home.*

First of all, *friendliness.* You can scarcely render a greater service to those with whom you associate from day to day than to be friendly toward them.

Be ye merciful, even as your Father is merciful.

—LUKE 6:36

GOD is merciful.

That was the new thing that Jesus brought. A merciful God was unknown to the then known world. The people of culture in those days vacillated between the belief of the Stoics in silent resignation and the doctrine of Aristotle concerning God as the heartless onlooker at the law-bound movements of the world in its course.

The common people looked upon God as a capricious and terrible tyrant.

And the Jews—of course they had the revelation of God and the sacred Scriptures. But the scribes and the Pharisees had obscured the meaning of the Word by their intricate interpretations to such an extent that people knew only a strict and zealous God who was so exalted above all things and all people in this wicked world that a human being did not even dare to mention His name.

Then Jesus came.

He did not only *say* that God was merciful. He *showed* it in His person, in His life, in His miracles, in His forgiveness of sin, in His sufferings, and in His death.

Like the Good Samaritan, He associated with the fearful and weary souls among humanity. And comfort and hope sprang up and grew along the way wherever He went.

God is merciful.

That is the good news which comes to every generation. Also to ours. For two generations people have been bending the knee to the immutable law of cause and effect, to the blind forces of nature, and to unmerciful natural laws. Modern humanity has lost sight of an almighty, loving, and merciful God.

Listen now to the glad tidings: God is merciful.

That I may know him, and the power of his resurrection.

—PHILIPPIANS 3:10

HERE we meet one who believed in the resurrection of Christ. Not only in such a way that he believed it had taken place, but in such a way that he made use of the power of Christ's resurrection in his daily life.

It is such disciples whom Christ seeks, that He may impart His supernatural, unconquerable powers to their lives and make them victorious Christians.

Resurrection power is a mysterious power. It conquers through defeat.

Never was the humiliation of Jesus deeper than when He died and was buried. But at that very time he won His greatest victory, the resurrection.

Dear child of God! You who suffer defeat at your own hands as well as at the hands of others, who suffer defeat in connection with both the joys and the sorrows of life, who have left a trail of lost battles behind you on every hand, listen: Jesus has a secret power which He would impart to you, resurrection power, a power which conquers through defeat.

Tell Him of your defeats. Acknowledge before yourself and before Him that your own strength is vain. And pray as Paul did that you may know Him and the power of His resurrection.

This power is at the disposal of the weakest of people. God Himself says: "My power is made perfect in weakness."

Therefore Paul said also: "I would rather glory in my weakness."

This is a glorious gospel for you and me, my defeated and discouraged fellow soldier.

Jesus expects nothing else of us but that we should permit our defeats to make us humble and to lead us to receive the power of His resurrection, that He may glorify Himself in our daily dying away from sin and in our daily living unto God.

But thou, O Lord, art a God merciful and gracious.
—PSALM 86:15

Yes, says the honest doubter, I, too, would like to believe in a merciful God. But war, suffering, sorrow, and distress, what do you do about them, you who believe? Do you close your eyes to these things?

No, but I *believe* in a merciful God, I cannot refrain from that. When He received me, miserable wretch that I was, and blotted out all my sins, taking my weary, frightened soul to His own heart, I met a merciful God. I know that He is merciful, even though I come upon many things in this world which I do not understand.

But, then, God has never demanded of me that I should *understand* Him and all that He does. All He expects is that I should *believe* in Him.

However, *some things* I do seem to understand.

I remember from the time that I was a little child that when my father disciplined me I thought at times that he was unmerciful. But now I thank him because he had the wisdom and courage to do so.

Our heavenly Father, too, is so merciful that He chastens us. And even though the chastening, *while it lasts*, seems hard, nevertheless, *afterwards*, we see His mercy.

Oh, how merciful! He gives us sorrow in the world, but joy in the Lord. He permits us to be ill in body, but well in soul. He makes us poor in the things of this earth, but rich in peace and hope.

Suffering child of God! It is not dangerous to suffer. In this world we *are* to suffer. Christ went before us also in this respect. We are to follow Him also in suffering. You are making good use of your time when you suffer.

You are suffering unjustly, you say?

Oh, well, neither is that dangerous. That is the way Jesus suffered all His life.

O Thou merciful God, teach us to know Thy mercy!

Be ye merciful, even as your Father is merciful.

—LUKE 6:36

BE merciful," Jesus tells us today.

Be merciful in your *thoughts* today! Do not think harshly or suspiciously of those with whom you are to associate. Put the best construction on everything, both on what they say and on what they do.

This is an act of kindness toward them.

You will not suffer any loss; you will reap great benefit from it.

Be merciful in *word* today! You will no doubt be tempted to use harsh or ill-humored words. Do not use them, even though you think the other person is so repugnant that you have a reason for doing so. Oh, what merciful words may mean! How they subdue the waves of a storm-tossed sea! What a balm they are to people's wounded souls!

Be merciful in *deed* today! Be willing to serve; do some little deed of kindness that you really are not obliged to do. You will surprise people and make them happy. Bring a little joy in this way to everybody in your home today.

Be merciful in your *whole being* today! Be friendly and kind toward all with whom you have any dealings. Be friendly when you are busy and when you are not. You scarcely know what grace you reveal to others simply by being friendly.

Be merciful for *Jesus'* sake! Is there anything that He needs more than friends who are merciful? They make His gospel irresistible.

Be merciful for your *own* sake!

"Blessed are the merciful." "With what measure ye mete it shall be measured to you again." Yes, "good measure, pressed down, shaken together, running over, shall they give into your bosom."

Judge not, that ye be not judged.

—MATTHEW 7:1

Not many passages of the Bible are quoted as often as this one, even by people who otherwise do not as a rule go to the Bible to learn the truth.

Nor is there any passage in the Bible which is misused as often and as grossly as this one.

People say: Here Jesus has once for all laid down the rule that we should not give expression to any judgment with respect to others and their relationship to God.

To point out some as children of God and others as children of the world is therefore not only presumptuous, but in direct violation of the words of Jesus: "Judge not."

Did Jesus mean these words in that way?

Any one who is somewhat acquainted with the Bible knows that the above interpretation is based upon a complete misunderstanding of the words of Jesus. Only a few lines farther on Jesus asks His disciples to beware of false prophets.

From this it follows that we not only have the right, but that it is also our duty to make up our minds about other people's relationship to God.

This is the way the disciples understood these words of Jesus.

John exhorts his readers to prove the spirits, whether they be of God. And Paul charges Timothy and Titus not to appoint elders without having inquired into their relationship both to God and to their fellow humans.

No, what Jesus wishes to get at here, as otherwise, is the *attitude of heart* with which we give expression to our judgments of others.

Why do we discuss the failings of others? Is it to injure them and to exalt ourselves?

If so, we are doing that which Jesus means by *judging.*

Judge not, that ye be not judged.

—MATTHEW 7:1

TODAY Jesus would speak to us about the way we speak about others. No doubt it is necessary for Him to do this. It is a very sensitive point in our life.

You have no doubt seen an orchard in which all the trees and bushes have been attacked by vermin. A very sad sight!

As Jesus stands today and looks out over the orchard which He has purchased with His blood, every plant of which He loves, even to the least, He sees many a plant that has been stripped of both its foliage and its fruit. Many have withered; others are dying; some are entirely dead.

It is love that has grown cold.

Heartlessness and lack of love spread like gangrene and destroy the tender shoots. If we realized how Jesus loves the little ones, the fact that we have, with heavy tread, trampled upon the little plants that He has purchased with His blood, would be unspeakably painful to us.

A brother has a little scratch and we spew poison into it instead of having it bound up and healed. Or our sister has an opinion different from ours about some Christian work, about ecclesiastical questions or something similar. And we pass unmerciful judgments instead of permitting her to stand before God with the opinions she has.

But must we not both see and speak about the relationships and mistakes of others? How then can we avoid injuring our Lord's tender plants?

Let us in the first place ask ourselves if it *hurts* us to speak of other people's failings, or if we experience a secret joy at presenting others in such a light that our own strong sides stand out the clearer. If so, then let us not speak.

In the next place: Have we prayed for those of whose faults we have spoken? If so, that love which covers a multitude of sins will be shed abroad in our hearts.

For the kingdom of heaven is like unto a man that
was a householder, who went out early in the morning
to hire laborers into his vineyard.

—MATTHEW 20:1

THE greatest work ever begun upon this earth was planned
and started by Jesus.

He seeks nothing less than this: to bring heaven down to
earth. He often spoke of it as establishing the kingdom of God
on earth.

In our Word today He speaks of it as God's garden on earth.

Humanity began its life on earth, too, in the garden of God.
But sin made of the earth a waste of thorns, thistles, and weeds
of all kinds. And now in order that there might be a garden
of God on earth again, it had to be watered with God's own
blood. It becomes very costly to have to purchase a garden site
with one's own blood!

He would have the most costly soil of all for His garden—
human hearts, where sin has wreaked its worst destruction.

It is a thought full of joy that Jesus is to transform the race
and the earth which have been cursed by sin into a very garden
of God again. That He will not stop until the new earth
stands there as God's perfect garden, gloriously laden with rip-
ened fruit.

And our hearts are filled with gratitude at the thought that
there is a garden of God here on earth, and that we, with our
little lives, have been planted within the divine hedge sur-
rounding this garden. Ever since our baptismal hour.

First, this, that I am under His *protection*. He cares for His
plants. My life shall be a success!

In the second place, that I am under the daily *supervision*
of Jesus. He directs the growth of His plants. He waters, dungs,
and prunes them.

What a joy to live one's life in the garden of God! Planted
in the sacred soil of Calvary, with the rain of heaven and the
sunlight of grace falling upon the heart-leaves of one's life!

But Simon Peter, when he saw it, fell down at Jesus' knees, saying, Depart from me; for I am a sinful man, O Lord.

—LUKE 5:8

PETER had known Jesus for some time. Down by the Jordan his brother Andrew had met Jesus and had come to believe in Him. And Andrew succeeded at once in bringing his brother to Jesus. Ever since that day Simon had followed Jesus faithfully, in order to hear His mighty words and see the miracles He performed.

On this day, too, he had heard Jesus speak. He had, as a matter of fact, lent Jesus his boat as a pulpit.

When the sermon was ended, Jesus would have had Peter launch out upon the deep for a draught. Peter was willing. But, experienced fisherman that he was, he could not help calling Jesus' attention to the unreasonableness of such a suggestion. They had fished all night and taken nothing. That left no hope, of course, for broad daylight. Least of all out where it was deep.

But he had gained such confidence in Jesus that he would have done it notwithstanding, since Jesus had commanded him. And he sat down to row, saying as he did so, with humility and strong faith: "At thy word I will let down the nets."

Then Jesus performed the great miracle for Peter.

Not the one relating to the many fish. It, too, was a mighty miracle. But Peter had seen Jesus do this often before. No, Jesus performed a miracle within the heart of Peter, as a result of which Peter began to realize his sinfulness. As never before. He was seized with fright and fell down at the knees of Jesus and prayed the hardest prayer of his life: "Depart from me; for I am a sinful man, O Lord!" Never had he needed Jesus as he did then. But he was so conscious of his sinfulness that he felt he had to warn Jesus not to stay in the same boat with him.

But Jesus raised him up and said: "Fear not, Simon, I am not leaving you."

And Jesus said unto Simon, Fear not; from henceforth thou shalt catch men.

W HEN Peter, in great distress because of sin, asked Jesus to depart from him, he did not feel that he was very well fitted to be a fisher of men and women.

But *at that very time* Jesus was *preparing* him for his great work. Peter had now become so small and insignificant in his own estimation that Jesus could use him. His was now the humble heart to which God gives grace. Grace also to win people.

Note also that Peter had now become *willing* to do the task to which he had been called and which entailed such great sacrifices. We have only the brief, but significant, word: "And when they had brought their boats to land, they left all, and followed him!"

Thus it is that the Lord prepares all of His workers.

Here we are undoubtedly in one of the most secret rooms of His great workshop. When I meet such men and women as these, I am seized with holy trembling: Remove thy shoes!

They are God's people, happy and contented. They take part in Christian work. Everything goes well. The friends of Jesus are happy. And these people themselves are glad.

But then something happens.

Suddenly or gradually all is changed. Heart and hearth become dry and empty. God seems far away, and sin seems strong and enticing. Christian work becomes a burden. These same people become weary of Christian people and of Christian gatherings. Perhaps adversity, illness, and sorrow augment their troubles.

It is then that everything goes to pieces for all half-souled people. They either give up or they become mere machines in the kingdom of God, permitting themselves to be swallowed up by their earthly tasks.

Honest souls, however, do as Peter did. They cast themselves down upon their faces at the feet of Jesus.

And the miracle takes place. The Lord raises them up and gives them their appointed task again.

> Who do men say the Son of man is?
> —MATTHEW 16:13

Yes, you have either read or heard it, have you not?

Some say that He never existed. Everything that has been written about Him is only hearsay and myth.

Others says: Yes, He did live. That fact has been so well authenticated historically that no person of sound mind can doubt it. But He was no God-Man. He was a human being such as we are; He was born as we are and He died as we do. His remains are in an unknown grave near Jerusalem.

Others again say: Jesus was the great religious superman. He stood in a relationship to God in which no one else has ever stood, and He lived for His fellow beings as no other person has ever done. His shining purity, His indomitable courage in telling the truth, His willingness to sacrifice and to suffer make Him the self-authenticated leader of the human race in morals and religion. He is the unattained ideal of all human generations, one whom we all should follow, one who will lead us all to God. But He was not God and did not pretend to be. His well-meaning friends are the ones who have made a God of Him.

Still others say: No, the Biblical record is true. The words of Jesus shall stand though heaven and earth pass away. But in their hearts and by their lives they do not speak thus. Jesus is not the main character in their daily life. They never mention His name except in swearing and cursing. They drink, commit adultery, defraud, and steal.

Strange! Yes, is it not strange that the Son of God came in such a form that opinions about Him *can* be so divided? We would rather have thought that when the Son of God came to our earth He would have come in such a way that there could be no division of opinion regarding Him.

But in this, too, we see the *Humiliated* One. His form was to be such that people *could* find an occasion of stumbling in Him.

191

But who say ye that I am?

—MATTHEW 16:15

To this question Peter made reply with fervor and conviction: "Thou art the Christ, the Son of the living God."

Whereupon Jesus said to Peter that he was the rock upon which He would build His church. By his faith and confession Peter became the beginning of the Christian church.

Since that day the church of the Lord has owned this faith in Jesus as the Son of the living God. This is the faith which has gathered and united the whole Christian church in every land and in every age, in all denominations and communions.

Here we are, gathered in our home. Can we all reply as Peter did? With the same fervor and conviction as he?

When Peter had answered, Jesus said to him: "Blessed are thou, Simon Bar-Jonah!" Yes, blessed are those who have attained to personal faith in Jesus as their Savior. No joy can be compared with that of believing.

They who by the grace of God have been given faith in Christ have found the fixed point which gives balance and poise to their whole lives. They know where to go with everything which before made their lives so distressing, burdensome, and hopeless.

Christ is their substitute. To Him they can go with all their sins and never be turned away, received by Him with love and forgiveness, raised up by Him to new courage and a new desire to strive against their sins.

Christ is their almighty Friend, to whom they daily turn with all that is distressing and burdensome, difficult and impossible. And Jesus is never at a loss as to what to do. He finds a way out, even when we have complicated matters as much as
possible.

Yes, we praise and worship Thee, Thou Son of the living God!

192

Speak, Jehovah; for thy servant heareth.

—1 SAMUEL 3:9

GOD spoke to young Samuel. But Samuel did not understand. Then the old and experienced priest taught him to reply: "Speak, Jehovah; for thy servant heareth."

God speaks to us also before we can understand Him. He began in Baptism. And we, too, learned from some man or woman of God to reply: "Speak, Jehovah; for thy servant heareth."

These words indicate the normal, the ideal attitude which we sinners should have toward our holy and gracious God. It is our salvation that God speaks to us and awakens us from the dead, telling us liars the truth in such a way that it pierces to our very bone and marrow.

We are thereby compelled to *choose.* And the choice involved in conversion really consists in praying from our hearts the prayer of Samuel: Speak, Lord; for Thy servant heareth. Speak to me as Thou wilt. I would know the truth, no matter how hard and exacting it may be.

And to live as a converted person is really nothing else than to pray from our hearts the prayer of Samuel: Speak, Lord; for Thy servant heareth. Tell me what you think of my Christianity and of me. Tell me about my sins in such a way that it hurts. Speak forgiveness to me in such a way that I believe it and give thanks for it. Make me to know Thy way and Thy will, for my own thoughts and ways lead me astray.

When we read the Bible, we should pray: Speak Thou, Lord, to me through Thy Word today. We should pray in this way particularly: Lord, help me, restless and preoccupied as I am, to hear when Thou speakest to me today.

And in our daily lives we should pray: Lord, help me to hear and to understand Thy message to me as it comes through the things Thou sendest me this day.

If we will pray this prayer each day, we shall hear glorious things. For there is nothing the Lord would rather do than *speak* to His children. He will speak unspeakable things to your heart.

> For what the law could not do, in that it was weak
> through the flesh, God, sending his own Son in the
> likeness of sinful flesh and for sin, condemned sin in
> the flesh: that the ordinance of the law might be
> fulfilled in us.
>
> —ROMANS 8:3-4

H ERE the apostle states briefly and clearly what the purpose of God's salvation is.

It is that the requirements of the law might be fulfilled, not only in *Christ*, but also in *us*.

At the same time he says that God could not secure the fulfillment of these requirements of the law through the law.

The law could not bring forth the *attitude of heart* which is the condition of all fulfillment of the law.

Because it was impossible for the law to change sinful humanity, either in peoples lives or their attitudes, God had to send His Son to save us. But the purpose of this salvation by the Son was that the requirements of the law might be fulfilled *in us*.

At our very awakening this becomes clear to us sinners. We proceed to fulfill the requirements of the law of God sincerely and without compromise. But to begin with we misunderstand. We think that we, by our fulfillment of the law, can make God kindly disposed toward us. But we soon discover our mistake, and then we begin to think that our fulfilling of the law is the condition upon which God can give us a part in the finished redemption of Christ.

And when this attempt on our part to fulfill the law has done its work, when we by the law have become dead unto the law, when the law has shown us our utter impotence, then we have acquired the inner qualifications for beholding the mystery of the gospel—that God justifies the ungodly, that God loves us in Christ even before we have as yet fulfilled a single commandment.

We see now that we have turned the matter upside down. We are not to fulfill the law in order to move God to love us and forgive us. God loves and forgives us in Christ, in order thereby to enable us to fulfill the requirements of the law.

> Do we then make the law of none effect through faith? God forbid; nay, we establish the law.
>
> —ROMANS 3:31

Is not the command of the law, "Thou shalt, thou shalt not," out of order in connection with the believer's new attitude of heart and willing spirit?

Are not duty and love irreconcilable opposites? Does not duty pass out when love enters in? And does not love go out when our relationship with God has become one based upon duty?

And if the law is written in our hearts, as the Scriptures say, is then any other commandment necessary?

Let us consider this briefly.

The new birth places a sinner in the right relationship to the requirements of God's law.

Old persons feel that the requirements of God are a burden, that they are strange and inimical to them.

New persons, on the other hand, love the law of God and, therefore, also their conscience, which in such a remarkable way brings the will of God into their very souls. Believers look upon their conscience as a friend helping them, with vigilance and without guile, both *to know and to do* the will of God.

It is this to which James refers when he speaks of the law of liberty, speaking of it as perfect.

Here he unites liberty and law. They seem to be mutually exclusive. But life unites them. For love is this very union of liberty and law. God is bound to the law of love to such a degree that He cannot act contrary to it. But He has bound Himself voluntarily.

The miracle of the new birth is that it frees us from the compulsion of the law and writes the law into our hearts, enabling us to feel that we are the free children of God when we do the will of God.

> For we know not how to pray as we ought; but the
> Spirit himself maketh intercession for us with
> groanings which cannot be uttered.
>
> —ROMANS 8:26

YOU who, like me, are not very well acquainted as yet in the realm of prayer, pray in a childlike way for the Spirit of prayer, a little every day. And you will make a number of discoveries in that realm which is so full of surprises.

Do you understand very little as yet of the deep and gracious significance of prayer? Then pray for the Spirit of prayer. There is nothing He would rather do than unveil to you the graciousness of prayer.

Do you feel that the difficulties in connection with prayer are so great that you become disheartened? Then pray for the Spirit of prayer. He will come to your assistance in your weakness, reveal to you wherein you misunderstand prayer, and make prayer simpler and easier for you to practice.

Does the work of praying seem heavy to you, do you feel prayer-weariness settling down upon you? Then pray in all simplicity of heart for the Spirit of prayer. It is written that the Lord will pour out the Spirit of prayer. It is therefore not necessary for you to work up a spirit of prayer or a prayerful mood within yourself.

If you recognize that you misuse prayer, resorting to prayer for selfish purposes, for the purpose of securing things to enjoy, and you are beginning to lose courage, then pray again for the Spirit of prayer. He will not only show you the true meaning of prayer; He will also lift you up and draw you close to the heart of God, where you will begin once again to pray according to the will of God and to desire nothing but that which God would give you.

Are you scarcely able to pray, even less able to thank God, least of all able to praise Him? Then pray for the Spirit of prayer. There is nothing He would rather do than *teach* you all these things.

Fight the good fight of faith!

—1 TIMOTHY 6:17

VICTORY over sin is from first to last a victory of *faith*. It is so from the very moment of conversion.

To be converted does not mean that you yourself have the power to free yourself from your old sinfulness, that you yourself have the power to change your heart and are therefore able to begin to hate sin and love God.

To be converted means rather that you in your distress turn to Christ and tell Him the whole truth: that you are hopelessly enmeshed in your old sins and that you love sin and not God.

Then you will receive from Christ the power which you yourself lack. And you will receive it by faith.

The daily struggle against sin takes place in exactly the same way.

However, this daily striving against your old sinful habits is perhaps the weakest point in your whole Christian life. You strive against your failings, suffer defeat, and become discouraged. Then you lose hope.

You will continue to suffer defeat until you learn to fight the fight of *faith* against your sinful habits.

To oppose my old sinful habits in faith means not to array myself and my own strength against these habits, but to turn to Christ and acknowledge that I will be defeated if He does not help me with His almighty hand.

The fight of faith which the believer wages is, therefore, a struggle to get *away from self and to Christ*.

It is then that we experience victory in the struggle against our old sins.

A calm and humble courage settles down upon our souls and forms a shield of faith which quenches all the fiery darts of the evil one.

> And having found one pearl of great price, he went
> and sold all that he had, and bought it.
>
> —MATTHEW 13:46

AMONG heathen peoples it never occurs to any one not to
be religious. It is as much a matter of course to share in the
religious life of the people as it is to accept their other customs
and habits.

Not until Christianity begins to affect the old religion of a
people do we note any change.

However, if Christianity becomes the prevailing religion of
a people, we observe the very remarkable thing that most of
the people within the nation do *not* share in the religion of
their people.

The reason for this is given us in this parable about
the pearl.

The Christian religion makes demands that are unknown
to other religions. It is a pearl of so great a price that most
people give up owning it personally. Whereupon they proceed
to provide themselves with imitations or to live entirely without
the pearl of life.

We are told here how costly it is.

They had to sell all they had in order to come into possession
of the pearl. This is a tremendous act of daring. Many conclude,
therefore, that it is less hazardous to do without the pearl, for
then they can keep what they already have.

But does it *cost* so much to become a Christian?

Do we not enter into the kingdom of God gratis? Is not the
grace of God free? Can we not receive it without money and
without price?

Yes, that is quite true. We need not *pay* anything to be
saved. But there are things we must *sell*.

God does not need to receive anything from us in order to
save us. But there are things He must persuade us to surrender.
"If thy hand cause thee to stumble, cut it off."

"Those who do not renounce all that they have cannot be
my disciples," Jesus says.

Thou didst encourage me with strength in my soul.
—PSALM 138:3

"THOU didst encourage me."

That is what took place when we became believers.

We stood there in the glaring light of the truth, overwhelmed by our sinfulness, grieved unto death. Then we *saw* Him, the friend of sinners, the Lamb of God who bore all our sins. And courage settled down gently and refreshingly upon our weary souls.

"With strength in my soul."

Yes, a wonderful and unexpected strength. With which to wage warfare against sin. Strength to serve God and others. To sacrifice time, effort, and money. Strength to confess the name of Jesus. Strength to meet and bear the difficulties of life.

His quiet, mighty presence imparted to us a peace in which we felt secure, even when the billows of life reached their crest.

And not only strength, but also rich and abundant joy.

Is there a deeper joy than that which holds in the dark days of adversity? The joyous spirit which cannot be subdued by distress of any kind because it sees the way of the Lord and His mercy in the very midst of adversity, poverty, sorrow, and death?

This courage is not the fruit of a natural endowment of a bright and cheerful disposition. Nor is it the product of outward circumstances, such as a strong body, or a good income, or reserve wealth.

No, it is the courage of faith. The courage which is ours through the *blood* of Jesus.

"Cast not away your boldness!"

Neither let your defeats rob you of your courage.

"Yes, come to the Savior whose mercy grows brighter
The longer you look at the depths of His love;
And fear not! 'tis Jesus, and life's cares grow lighter
As you think of the home and the glory above."

199

> Gather up the broken pieces which remain over, that
> nothing be lost.

—JOHN 6:12

THE disciples experienced many surprises the day Jesus fed the five thousand out in the wilderness. And now Jesus told them that they should pick up every piece that lay scattered on the hillside. Which was also a surprise.

This is a message that all of us need—especially in our day.

In olden days thrift was rated more highly in our nation than it is today. Then people said: "Crumbs are also bread." The least portion of food that fell on the floor was treated with respect; people bent down at once and picked it up in order not to trample upon "God's gifts," as they said.

God would have nothing go to waste, our Word says today. When this becomes clear to us, thrift will become a part of our spiritual service.

Thrift has a hard struggle with *greed.* Greedy people will at times excuse themselves by saying that they are only thrifty. At other times thrifty people will be accused of being greedy.

What is the difference between thrift and greed?

It is this: The greedy save in order to have everything for themselves. The thrifty save in order to have something to give others.

Those person who practice contentment are not sparing in their giving nor in the wages they pay to those who are working for them. No, they are sparing in their own personal requirements; they reduce them to a minimum and try to persuade their near of kin to do likewise.

The young person who goes out into the world with a personal will and capacity to practice thrift is a rich and happy youth indeed.

Our nation needs such young people now more than ever before.

Especially such as practice this for God's sake.

One thing I know, that, whereas I was blind, now I see.

—JOHN 9:25

CHRISTIANITY is the only religion which leads people into full assurance concerning their relationship to God.

In this also, then, it shows itself as the true religion.

It fulfills what the others promise, namely, to lead people to a personal meeting with God, face to face.

The other religions tell about God, point up to Him, and ask people to stretch themselves up toward God.

In Christianity, on the other hand, God comes down into the very midst of our world, as a human among humans. We can meet Him, speak with Him, and live our life with Him. We need not stop with only hearing and reading about Him and longing for Him.

But why then are most people uncertain about their relationship to God?

In Christian lands you will find one little flock of those who know that they were blind before but that now they see. On the other hand, you will find another little flock which knows that it lives in an unconverted state.

Midway between these two little flocks you will find a great mass of people whose relationship to God may be characterized in the following manner: they *know* nothing but *hope* for the best.

Some of the latter are of the opinion, moreover, that it is not possible in this life to gain assurance with respect to this relationship.

Where do you stand?

There are many who hoped themselves down into eternal perdition because they have never had a real meeting with God for the purpose of becoming reconciled to Him.

You, too, have a restless and longing soul in your bosom.

Follow the longing God has given you!

It leads to the very bosom of the Savior.

Lord, have mercy upon all half-hearted souls!

201

One thing I know, that, whereas I was blind, now I see.

—JOHN 9:25

THIS man who had been born blind did not know *a great deal.*

But what he did know, he knew with certainty: I was blind, now I see.

Perhaps you are saying the same: I was blind, but now I see. I see now that I have never received that which I need and which God offers to give, namely, assurance.

I see now that I have deceived myself by hoping for the best instead of making every effort to be clear in my relationship toward God.

Now I will not give up until I know what it is that has been acting as a barrier between God and me.

Jesus met the man born blind and helped him to personal faith in the Son of God, a faith which led him to fall down before Him and say, "I believe, Lord!"

Jesus would have a meeting with you also.

If you will enter into your room, close the door, and begin to speak in all sincerity and confidence with your Savior, you will find that He will meet with you and answer you.

Then take your Bible and read, and He will make clear to your conscience what it is that shuts you out from Him day after day. Every time you feel that you have done anything against Him, tell it to Him.

He tells you in His Word that if you will confess He will forgive you your sin. When you look to Him in His suffering and death, you will receive courage to believe His Word.

If you will begin thus to go in and go out each day with your Savior in the privacy of your own room and of the Word, you will soon be able to say with a new meaning: "One thing I know, that whereas I was blind, now I see." You will see not only your sins, but also the Lamb of God who bore all your sins.

Then you will have received the gift not only of *faith,* but also of *assurance.*

> Whence are we to buy bread, that these may eat?
> And this he said to prove him: for he himself knew
> what he would do.
>
> —JOHN 6:5-6

Whence Jesus takes His friends aside, difficulty always arises.

As the disciples journeyed together with Jesus in the mountains toward the east, the great company of Passover pilgrims that was to go south to Jerusalem for the feast was gathering little by little. They had heard that He was to travel that way and, without hesitation, they took the same road themselves.

When Jesus saw them, He understood at once how precarious the situation was; they had not taken food along.

At once Jesus turned to His disciples. He shared everything with them.

And they tried every way they could devise to cope with the situation.

But to no avail.

Even though they had *money* enough they were helpless; there was no bread to be bought here.

The disciples did not know what to do; but He Himself knew what He would do. Whereupon he performed His great miracle with the five barley loaves and the two small fishes.

This is good news for you and me, we who so often in our daily lives are helpless and do not know what to do. No doubt such is the case a great deal oftener than folk think.

The difficulties which Jesus sends us, all of us, are forerunners of Jesus' miraculous dealings. Rich blessings hide behind our difficulties.

When Jesus has persuaded me to acknowledge that I do not know what to do, then a miracle on His part is near at hand. A glorious surprise awaits me.

Oh, how unspeakably good the Lord is!

And when he had said this, he showed unto them
his hands and his side.

—JOHN 20:20

MANY a disciple of Jesus sits alone with his sorrows and
doubts. He has lost sight of Jesus.

Worst of all, you yourself are to blame for it all. It is your
unfaithfulness and disobedience which are responsible for His
disappearing from you, and they are the reason why you do
not receive answers from Him any more.

You feel lonely and forsaken, as though every door were
closed to you—even the door of heaven.

Yes, without any doubt you and I are ourselves alone to
blame that we have lost sight of Jesus. If we were to receive
according to our own merits, we would be *forever* excluded
from the presence of God.

But He does not deal with us according to our sins. And
therefore He comes through closed doors to His frightened
disciples. He points to His wounds and says: "Behold, I have
atoned for the evil that you have done. Therefore I can now
forgive you all that you have done without upbraiding you. If
a mother could forget her infant child, I could not forget you.

"The disciples therefore were glad," it says—so glad that
they went out and preached the gospel of the crucified and
risen Savior. They did it even in the very midst of Jerusalem
where the bloody executioners of Jesus were breathing out
threatenings and murder.

Jesus needs confident and glad disciples today as well as
then. Especially in our God-distant and doubting generation.

The world is waiting to meet disciples who come directly
from a meeting with their Savior and who can say: "We have
seen the Lord!"

Believing friends, let us ask the Lord to breathe upon us
every day, that we may bring a direct message from Him to
the people we meet on our way. That we may be a savor of
life unto life in this dying world.

Surely goodness and lovingkindness shall follow me
all the days of my life.

—PSALM 23:6

THIS is a remarkable passage.

It is remarkable simply for the reason that most people do
not agree with it. Our anxieties show this. The fact that we
are anxious nearly every day shows that we feel that we are
being followed by sorrow and trouble all the days of our life.

David, on the other hand, said that only goodness and mercy
followed him every day.

It would be wonderful to live under such circumstances, you
reflect. Without anxiety, without that gnawing uneasiness with
respect to the future! Yes, it is wonderful to live in that way.
It is concerning this very thing that this psalm speaks. Turn
to your Bible some time today and read this little psalm, the
pearl of all the psalms of the Bible. You will learn to know
what a rich and blessed life it is possible to live by believing
in God.

Do not think that the writer of this psalm was a sentimental
dreamer. No, he was a king who had been severely tried, who
had been compelled to experience more of life's trials than
most people. He also knew what it was to sin and to fall.

Yet through it all he had learned to have faith in God. He
had learned to know that the Lord was his faithful shepherd,
who tended him and saved him from great dangers.

David had enough enemies, both at home and abroad—
yes, even in his own household; but he also knew what it was
to have the Lord prepare a table before him in the very presence
of those enemies.

In the greatest trials of his life he felt that the Lord refreshed
his soul in wondrous ways. He was made to lie down in green
pastures and was led beside still waters.

Yes, even his last enemy, death, he faced courageously;
because the Lord was with him all the way.

> In nothing be anxious; but in everything by prayer
> and supplication with thanksgiving let your requests
> be made known unto God.   —PHILIPPIANS 4:6

IN nothing be anxious," says the apostle.

Indeed, it would be pleasant to live then; for one of the things that cause us most distress is our anxieties.

What are anxieties?

Well, they are the anxious thoughts we think concerning things we have not as yet experienced but which we see coming or think will come. We picture these things vividly to our imaginations and live them out *inwardly* so completely that when they finally do come in actual life they are not nearly as bad as we had imagined they would be.

Think how bright and carefree our lives would be if we did not have these anxious cares! It would almost be heaven on earth.

"In nothing be anxious," says the apostle. Can he mean that literally?

Yes; but of course he says this only to the children of God. A child of God is one who sits, as it were, in the lap of God, held by the eternal arms. God Himself whispers in our ears: "You are my child; and I care for my children. Simply come to me and ask for the things you need.

"I protect my children. Neither people nor any devil shall be permitted to touch you without my permission; and they shall not be permitted to do anything to you but that which is beneficial to you."

Is it not thus that God whispers into your ears also?

> "In Thine arms I rest me,
> Foes who would molest me
> Cannot reach me here;
> Though the earth be shaking,
> Every heart be quaking,
> Jesus calms my fear;
> Fires may flash and thunder crash,
> Yea, and sin and hell assail me,
> Jesus will not fail me."

For as many as are led by the Spirit of God, these are sons of God.

—ROMANS 8:14

How can I be certain that I am led by the Spirit of God?

You understand, of course, that the Spirit is known by what He does with us. When He leads us, He does something that no one else can do.

The Spirit leads us *to God*.

No one else can do that. Not the devil; not we ourselves either, for we are enemies of God.

However, there are religious people who are not led by the Spirit of God, are there not?

Yes, that is true. And for that reason they are not led *to God* either. They are, on the contrary, afraid of God and of His message of repentance.

The Spirit, on the other hand, leads the sinner *out into the light*, onward to *reconciliation*.

We ourselves oppose this as long as we can and dare.

If you have been reconciled to God, you have certain proof that you are led by the Spirit of God.

The Spirit leads *to the cross*.

But does not dead faith also put its trust in the grace of God? Yes, but it never seeks the cross to *confess* sins, only to seek comfort in sin.

But with me everything is impossible and meaningless. There is no real prayer, no sincere remorse, no real striving against sin. As a result my life is merely one defeat after another.

My friend, who has shown you this? God's Spirit, who leads sinners *to the cross* in just that way.

As many as are led by the Spirit of God, these are children of God.

> "How blessed is the little flock,
> Whom Jesus calls His own!
> He is their Savior and their rock,
> They trust in Him alone."

207

So teach us to number our days,
That we may get us a heart of wisdom.

—PSALM 90:12

TIME is inexorable.

It is like a stream which never stands still, which cannot be stopped.

You can stop the clock; but you cannot stop time.

There are many who would like to stop time. They do not care to grow old.

But even though they cannot stop time, they do stop the clock. They dye their hair and rouge their faces.

However, no one can halt the advance of age. We must all follow the dream of time; and this stream flows steadily and briskly.

How fast it goes!

When we look ahead, time seems so long; but when we look back we see how fleeting it is, how rapidly it goes.

Time is the beginning of eternity.

It leads us all into eternity, whether we wish it or not.

There are two ways into eternity. They cut across each other at the portals of death, never to meet again. The broad way leads downward into eternal woe. The narrow way leads to eternal bliss.

Which way are you taking?

What a horrible thing to drift along on the stream of time, going downward continually and inexorably into eternal perdition!

What a joy, on the other hand, to be borne upon the stream of time to the fair homeland of heaven!

Child of God, every time the clock ticks, time pulls the oars of your little life-boat.

Look up as you move along and thank Him who has opened a channel for you through His blood.

For narrow is the gate, and straitened the way, that leadeth unto life, and few are they that find it.
—MATTHEW 7:14

JESUS does not conceal the fact that the gate is narrow. To get through it, therefore, is not easy.

Therefore also it is an unspeakable joy to have passed through the narrow gate. I wish you success, you who have chosen, you who have cast your lot, you who have taken life's most decisive step.

I know, of course, that this is not all. Begun is not done! But, after all, to have made a beginning is of decisive importance. Those who do not make a beginning upon the narrow way naturally can have no hope of reaching the goal.

Yes, you who have entered upon the straitened way are fortunate!

But remember that it is the *way* that is your good fortune. Your walking upon the way brings you more sorrow than joy. You are often ungrateful and unhappy, often unwilling and slow, often tired and discouraged. Oftentimes you look back, yes, are on the verge of turning back. Many times you stumble and fall; and sometimes you lie there rather long before you rise again to your feet.

All this makes you feel ashamed and sad; in fact, you are often in despair.

You wonder if any one who stumbles again and again as you do will ever reach yon beautiful shore.

Sit down by the wayside a little while today, notwithstanding it all, and thank God because you *are* on the straitened way, that the Lord has been permitted to preserve within your heart that sincere spirit which is willing to face sin and is willing also each day to be driven to the cross of Christ.

Arise and proceed on your way with courage. But walk carefully! Do not make the straitened way any broader than the Lord has made it.

Wide is the gate, and broad is the way, that leadeth to destruction, and many are they that enter in thereby.

—MATTHEW 7:13

WHY do not the many seeking, longing souls go *through* the gate?

The gate is narrow. That is the reason.

They make a compromise. They cannot live entirely without God, and therefore they *seek* God.

They would like to be *religious.*

But they will not permit religion to create any sort of disturbance in their daily life, their life of ease, comfort, and pleasure.

They do not want it to embarrass them in their contacts with the world. They avoid speaking of their relationship to God, maintaining that no normal person can do so without violating spiritual modesty. It is such a personal and sacred matter.

Their religion consists in negotiating and bargaining with God. They would believe in God at all costs and yet be in charge of their own lives. They would have God's favor without being reconciled to Him. They would have forgiveness of sins without acknowledging sin and striving against it.

So they take the broad way and are recognized by the world as considerate and discreet "Christians."

God does not answer their prayers. Their religion is a monologue. Since God does not declare to them the forgiveness of sins, they declare it to themselves.

Listen to Jesus' cry of warning today. Turn aside from the broad and easy way that you have made your way. And enter in by the *narrow* gate.

> "God calling yet! I cannot stay;
> My heart I yield without delay:
> Vain world, farewell! From thee I part;
> The voice of God hath reached my heart!"

He that eateth my flesh and drinketh my blood hath
eternal life.

—JOHN 6:54

JESUS stands in the midst of the race which has been poisoned
by sin and cries out: "He that eateth my flesh and drinketh
my blood hath eternal life."

This is something for you and me to hear, we who feel the
virus of sin in soul and in body.

What a world of poisoned desires, thoughts, and imaginations! What a world of open and secret antipathy toward
God, of conscious and of unconscious opposition to Him!

My companion in suffering!

We who feel continuously the virus of death in our hearts,
we have only one antidote. Jesus says to us: Eat my flesh and
drink my blood.

We are to satisfy the hungering and thirsting after righteousness which He Himself has awakened in our hearts with
the living bread given to us in the Word and in Holy Communion. The life which we now live we live by faith in the
Son of God who loved us and gave Himself for us.

God has many children in our day and age, perhaps more
than at any previous time.

But I fear that He has more *stunted* children now than ever
before also—spiritually overstrained, restless, powerless, joyless.

No doubt there are various reasons for this condition; but
the main cause is undoubtedly spiritual *undernourishment.*

All those who unceasingly inhale the pure air of free grace,
who live at all times by the life and the death of Christ, who
sustain themselves by the bread which waits for them in the
Word like fresh manna from heaven will each day experience
the power of that antidote which drives out the poison of sin.

The pure and fresh air at the cross of Christ is too penetrating
for our old ego; but in this atmosphere our new self grows and
we live our lives humbly, quietly, and gratefully.

211

Even so there shall be joy in heaven over one sinner that repenteth.

—LUKE 15:7

GOD loses human souls every day.

He Himself says that one single soul is worth more than the whole world.

This is hard for us to grasp. We do not look upon souls in that way, at least not unless they are very close to us—such as our children, our spouse, our parents, our brothers or sisters.

God, however, feels that way about every soul. To Him each one is worth more than the whole world. This means that nothing can compensate for the loss of a soul.

Hear this, you who have wandered away from God.

He misses you.

As long as you are away, there is one missing from the flock. Therefore He seeks you. He tells us today how happy He will be when He finds you again. Indeed, He says all heaven will be glad. You have some one there waiting for you. No doubt you remember your father's last words to you. You will never forget your mother's tear-filled look before she closed her eyes in death.

You fathers and mothers whose children are out in the wilderness of sin, you who weep so often and sigh so deeply as you see the wildness of their ways: do not forget that Jesus is seeking them. He tells you today that He searches for His lost sheep *until He finds them.*

Friend of Jesus, do you help Jesus seek after the souls that have gone away from Him?

There are some souls that He will not find unless you come along and seek them.

Are you living your life in your home and doing your daily work with the purpose in mind of winning souls for Jesus?

God bless you! They who seek shall find.

He that is faithful in a very little is faithful also in much.   —LUKE 16:10

Many young people pass through a great deal of doubt and distress before they see clearly which vocation in life they should choose.

Others have no choice. They are compelled to accept whatever comes. They are very dissatisfied with the positions they have and are constantly looking for something else. They feel that they have talents, abilities, and interests which qualify them for work of a far higher order than that in which they are at present engaged. They feel that it is not only a burden to them but also downright wrong to waste the precious years of youth upon a task as insignificant as the one they have been compelled to assume.

There are also Christian young people who find themselves in such situations.

My young friend! It is very possible that you have capacities and talents for some other vocation in life. In that event it is only natural that you long to get into that type of work and even try to find a way to do so.

But be careful. There are many young people who have never been able to reach the goal they desired in this respect. And the reason was simply this: they were not faithful in little things. They were not faithful and conscientious in the position they did have. They took the attitude that it was an insignificant, a menial task, and never put their whole soul or all their energy into it, performing it only in a careless and heedless manner. As a result, they were never put in charge of *greater* things either by God or by other people.

Now do not do this, but be faithful in your present position. Thank God for the work He has given you to do. Do your duty every day as though you were in His presence. Be industrious, capable, dependable.

Meanwhile pray in all confidence to God that He transfer you, if it be according to His will, to the position to which you desire to attain.

Then these words will be fulfilled also in your life. Thou hast been faithful in little things, I will set thee over *greater.*

Except ye turn, and become as little children, ye shall in no wise enter into the kingdom of heaven.

—MATTHEW 18:3

W e who are sitting here together in our home are attached to one another by life's finest and most tender bonds. Let us not forget to thank God for this.

We also have in common the desire to reach heaven. And it is God's will that we should all be gathered in His great home above. God grant that none of us may be missing on that day!

We are alike also in this, that we have all done certain things in order to get to heaven. He who speaks to us today knows us all very well. He knows the innermost recesses of our hearts. He has followed us in our greatest struggles and heard our deepest groanings. He is our friend.

And He would help us in this most important matter of all in life, that of reaching our home with God above.

Now He says: Except ye turn, ye shall in no wise enter in. Herewith the question is directed to all of us: Have you turned? Are you converted?

If you are not converted, you cannot enter in, even if you desire to do so, think of doing so, and hope to do so.

Perhaps you do not like this question.

You think that all this talk about conversion is too easy, too schematic, too pietistic.

That does not surprise me. There is something offensive about conversion; but I would have you reflect upon the fact that it is Jesus who has spoken these words about conversion. And He is the only real expert in this field. It is impossible for Him to tone down the truth, even though you and many others take offense at it.

At the same time, remember that Jesus speaks these hard, strict words in most tender love. He would help you, so that you will not deceive yourself and become eternally lost.

And I say unto you my friends, Be not afraid!

—LUKE 12:4

HERE again Jesus tries to help His disciples to believe in God. We have seen before how He tried to give anxious souls courage to believe in the forgiveness of sins. Today He would help us believe in God in all of life's relationships, enabling us to dare to live our lives according to His Word.

He would tell us that it is not hazardous to live according to the Word of God. It only appears that way.

Do not be afraid of *being considered unimportant* in the estimation of others; for they who humble themselves shall be exalted.

Do not be afraid of *serving* others! Be humble in the presence of your associates. No one will lose by this, you least of all.

Do not be afraid to *suffer injustice!* It seems to involve a risk to yield one's rights; but such is not the case. God will avenge His elect.

Do not be afraid to *suffer!* It will not be inimical to your happiness. Suffering will make your joys purer and deeper. Your life will be made stronger and more useful as a result of suffering.

Do not be afraid to *sacrifice!* Give confidently of your time, your efforts, and your means. There seems to be a risk involved in this, too. And that is why we are so careful about giving. But Jesus tells us that it is not dangerous to give.

He says: Fear not!

It takes courage to have faith. There is nothing more courageous in all the world than to believe in God; that is, to believe in God in such a way that we dare to order our lives in accordance with His Word in spite of our fears and our own wise calculations of all kinds.

> "Seems a thing to me a treasure,
> Which displeasing is to Thee,
> Then remove such dangerous pleasure;
> Give instead what profits me.
> Let my heart by Thee be stilled,
> Make me Thine, Lord, as Thou wilt."

215

Ask, and ye shall receive, that your joy may be made full.

—JOHN 16:24

THE other day we said that the real purpose of prayer is to glorify God. Today we are told that prayer has still another function, that of making us happy—yes, of making our joy full.

However we cannot experience this prayer-joy before we have learned to make use of prayer, not to gain some advantage for ourselves but as a means of glorifying God.

The reason why we experience disappointment and weariness rather than joy in connection with prayer is that we strive against the Spirit of prayer when we pray. On the other hand, when we want only to glorify the name of God by our prayers, we are in complete harmony with the Spirit of prayer. Then there is peace and joy in our hearts, both while we pray and after we have prayed; for we have sought by our prayers only those things which would glorify God.

Then we can also *wait* for the Lord.

He Himself must of course determine what will glorify His name most, either an immediate answer to our prayers or a delayed one.

When we have learned to pray like this, even in a small way, we can also experience the joy of having everything that occurs in our daily life take the form of prayer and thanksgiving—even the things that are hard and unpleasant.

We do not expect anything of ourselves alone. Therefore we tell everything to the Savior and wait for *His* strength to assert itself through our *weakness*.

If we bring to Jesus all the failures round about us in connection with people, conditions, and institutions, we shall see the heavenly light of hope shining upon everything that is wrong and awry. Then we shall not be indifferent toward, critical of, or impatient with, everything we see and hear.

> "What a friend we have in Jesus,
> All our sins and griefs to bear;
> What a privilege to carry
> Everything to God in prayer!"

> He that is faithful in a very little is faithful also in much.
>
> —LUKE 16:10

SOME Christians get very far.

When we learn to know them, we discover that it is neither their ability nor their knowledge, nor favorable circumstances which have won for them the high respect in which they are held. No, it is their *person* itself which wins such remarkable respect and confidence from those with whom they associate.

If we had occasion to inquire further, we would soon discover the secret of these people. They are *faithful in little things.*

They have learned to know that unfaithfulness is the hidden leak through which blessing and grace quietly ebb out of the heart. And therefore they have taken up the battle against unfaithfulness in *prayer* and in meditation upon the *Word.* How these people guard their *quiet hours* from all disturbance!

In their warfare against sin they are equally anxious lest they be unfaithful. They are afraid lest they dress up their sins in some attractive manner, or explain away their disobedience. They strive against fine and unnoticed sins just as energetically as against the obvious ones.

In such a literal sense are they faithful in *little things* that they do the little and unnoticed things that other people prefer not to do. There is no work that they consider themselves too good to do. Nor do they sacrifice only on important occasions. On the contrary, they avail themselves of the thousands of lesser occasions in their daily life to say "no" to themselves and to render service to others.

Their life is occupied with those daily *little* acts of kindness which are of most value to those with whom they associate and which require most of those who perform them.

They are not sinless. But their faithfulness comes to light also when they err. How they humble themselves both before God and others when they have done wrong! Wherefore their lost peace and power are quickly restored to them.

> And whatsoever ye do, in word or in deed, do all in
> the name of the Lord Jesus, giving thanks to God
> the Father through him.
>
> —COLOSSIANS 3:17

THIS is one of the many passages of the Bible about our daily life and our daily work.

The Scriptures tell us that our daily work is a service unto God, yes, a means by which others may be saved—even those who are hard to win.

In Luther's day to marry and establish a Christian home was not considered holy, but to remain unmarried and enter a cloister, on the other hand, was holy. To be a *mother* was not holy, but to be a *nun* was. To do one's daily work was not holy, but to make pilgrimages and give gifts to monasteries and churches was.

In this connection, too, Luther brought to light once again the Biblical view: God looks on the *attitude of our hearts*. In the daily life of the faithful Christian there are therefore no acts which in themselves are holy and others which in themselves are unholy. No, all our deeds are well-pleasing to God if they are done in the right attitude of heart; to the glory of God in Jesus' name, in love toward God and in zeal for the welfare of others.

Luther says therefore that it is just as well-pleasing to God that we sweep the floor as it is that we preach the Gospel, provided that both are done in the right attitude of heart. Whether we are to sweep or to preach is simply a question of the gift of grace that God has given us.

Do your ordinary daily work, therefore, and rejoice that through it you are rendering a spiritual service every day. By so doing you shall also win souls for God, even the hardest. You shall win those who, the Scriptures tell us, cannot be won by words.

> Who comforteth us in all our affliction, that we may
> be able to comfort them that are in any affliction,
> through the comfort wherewith we ourselves are
> comforted of God.
>
> —2 CORINTHIANS 1:4

THE apostle here mentions one aspect of the blessing which our sufferings bring to others. We have afflictions in order that we may be able to comfort those who are in affliction of any kind.

Unquestionably the apostle is thinking of profound and sacred experiences in his own life. In the eleventh chapter of our epistle he tells us a little of what he has suffered for Christ's sake. It is terrible indeed; but he also reminds us, in our verse today, of the abundant comfort which he received from God in these terrible afflictions. We need think only of Paul and Silas in prison at Philippi with their feet fastened to the stocks. God comforted them in such a way that they sang songs of praise. The apostle knew now that the comfort which he received enabled him to comfort others.

Child of God, this is for you—you who have so many tribulations and afflictions. You are not disturbed so much by the fact that you suffer as you are by the fact that your sufferings seem to you to be so devoid of meaning. The apostle here tells you that you are being trained by God to comfort other sufferers. You cannot comfort others with any other comfort than that with which God has been able to comfort you. You remember, no doubt, how blessed it was when you met some one who had gone through the same sufferings that you had and had been comforted by God.

Remember that you who have suffered and have been comforted of God are privileged to comfort more people than you know. Not only by speaking with suffering people directly. Only a few will speak to you about their sufferings. However, all people suffer. And they need comfort. And hunger for comfort. And it has been so ordained that there is something unspeakable about a person who has suffered a great deal, but who has also been abundantly comforted of God, something which is of great comfort and help to all suffering souls.

Upon this many of his disciples went back, and walked no more with him.

—JOHN 6:66

Is it not strange that it is so difficult for us to speak naturally about spiritual things? This too tells us something about how sin has estranged us all from God.

But the most unnatural thing of all is the fact that people will not even speak about God. Many look upon speaking about God as being uncultured, saying with great agitation that those are immodest spiritually who speak with others about such holy things.

If we could have a conversation here today, could speak confidentially with one another about the deep things of life, I would propose that you who are not Christians tell us why you have not become Christians.

Our text today invites you to such a conversation; for it tells us of some who would follow Jesus no longer, and why they would not do so.

You, too, have your *reasons* for not doing so. You *must* have reasons.

You are unable to withstand Jesus unless you have one or more reasons which you can draw upon as a means of comforting yourself when your conscience becomes too restless.

Some offer as a reason that they are too young, and say as Felix did: Go thy way for this time!

Others maintain that they are living in difficult surroundings, and say to themselves: As long as I am compelled to live with such difficult people, it is impossible for me to become a Christian.

Others are too busy. They work day and night for themselves and their dependents. They say that they will turn to religion when they become old or ill.

My dear friends! You yourselves are no doubt aware that these are not the real *reasons* why you are unconverted. They are only *pretexts*.

Do you know what the real reason is? If you will not tell, I shall tell you: You *will* not.

220

Jesus said therefore unto the twelve, Would ye also go away? Simon Peter answered him, Lord, to whom shall we go? thou hast the words of eternal life.

—JOHN 6:67-68

YESTERDAY we spoke of those who try to find a valid reason for postponing their conversion.

These people differ greatly in many respects and therefore offer different reasons.

But they have two things in common: They want to be Christians, and feel that they must become Christians some time; otherwise they cannot be saved. But they also feel certain that Christianity will deprive them of their joy in life. And therefore they postpone their conversion as long as possible.

If you would tell us the whole truth, however, we would no doubt hear that the joy you have outside of Christ is not very great either.

Let us take it for granted that you are one of the fortunate ones who have had everything in their favor. You have succeeded in nearly everything you have set out to accomplish.

However, in the very midst of your successes you experienced something very remarkable. Every now and then everything seemed to become meaningless to you. The hideous emptiness of your life grinned and stared you in the face. A peculiar weariness and ennui threw a shadow across all your joys, even your best and richest ones.

Then you began to long for God. Perhaps in all quietness you began to pray to Him occasionally. It felt good to bend the knee. How you longed to weep out at the feet of One who understood you! How you longed to make an accounting before God of all your sins! How you longed to have a good conscience again!

Yes, this is what we find in our Savior. He sets us free from our sins and binds us unto Himself.

We, too, say with Peter: "Lord, to whom shall we go? Thou hast the words of eternal life."

You who continue to long for God, what are you waiting for? Follow your deepest longings—to the foot of the cross!

221

And when he drew nigh, he saw the city and wept over it, saying, If thou hadst known in this day, even thou, the things which belong unto peace! but now they are hid from thine eyes.

—LUKE 19:41-42

THERE was a feast in Jerusalem, a great religious feast. Pomp and solemnity prevailed in the temple; festively attired people were present everywhere in the city.

Up on the Mount of Olives Jesus sat weeping.

He loved this people, and especially this city—this city in which God had revealed His glory down through the centuries.

For thirty years now Jesus had shared weal and woe with His people. Their joys were more distressing to Him than their sorrows. He saw their noisy festivals, their slavishness under the law, their false Messianic hopes.

He saw that they did not recognize Him as the Messiah, having decided to put Him out of the way.

He saw farther.

He saw the day when God's threats would be carried out and punishment would be visited upon this rebellious people, the time when their enemies would surround the city and overthrow it.

Jesus stood helpless.

He no longer had any means of helping His people. And when love can no longer come to the rescue of the loved one who is in mortal danger, love weeps.

Since that day Jesus has wept over many cities and over many human beings.

Is He weeping over any one in our home today?

If so, He weeps because the things which belong to your peace are hidden from your eyes.

Friend, can you take that sin lightly over which Jesus weeps?

> Be ye yourselves like unto men looking for their lord,
> when he shall return from the marriage feast; that,
> when he cometh and knocketh, they may straightway
> open unto him.
>
> —LUKE 12:36

J ESUS is waiting for the day when he is to return.

He takes for granted that all His real friends are doing likewise. This runs like a red thread through all His sayings about His second advent.

If I understand Jesus correctly, to await the return of the Lord is one of the signs that we are true friends of Jesus.

Are *we* awaiting His return?

Or has something gone to pieces within us, as a result of which the day which Jesus looks forward to with rejoicing has become distant and unreal?

I remember from the time that I was a lad how we children looked forward with joy to the return of faith and mother when they had been away. But I remember also that there were times when I did *not* look forward with joy. I had not behaved properly. I can still remember the anxiety I felt when I heard the sound of the wagon in the distance.

Nothing is harder for Jesus to bear than that His return has become a thing to be feared. There are many who *did wait* for His return years ago, but who no longer do so.

One awaits with joy those whom one loves.

At the railway station we see the station master. He is all ready; the flyer can come whenever it will. But whether it comes or not makes little difference to him.

But look at old Anne over there. She is listening for the train and asking about it. For she is *waiting* for it. Andrew, her son, is coming on that train. And she has not seen him for twenty years.

> "Bear through the night
> Your well-trimmed light,
> Speed forth to join the marriage rite."

For whosoever would save his life shall lose it: and whosoever shall lose his life for my sake shall find it.
—MATTHEW 16:25

W E said the other day that willingness to suffer was the secret of Jesus' life, not only as the Son of man, but also as the Son of God. To *will* to suffer is the secret of God's life, is the peculiarly divine element in the love of God.

Suffering is therefore also the secret of the believer's life. The apostle who gained the deepest insight into the mystery of the Gospel of Jesus is the one who knew of no greater desire than to share in the sufferings of Jesus by the power of His resurrection. He considered as fortunate his friends who were permitted not only to believe in Christ but also to suffer for His sake.

We often wonder why we do not grow more than we do as Christians. The answer, as far as most of us are concerned, is no doubt this: We accept the unmerited grace of God and use it as a means of adding to our own well-being instead of using it as a power which will enable us to suffer with Jesus.

Let us acknowledge this: We are afraid of suffering, both physical and spiritual. None of our prayers are so sincere and earnest as those we pray when we ask God to deliver us from adversity, sorrow, and suffering. Fortunately God does not fulfill all these petitions of ours.

We *are* to suffer and we *must* suffer—all of us—in this world of sin. But salvation should enable us to *will* to suffer, for through salvation we receive the mind of Christ.

But what shall we do then, we who see daily that we do *not* will to suffer?

There is only one thing for us to do: pray for *grace*. First that we may be forgiven for the sin of not believing in the Christ who says that it is good to suffer.

And then for *grace to suffer.*

224

Lo, I am with you always, even unto the end of the world.

—MATTHEW 28:20

THIS Word is to you who, by the grace of God, are His child. You have an unseen friend near you wherever you go. He loves you so much that He gave His life for you. He has all power; He is never helpless. No one can frustrate His plans. He never grows weary.

He lives with you, feels with you, rejoices with you, grieves with you, and suffers with you. He shares your struggles, both when you pray and when you are tempted.

He says to us today: "Lo, I am with you!"

Do you see Him in your daily life? In the realm of the Spirit we cannot see with our physical eyes. But the Scriptures tell us that God's children received spiritual eyes, eyes of the heart, with which to perceive the spiritual realities all around them. A servant of one of the prophets was also permitted for a moment to behold the spiritual realities which surrounded him. He saw horses and chariots of fire. It calmed his spirit and made his heart glad.

You, too, should pray that you might see this as you go about your tasks from day to day feeling lonesome, restless, anxious, and unhappy.

"Lo, I am with you *always*."

Some days are unusually hard. So many things can darken our lives. The hardest of all is to feel that we are far away from our heavenly Friend.

At such a time remember the word of Jesus: "Always."

He is never closer to you than when you feel lonely and heavy of heart. Tell Him how you feel. And pray that the eyes of your heart may be opened so that you see Him.

> "The world may seek and love its own;
> I love my Jesus, Him alone."

Fight the good fight of the faith.

—1 TIMOTHY 6:12

LUTHER says somewhere that faith lives only as long as it strives. He had in mind this very fight of faith to hold fast to the grace of God when our heart condemns us because of our daily life.

This tension is inherent in living faith and can never be removed. If this is eliminated from faith, we have a *dead* faith which holds fast to the grace of God with the intellect and does not give the conscience an opportunity to condemn sin.

This struggle and this tension in connection with faith can therefore never be obviated by theoretical insight into the mystery of the Gospel. Not even a long *experience* of the grace of God can eliminate it.

The people who experience these difficulties in connection with believing the grace of God are not Christians of the poorest type. Luther himself, a great hero of faith, often had great difficulty even in believing the forgiveness of sins.

The more sensitive and keen our conscience becomes, the *more* it will accuse us, the *deeper* it will prick us.

A rich and long experience of the grace of God will also sharpen the conflict: Can you be a child of God when so much of His grace has been so fruitless in your heart and life? Is not this proof that your faith is dead, that you are misusing the grace of God?

Here, too, living faith will win the victory and again *rest* in the grace of God.

But only after a *struggle*.

The distress of conscience caused by sin is therefore not only the mother of faith; it is this distress which each day preserves the faith of a child of God as a *living faith*.

"Redeemed, restored, forgiven
Through Jesus' precious blood,
Heirs of His home in heaven,
Oh, praise our pardoning God!"

A man had two sons; and he came to the first, and said, Son, go work today in the vineyard.

—MATTHEW 21:28

WHEN we look at the great ocean of humanity, even just that little portion of which we have a view, a feeling of impotence often comes over us.

Here they swarm about one another: punished and unpunished criminals, people living in open and people living in secret vice, folk living in a form of ungodliness sanctioned by society, and finally the many other quiet, upright, industrious, and capable people—all *without* God.

It is true that there are oftentimes many people present at services in church and at other Christian meetings. But the number of those who do not come is nevertheless many times greater.

It is these that weigh so heavily upon our minds. We ask ourselves: Is it not possible any more to get people to listen to the Word of God?

Our Word for today tells us also, among other things, that all of us have our own inner history of our relations with God. And it is this which determines our outward life.

God speaks quietly and lovingly to each individual in our beloved nation.

Oh, how happy this makes us! God is speaking to all His wayward sons and daughters.

Also to you! You *had* to listen to Him because you felt some of the gracious love inherent in the words: My son! My daughter!

As you heard the call of God, life became a heavy burden to you. You felt that your whole life was nothing but an unending sin against the Father in heaven.

Whereupon you made Him some fervent promises.

Did anything more come of them, or were they only promises?

Son, go work today in the vineyard. And he answered and said, I will not: but afterward he repented himself and went.

—MATTHEW 21:28-29

ONE of the brothers answered in the affirmative immediately. But all it amounted to was a generous promise. Many are they who do likewise. When they hear the gracious call of God, they are immediately moved by it and make the Lord some well-meant and fervent promises. As long as they feel the call of God strongly and clearly in their hearts they are completely convinced of the one thing needful, and it is really their wish to become new men and women.

But when they encounter contempt and opposition and are called upon to make daily renunciation of sin, they give up and quietly slip back into their former manner of life.

The other of the two replied in the negative but afterward regretted his decision and yielded to the call.

Yes, that is the way it has gone with many of us.

We would not heed when God called us.

But afterward, when the call began to grow fainter, an unspeakable anxiety came over us: Suppose this should be God's last call! What if He could never again get us to hear His call!

So we turned, and prayed God humbly to receive us and not cast us away, even though we had despised His call so grossly.

Yes, we all have our own inner history.

It is lived on earth, but written in heaven. It is replete with incidents.

Some day it will be read to us in its entirety.

Then no part of this history can be changed.

Now, on the other hand, we who so often have said "No" to God can repent of this decision; our life can become a daily "Yes" to Him by the grace of His Spirit who works in us both to will and to do according to God's good pleasure.

Fear not, little flock; for it is your Father's good
pleasure to give you the kingdom.

—LUKE 12:32

HERE Jesus seeks to give us courage to believe in God. As
a matter of fact, He does this often. We could no doubt say
that the aim of all that Jesus did was to persuade us to believe
in our Father in heaven.

This seems easy enough to a conscience which is asleep,
which is not aware of its guilt nor of God's burning wrath
against sin. But to the soul that is spiritually awake, that has
become aware of the seriousness of sin, nothing is as hard, in
fact, as impossible, as to believe that God forgives.

Indeed, such souls do not get courage to believe until they
see Christ in the Word, the only one on earth who can give
a sinner courage to believe in the forgiveness of sins.

"Fear not," says Jesus today to all the fearful souls who
condemn themselves. It is your Father's good pleasure to give
you the kingdom. He does not simply endure you; He rejoices
to give you the kingdom. He who spared not His only Son,
how could He do anything else but give you all things together
with Him?

"Little flock," He says.

He knows that we often feel discouraged and fearful just
because we are so few and so weak. The contempt and opposition of the world would deprive us of our courage. It seems
as though both we and God's whole cause seem destined to be
defeated by the mighty powers which are at the disposal of our
opponents at all times.

Then He comforts us. He tells us that it is not dangerous
to be the little flock. It is not dangerous to be in the minority.
It is not dangerous to face adverse winds. It is not dangerous
to encounter super-mighty opposition. It is not dangerous to
be despised! For it is thus that it has pleased God to further
His cause in this world.

"Fear not, little flock."

> Everyone that committeth sin is the bondservant of sin. If therefore the Son shall make you free, ye shall be free indeed.
>
> —JOHN 8:34, 36

J ESUS speaks here of bondservants and of those who are free.

A bondservant is a person who is owned and used by another and therefore has no rights or prerogatives of his own.

True, slavery has been abolished.

To buy and sell human beings is now punishable by very severe penalties.

Still slavery flourishes throughout the world. Most human beings spend their lives in slavery. There are people who sell themselves every day. Worst of all, they sell themselves as slaves, not to other human beings, but to humanity's most bitter enemy, Satan. To him who exploits and oppresses his slaves, not only during their brief earthly span of years, but in an everlasting hell.

Young boys and girls sell themselves with a smile on their faces.

To them sin is fascinating amusement. "It is not as dangerous to sin as the old folk think," they blaspheme.

But they have found that sin is something else besides fun. Lust soon becomes the lord of their lives. They resist, it is true, but the desire becomes too strong. It whips them into sinning more and more against the clear convictions of their consciences.

As a result they go through life bound by the chains of sin. Some by the heavy manacles of vice. Most of them by the glittering but strong fetters of worldly-mindedness.

What makes this slavery so terrible is the quiet voice within the bosom of the slave which says that she was never ordained to be a slave.

She was created to *have dominion* over herself and over her enemies. She was created to be *free.*

My friend, chained to sin, would you be free?

And when Jesus saw her, he called her, and said to her, Woman, thou art loosed from thine infirmity.

—LUKE 13:12

THE woman with the spirit of infirmity is a mighty sermon to us all.

Our infirmity comes to light most clearly in our relationship to our old ego. It is in that connection that we can most readily discern our spiritual condition, whether we have the spirit of *power* or the spirit of *infirmity*.

There are, for instance, the people who gladly make great sacrifices for the sick and the poor, but neglect their own. To them the daily sacrifices connected with their own home life are too small and insignificant.

There are people who go long distances to preach, to testify, or to sing of God. But in their own homes they do not even conduct devotions for the family.

There are people who are congenial and interesting when among strangers, but who at home, among their own, are taciturn and sullen, yes, even contrary.

What I have here mentioned is not *hypocrisy*. It is spiritual *infirmity*.

A Christianity with much flame but little power. A Christianity with much human spirit but little of the Spirit of God. Paul would no doubt have called it *carnal* Christianity, regardless of how spiritual it might seem in the eyes of many people.

We hear today, however, not only of the spirit of infirmity, but also of Him who can heal us. But first He must show us how "bowed together" we are.

O friends! Let us go to the Lord with our inflated ego and confess this hideous sin of ours against Him, against one another, and against His cause in this world.

The oftener our old self is made to take its place beneath the cross of Christ, the more assuredly will it lose its vitality.

Walk while ye have the light, that darkness overtake you not.

—JOHN 12:35

TODAY Jesus would speak in all earnestness to you who have postponed your conversion every time you have been called of God. He would speak to you about the greatest danger involved in living as an unconverted person.

What do you think is the greatest danger facing you? In all likelihood you fear sudden death more than anything else. It would prevent you from repenting at the very last.

But that is not the greatest danger, says Jesus. For God can ward off sudden death. But there is one danger that He cannot ward off from you. The Bible calls it *hardening* of the heart. This refers to the cumulative though quiet effect that seeing the light without yielding to it has upon your soul.

Hardening of the heart means that you harden yourself against your conscience, that you have convictions without following them. By so doing you first lose your capacity for following your convictions and then your faculty for possessing a conviction.

When the latter state is reached, almighty God Himself has no way of helping you.

Why are you unconverted today?

Because there was always *something* hindering you, something which prevented you from following your conviction.

Why do you not repent today? There is not a great deal that is keeping you from doing so.

But these *little* things are enough to keep you from following your convictions.

Have I not already hardened my heart, some one may ask.

No, your fear of this shows that the Spirit of God is still at work within you. But do not permit this to become a new temptation to you to postpone conversion.

Thy word is a lamp unto my feet,
And light unto my path.

—PSALM 119:105

MANY children of God think that this promise is not being fulfilled in their lives. They pray for light and desire earnestly to know the will of God. But they do not think that they receive a definite answer.

The reason is in many instances that they misunderstand the light that God does give them. They forget that it is a lamp unto our feet.

On a dark autumn evening, a little lantern in our hand, we stand ready to start out upon the mile-long road through the wood. One without any experience would no doubt ask: "You do not expect to get along with that little light, do you?"

But everything goes all right. The lantern does not light up a great deal more than one step at a time. But since I am carrying it in my hand, it lights up every step I take until I have reached my destination.

Thus God lights up our pathway. Step by step.

We are not always satisfied with this light. And would rather that God would employ His heavenly search-light in order that we might be able to see all the way to the end of life all at once. Especially would we have Him project His light through the dark veil of death and into the invisible realm beyond.

But it is grace from God that He does not open the book of the future to us, that He gives us His light only step by step.

True, this oftentimes becomes an earnest trial of our faith. We become restless when it seems that God delays too long before shedding His light upon the situations in which we find ourselves.

However, as we look back upon our life with God, I think that we must all thank and praise Him because he has so graciously led us upon the right pathway, notwithstanding all our restlessness and impatience. Wherefore we say:

"Hitherto the Lord hath helped us!"

Whether he is a sinner, I know not: one thing I
know, that, whereas I was blind, now I see.

—JOHN 9:25

THERE is something remarkable about this blind lad.
First, that he was healed although he had been *born* blind.
Next, what he *then* experienced.

Instead of meeting him joyfully and with good wishes, people
began a veritable cross-examination of him, as though he had
done something wrong. They wanted to explain away the whole
matter. So they turned first to his parents. But they were such
cowards that they wriggled away from the whole affair, saying:
"Ask him; he is of age!"

Then they tried to bewilder the boy by asking him various
questions. But he would not permit himself to become confused.
He held clearly and definitely to what he knew: "One thing
I know, that, whereas I was blind, now I see."

Thereupon he turned upon them with counter-questions
and stopped their mouths completely. Whereupon they became
furiously angry and cast him out of the synagogue.

Many since that day have had similar experiences.

Jesus has come to them without their asking Him to do so.
He has opened their eyes and they have seen their sinfulness.
It is all so remarkable. They have experienced such distress
that they could not endure to live their former life any longer.
They have felt that they must care for their immortal soul and
yield to the merciful Savior who has opened their eyes.

Then difficulties have arisen.

Their old friends have become malicious: "Would you teach
us? Would you be better than we are?" They have carried on
a veritable campaign of espionage against the new convert in
order to find faults about which to talk. Yet, many have even
had the experience of having evil reports spread concerning
allegedly base sins which they are supposed to have committed
after their conversion.

Do not despair, my dear friend. He who opened your eyes
will defend you as He defended the man born blind when
trouble broke in upon him.

> And he charged them that they should tell no man:
> but the more he charged them, so much the more a
> great deal they published it . . . saying, He hath done
> all things well.
>
> —MARK 7:36-37

HERE we meet some happy people, people who speak enthusiastically about Jesus, who cannot refrain from doing it.

Most people never say anything about Jesus.

No doubt they think about Him, and perhaps think a great deal. But they do not speak. They never start a conversation about Jesus. And they never participate in one started by others.

Others speak about Jesus, and write about Him also. Some even write a great deal.

But they never say, "He hath done all things well." They are never really satisfied with Him.

Of course there are many things about Him which they value highly: His purity and goodness, His undaunted courage in standing for the truth, His willingness to sacrifice and to suffer. Nevertheless, there are some things with which they are not satisfied.

That He is the eternal Son of God, that He was born of a virgin, that His death is a vicarious atonement for our sins, that He arose bodily from the dead, that He speaks of a personal devil and an eternal hell—of course I am not surprised that they object to these things.

For Jesus is not only the world's greatest Man; He is also its greatest stumbling-block. Even during His days here on earth He encountered doubt and criticism. Think of the Pharisees and the Sadducees! And do we not remember His doleful words: "Blessed are they whosoever shall not be offended in me!"

May I say to you who doubt: Let Jesus come into your life, and He will perform the great *miracle* also in you. That is the way *we* were cured of our doubts.

You are standing a little too aloof. You are looking *down* upon Jesus. When you kneel before Him, as the rest of us have done, you, too, will see Him as your *Savior.*

> And I say unto you, that every idle word that men shall speak, they shall give account thereof in the day of judgment.

—MATTHEW 12:36

J ESUS seldom uses such strong language as He did in the conversation from which our text was taken.

It was a conversation with the Pharisees during which He referred to them as the offspring of vipers. He also brought them face to face with judgment more earnestly and forcibly than He had ever done before.

From this it is clear that He was speaking about something exceedingly important, something to which we must therefore give heed most earnestly.

He was speaking of the sins of the tongue, which constitute such a large and significant proportion of the sins we commit. And this strikes all of us.

Jesus says in our text that we are to give account on judgment day of every *idle* word that we have spoken. What an accounting it will be for every one of us!

Think of the *thoughtless* words. We did not intend any evil, but because of the thoughtlessness of our words a great deal of harm was done to those about whom we spoke. Or think of the *cold* words. We ought rather to warm people's icy souls by our words; instead, our words are like ice-cold polar air to our surroundings.

Or think of all the *sly*, cunning and false words which make for insecurity among people. Or the *unmerciful*, harsh, and bitter words which pierce wounded souls like daggers. Or the *slanderous* words which buzz around like poison bacilli wherever we turn. Or the *untruthful* words, not only those that are deliberately false, but all the unreliable and irresponsible talk about persons and things concerning which people have no knowledge.

Let us bow humbly beneath the judgment which Jesus pronounces today. And pray for forgiveness. Also in this connection the blood of Jesus Christ is our only consolation.

And if we will permit ourselves to be humbled, Jesus will heal us and teach us the rightful use of our tongues.

Out of the abundance of the heart the mouth
speaketh.

—MATTHEW 12:34

W HEN Jesus speaks to us about our sins, He always directs
our attention *inward.*

Our words reflect our heart-life, He says. "Out of the abundance of the heart the mouth speaketh."

The great amount of false, flattering, wheedling talk of our day corroborates this. The falseness of people's hearts comes to expression in their false words.

If you will give heed to your words, if not for more than one day, you will learn to know the condition of *your heart.* Because there is this inner connection between our words and our hearts, Jesus speaks to us with such earnestness about our tongues.

Let us listen to Him carefully as He speaks, and prove ourselves.

The generation of Christians to which we belong is a superficial and thoughtless generation. We could perhaps without exaggeration use an even stronger expression: a frivolous generation. I believe that our speech is irrefutable proof of this.

The Christians of the past generation were quite different in their daily speech and in their social relationships; they were exceedingly careful. They took cognizance of Jesus' statement about every *idle* word. There was a certain seriousness and dignity about them in all their ways and in all their conversation.

Our generation of Christians thinks that the older Christians were too serious and legalistic. Whereupon they proceed to show their Christian liberty in their associations with others and in their speech. And, it is true, a Christian should be happy and jovial. However, the line between *joviality* and *frivolity* is not always easy to observe. And then we have so much nonsense and worldliness, so much thoughtless and frivolous speech, when Christians meet. Both among the clergy and the laity.

Lord, forgive us! Lord, teach Thou us how to speak!

> And whatsoever ye do, in word or in deed, do all in
> the name of the Lord Jesus, giving thanks to God
> the Father through him.   —COLOSSIANS 3:17

SOME people have misunderstood the sayings of Jesus about idle words.

They have taken them to mean that they should say nothing more than that which is absolutely necessary. Anything beyond that they consider idle. The result is, of course, that they become reticent and taciturn. Eventually it becomes difficult to live with them, even though they otherwise are good, conscientious people.

God has given us the gift of speech in order that we might *do good* with it.

In daily life, for instance, to chat with one another has a salutary effect upon us, whether we are working, relaxing, or visiting with one another. The things we say need not always be profound or weighty. It is the free, spontaneous conversation which makes the home such a good, cozy place. Only let us be careful lest gossip enter stealthily into these quiet, confidential chats.

Furthermore, God has given us the gift of speech for the promotion of *friendliness.* Remember that friendly words are among the best things that you can give to those with whom you associate. Make it a rule to speak in friendly terms to all with whom you speak.

Moreover, try to speak *encouraging* words to those with whom you associate. There are many things that weigh people down, annoy and irritate them. A word of encouragement does a great deal of good. Yes, even though you must reprimand some one, do not do it without at the same time saying something encouraging.

And turn the conversation into spiritual channels. Say a little about the great things the Lord has done for you. Not only to the unconverted, but to believers also. How we need it! I have learned to love more than any others those people who, by speaking a word to me in my daily life, help me in the accomplishment of the most difficult of all tasks, that of living as a Christian.

> And blessed is he, whosoever shall find no occasion
> of stumbling in me! —MATTHEW 11:6

JESUS sent these words as a greeting to John the Baptist while he was in prison, at a time when he was finding an occasion of stumbling in the humble personality of Jesus. Even the Baptist, this greatest of all the prophets of God, was really taking offense at Jesus. The fact of the matter is that there is something offensive about the person of Jesus which cannot be removed. It can only be overcome by faith.

Jesus Himself knew that He was such a stumbling-block. There is something mild, yes, even tender, in His words to John: "Blessed is he, whosoever shall find no occasion of stumbling in me!"

Jesus was not more than eight days old when the aged Simeon saw the occasion of stumbling: "Behold, this child is set for the falling and rising of many in Israel."

In our day people speak mostly of the offense which Christ is to our *intellect*. And this offense is great. But the occasion of stumbling to our *wills* is much greater.

Consider a person who is young and who is enjoying life, who lives, and laughs, and plays, and dances. And thinks of everything else but God. Jesus comes to such a one and says: "You must be converted!" Is there not something irritating about this, something which incites to contradiction and opposition?

Jesus no doubt felt it Himself also. One notices it as He says: "Blessed is he that is not offended in me!"

Or take the religious people who live their pious lives from day to day in prayer and meditation upon the Word of God, who struggle bravely against their sins and who are friendly and kind-hearted in every way. Christ comes to them and says: You are not converted. And if you are not converted you will be forever lost, notwithstanding all the morality and religion that you have.

Is not this offensive?

And still Christ can make reply in none other than these mild and tender words: "Blessed is he, whosoever shall find no occasion of stumbling in me!"

> But unto you that fear my name shall the sun of righteousness arise with healing in its wings.
>
> —MALACHI 4:2

W E spoke some time ago about "light treatments" for the soul, beginning with spiritual awakening and conversion. These stop the ailment which is afflicting the soul. But as yet the soul is not entirely *healed*. The light treatments must continue daily.

Our quiet hours in secret prayer should be such daily light treatments. But we do not often make use of them in that way.

We devote these hours to *speaking*. We speak with God about so many things. We talk all the time. And after we have talked a while, we say, "Amen!" and leave.

Suppose you did that to a doctor. You came into his office; he offered you a chair; you began to tell him of all your pains and ailments. And when you were through with this, you arose, bowed in adieu, and went. What would he think? Oh, he would most likely assume that some deranged person had come into his office by mistake.

God has patients such as these visiting Him every day. And this is one reason why our seasons of prayer mean so little to us.

If you know where your conscience hurts you, point it out to the Great Physician. He will heal all your diseases.

Oftentimes, however, we do not know where it hurts; we know only that we have no peace and that there is distress within. Let us then take time to permit Him to examine us with His light and place His finger on the sore spot, that we may know clearly what it is that has deprived us of our peace.

Then something will happen in our prayer room. We will see the things in our hearts and lives which are injuring our life in God or which are doing damage to the work we are doing in the vineyard. We will make an accounting before Him with tears and rejoicing. And the sun of righteousness will arise again with healing in its wings.

Rejoice in the Lord always; again I will say, Rejoice!

—PHILIPPIANS 4:4

ARE *you* happy in the Lord?

I am not asking whether you are *seeking* God, *praying* to God, *reading* about God, *hearing* about God, *talking* about God, *debating* God, nor am I asking you whether you have an *awe* of God or whether you *fear* Him.

I am asking: Are you *happy* in God?

Perhaps you must answer in the negative.

Tell me one thing: Have you never wondered at this?

You enjoy other people. You enjoy animals. You enjoy nature and art. And you enjoy money. But God, your Creator, your Father, Him you do *not* enjoy.

Have you never said to yourself that this shows that there must be something wrong with you, in fact, something *radically wrong?* Have you never felt that this is abnormal?

Undoubtedly you know that the Bible says that you are an *enemy* of God. "The mind of the flesh is enmity against God," it says.

No doubt some people here and there are in their own minds quietly protesting against this and saying: "No, it cannot be said that I am an enemy of God, even though I am not particularly intimate with Him."

But some will acknowledge the truth and say: "I am not happy in God. I have tried to enjoy God, but I do not succeed. And I do not know what to do about it."

God will take care of that for you, my friend.

You just do what He asks *you* to do: acknowledge before God that you do not love Him. And He will forgive, for Jesus' sake, this great sin of yours, the most terrible sin of all! The basic sin, the sin for which Jesus shed His lifeblood.

And when He has forgiven you your sin, He will give you His Holy Spirit. And an entirely *new* joy will enter into your life: rejoicing in the Lord. Rejoicing that your name is written in the book of life!

241

And behold, a certain lawyer stood up and made trial of him, saying, Teacher, what shall I do to inherit eternal life?

—LUKE 10:25

Here we meet Jesus and one of the lawyers of His day. The latter wanted to set a trap for Jesus; and with that in mind he put to Jesus the question cited above, a question which he himself considered very difficult and dangerous to answer.

When Jesus answered very directly by referring to that which was written in the law, the man apparently became disconcerted for a moment. He, an expert in the law, put a difficult question to an untrained rabbi, and Jesus replied by showing him that he, the expert in legal matters, did not know the law.

But the lawyer within him came to the rescue. Jesus had mentioned the word "neighbor." This was a much-debated concept among the learned of that day. Accordingly he seized upon the word and asked Jesus: "Who is my neighbor?"

How he resembles us!

We are all lawyers, born lawyers, eminent lawyers! Notice even little children. They cannot talk well as yet, but how they can excuse and defend themselves when they have done something wrong! And we adults, even though we are not exceptionally gifted, all do have one gift, namely that of defending ourselves. Listen to our speeches in defense of ourselves! Notice how we bring out all the mitigating circumstances— fully as capably as any attorney in court.

And not only *before* our conversion. We Christians, too, carry on a persistent defense of ourselves. Nor do we do it only before others. How seldom we meet a person who acknowledges his mistakes without attempting to excuse himself.

But we try to excuse ourselves before God also. To make immediate acknowledgement of our sins, without excusing ourselves before God, involves us in a great struggle every day.

But he, desiring to justify himself, said unto Jesus,
And who is my neighbor?

—LUKE 10:29

THIS lawyer resembles us most in this that he, by raising difficult theoretical questions, sought to argue himself away from the insistent truth with which Jesus was confronting him.

We all argue with God.

Not only because we do not agree with Him, but also to wriggle away from the truth of which we have been convicted and to which we refuse to yield.

Many people do nothing else all their lives but dispute with God. Some do it loudly and bombastically, in newspapers, magazines, and books. Others do it quietly, but their dispute with God may be equally passionate.

They endeavor to prove to themselves that they have valid reasons for living their old selfish life.

Some people have ceased such disputing. The Bible calls them children of God. For God's children are the people who have yielded, who will no longer argue with God. They have admitted that God is right, and have confessed, not only their sins, but also that they have been stiff-necked in their dispute with the good Spirit of God.

Children of God are those people who *each day* yield to God, who each day cease to dispute with God. Every time the Spirit speaks to them through their consciences about their sins, they yield and creep to the cross, to the cross of Christ. There they find *peace* with God instead of unending *conflict* with Him. And those who yield, God draws to His heart and gives unspeakable consolation and rest.

The Bible speaks of unconverted people. They are the people who continue to dispute with God and will not yield.

My friend, yield now and acknowledge that God is right!

243

And they were all filled with the Holy Spirit.

—ACTS 2:4

To be filled with the Spirit of God is the greatest thing to which we human beings can attain. And unto the attainment of this we were all created.

Many desire and even pray for the fulness of the Spirit without experiencing it. That is serious. However, even more serious is the fact that many Christians do not pray for the fulness of the Spirit.

Do not all, then, receive the Spirit of God when they pray for it?

Yes, Jesus tells us that no earthly parents give their children good gifts as willingly as God gives the Holy Spirit to His children.

Yes, God hears their prayer. They receive the Spirit. But they are not filled, because they cannot endure the Spirit's fire.

They looked for the fulness of the Spirit and expected, when they received it, to experience supernatural joy and liberation from all spiritual struggle and toil. But the Spirit was given for the very purpose of accentuating this struggle. He comes to convict of sin and to ask Christians whether they are willing to break with everything sinful, according to the new light which they have received from the Spirit.

Believers never feel so unhappy as when the Spirit has convicted them of the sinfulness of their hearts.

Be not dismayed, therefore, you who prayed for the fulness of the Spirit, but who experienced it as scorching fire in your soul.

Your prayer has been heard. The Spirit has shown you your sinfulness and your helplessness as never before.

But the Spirit does not expect that you can set yourself free. He will liberate you. With consuming fire He will burn you loose from the bonds which have kept your heart closed to God.

Then He will fill you with humble rejoicing that Jesus has died for your wicked heart and that you need only deliver it up to the Spirit's fire every time you note that it opposes God.

> At that season Jesus answered and said, I thank thee,
> O Father, Lord of heaven and earth, that thou didst
> hide these things from the wise and understanding,
> and didst reveal them unto babes.
>
> —MATTHEW 11:25

W E are not told a great deal in the Bible about the inner life of Jesus.

We are told a couple of times that He became angry. Once He said Himself that He was sorrowful. Twice we are told that He wept. But only once are we told that Jesus rejoiced.

And it is our text today that tells us this. Luke is the one who has preserved this incident from the life of Jesus. He begins his account as follows: "In that same hour he rejoiced in the Holy Spirit and said . . ."

Let us first notice *how* He rejoiced. He rejoiced in the Holy Spirit, it says. Let us examine our rejoicing.

Is it in the *Spirit?* We can ascertain this most readily by noting the other characteristic feature of Jesus' rejoicing: He had to go to His heavenly Father with it. Is our joy of the kind that it drives us to God? That makes us feel a desire to pour it out before our Father?

Jesus tells His Father here *what* it is that causes Him to rejoice, namely, that the Father has hidden these things from the *wise*, from those who think they are so wise that they do not need any revelation from God. And that He has revealed Himself to *babes*, to those who acknowledge that they do not know God, and who therefore are humbly receptive to all that God reveals to them of His salvation.

We *hear* of this rejoicing on the part of Jesus only on this one occasion. But from His life we learn that it followed Him wherever He went. Wherever His pathway led He met such "babes" as these to whom He could reveal Himself and His Father: the twelve poor fishermen, the woman taken in sin, Zacchaeus, the sick, those possessed with demons. And last, but not least, the thief on the cross.

Has He been permitted to reveal Himself to you?

Come unto me, all ye that labor and are heavy laden, and I will give you rest.

—MATTHEW 11:28

W<small>E</small> spoke yesterday of Jesus' rejoicing.

Today we hear a little more about it. It was a joy to Jesus to call unto Himself all who labored and were heavy laden and to give them rest.

He knew what He had to give these people. And He knew of no greater joy than seeing that the Word awakened their sleeping souls and that they began to reach out toward Him because they knew not what else to do but commend themselves, body and soul, into His loving and mighty hands.

Awakened and restless soul, do not be afraid to go to Jesus.

It is true that both you and I have deported ourselves in such a way that we have no right to appeal to Him. The Prodigal Son also was afraid as he journeyed homeward. But read in Luke 15 about the father's rejoicing when the son came home.

You labor with your heavy burdens. But listen today: Jesus has borne all your burdens for you. He has paid your debt.

It is He who has wooed and drawn your soul. He rejoiced every time he saw that you were becoming one of the "babes" who knew not what else to do but to go to Him. He rejoiced when He saw that your mouth was stopped and that you acknowledged your guilt before God.

And now that He has drawn you unto Himself and you lie at His feet, He rejoices to give you that for which you are longing so earnestly, that which He has won for you by His blood, namely, *rest* for your longing, weary, and despairing soul.

> "Come, come to His feet, and lay open your story
> Of suffering and sorrow, of guilt and of shame;
> For the pardon of sin is the crown of His glory,
> And the joy of our Lord to be true to His name."

> For the eyes of Jehovah run to and fro throughout the whole earth, to show himself strong in the behalf of them whose heart is perfect toward him.
>
> —2 CHRONICLES 16:9

THE Word of God is two-edged. This word also. And very sharp. It cuts to the very heart, for it speaks of the heart which is *perfect toward the Lord*. And puts to all of us the very pointed and persistent question: Do you fear God with all your heart?

Is your heart in your *prayers*? Or is it habit and duty which drive you to pray?

Is your heart in your *reading of the Bible*? Or do you read a chapter merely for the sake of having read it?

Is your heart in your *striving against sin*? Or do you fight against sin simply because you fear its consequences, your heart meanwhile clinging to sin?

Is your heart in your *remorse*? Do you grieve because you sin, because you act contrary to the will of God, or do you grieve simply because you fear the consequences of sin?

Is your heart in the *sacrifices* you make? Are you glad to give of your time and your money, are you glad to forego your own comfort and convenience?

What is *your* answer to these searching questions?

I imagine some one will say: "My heart is cut to the quick by all of these questions. My heart is so wicked that, alas, I do not know what to do."

My friend, I shall preach the Gospel to you today, the glad tidings that you, yes, you have a heart that is perfect toward Him.

"No, you are mistaken," you will reply. You will say: "My heart is divided; I am half-hearted, lukewarm."

Yes, all people have hearts like that, but all those who make known their lukewarm and divided hearts before the Lord, all those are perfect toward Him.

Draw nigh to His heart which broke in death for your divided heart. And give thanks to Him that you may rest *in Christ* with everything—also with your heart.

Were there none found that returned to give glory
to God, save this stranger?

—LUKE 17:18

OUR children pray more than they give thanks. Indeed, it
is a very difficult task to teach them to return thanks.

This is also the case with God's children.

It is true, of course, that we also pray too little. We do not
understand, and therefore do not make use of our prerogative
as God's children to come to the mercy seat, regardless of what
it may be that is troubling us, and say, "Father, Thou must
help Thy child!"

But we know even less how to thank Him as we ought. Nor
is it easy for our heavenly Father to teach us to give thanks.
A cordial and joy-filled giving of thanks seldom rises to the
heights of heaven from the vales of earth.

Still God would have us give thanks to Him.

Our text tells us how disappointedly Jesus inquired for the
nine lepers who had been cleansed, but who left without returning thanks. At the same time we hear how happy Jesus
became when one did return to thank Him.

Why did Jesus become so happy? Because to thank God is
to give glory to God, He says.

In heaven we shall all give thanks unto God.

But if we would become fitted for heaven, we must learn
the customs of heaven here on earth. And if we are to learn,
we must practice.

If practice of any kind should be easy for us, this certainly
should be. Day and night we are the recipients of nought but
lovingkindness at the hands of our heavenly Father. Should it
not be natural then for our days and our dreams at night to
be filled with thanksgiving and jubilation?

Only goodness and mercy shall follow us all the days of our
life, yes, throughout all the eternities, say the Scriptures and
our own experience.

O Lord, forgive us because we do not thank Thee more!

In the world ye have tribulation.

—JOHN 16:33

W E know that all the children of God are to have tribulation in this world. Nevertheless we are all surprised every time tribulation comes to *us*.

If the tribulation becomes severe and protracted, many a painful question begins to burn in our weary and wounded souls.

Let us see what answer the Scriptures give.

We do not learn *obedience* without tribulation. Even Jesus had to learn obedience by the things which He suffered. We cannot learn it by anything less. And obedience is better than sacrifice. Remember this, you who seem to get nothing else done but to suffer for the Lord.

Tribulation worketh *steadfastness*, we read further. We are all hasty and impatient. Tribulation makes us aware of this, that we may be saved from it by the grace of God.

Tribulation worketh *approvedness*. The fires of tribulation purge us by melting away the dross, all that is not genuine within us. And these fires are hot, though not dangerous.

Tribulation worketh *hope*, says the apostle. We all have a tendency to allow ourselves to become attached to this world, making our heavenly fatherland seem distant and alien to us. But "our tribulations make us weary of the bondage of worldliness and, on the other hand, make it easier for us to walk in the way of life," says Brorson.

The more familiar I become with the Scriptures and with life, the clearer it becomes to me that tribulation is the silent dynamic of all Christian life. As the old wall-clock stops when we remove its weights, so also would our life in God come to a stop if the weights of tribulation were removed.

Oftentimes it seems to you that the weights are heavy. But do not forget that he who places them upon you knows of what you are made. He will make both the temptation and the way of escape such that you can endure. Remember this also: you honor God through suffering.

As sorrowful, yet always rejoicing.

—2 CORINTHIANS 6:10

Many in our day misunderstand the joy which believing souls possess.

They think that it consists of spiritual states that are entirely free from pain and full of exalted sentiments. And since *such* joy does not come of itself, except in isolated moments, they try to bring forth in themselves and in others these intense and highly strained spiritual experiences. By various outward as well as inward means.

As a result, their joy becomes an unnatural and affected joy, which has a detrimental effect both upon them and upon their surroundings.

Fortunately, Christian joy is something different from this.

In the first place, it is natural and genuine. It needs no false stimulation, no exalted auto-suggestion.

In the second place, it is like life itself: it is in continuously surging motion, not like a monotone. It is this movement the apostle depicts in our Word for today: "As sorrowful, yet always rejoicing."

The Christian's joy may vacillate strongly and rapidly between sorrow and joy, between fear and calm, between smiles and tears. Life is complex; life in God is more so than any other kind. It contains within itself the strangest contradictions.

Experienced Christians know that their joy in the Lord can neither be won nor kept without sorrow. Their joy does not consist therefore in being free from sorrow. They see that to be deeply grieved because of themselves, because of their own self-love, wilfulness, worldliness, slothfulness, and unwilling spirit, is the only soil in which their joy in the Lord can grow and thrive.

Their joy consists in experiencing God and His unspeakable grace, both in joy and in sorrow, in fear and in calm, in anxiety and in blissful rest.

Awake, thou that sleepest, and arise from the dead,
and Christ shall shine upon thee.

—EPHESIANS 5:14

PAUL wrote all his letters to believers.

Consequently, this Word, too, is written to believers, although not only to them.

Is it necessary to write to believers: "Awake, thou that sleepest!"

Yes, otherwise it would not have been written.

Both the Scriptures and experience teach us very clearly that believers can go to sleep very easily and very quickly. Think of the three disciples in the garden of Gethsemane. They went to sleep even though Jesus admonished them very urgently to watch with Him.

Or think of the ten virgins. They all went to sleep. However, five of them were saved because their sleep had not become spiritual death.

Many of God's children have gone to sleep down through the years.

The sad thing in connection with this is that people go to sleep without knowing it. This is the case also with natural sleep. We are never aware of the exact moment when we go to sleep.

Spiritual sleep, too, comes quietly and unnoticed. The world becomes dear to us, sin becomes innocent and harmless, prayer becomes tedious and a matter of habit.

Lo, sleep has made its quiet advent.

Now, as of yore in Gethsemane, our gracious Savior would awaken His sleeping friends.

He would arouse us to *self-examination.*

I shall never finish my apprenticeship in the art of proving myself. I know of nothing more edifying than to sit down quietly with tried and tested children of God and confer with them about this aspect of Christianity.

During the remainder of this week we shall speak briefly of these things.

251

Try your own selves, whether ye are in the faith.
—2 CORINTHIANS 13:5

IN order to try ourselves it is necessary for us to know the things in our lives which constitute our greatest weaknesses, and which are therefore most dangerous to us.

I would mention first our *secret prayer life.*

Jesus says, "When thou prayest, enter into thine inner chamber, and having shut the door, pray."

Why would He have us close the door?

He would afford us *quietude,* of course. And that we need this is certainly true.

But from the context it is clear that Jesus would have the door closed also for another reason: to free us from *listeners* and *lookers-on.*

He knows us well; He knows how regrettably dependent we are upon auditors and spectators. In all our human relationships and in our relationship to God.

Even in our prayer life.

Is there any one who can pray to God while others look on and hear without its influencing his prayer?

I take it for granted that you enter into your inner chamber and close the door.

Now I ask you, "Do you experience anything with God when you are entirely alone with Him?"

I am not asking you if it seems pleasant to be in the inner chamber. For I know that it is necessary for us to have unpleasant times there just as often as pleasant ones, if all is to be well with us.

There are Christians who do not experience anything from God when they are alone. If they are to experience anything, they must be stimulated by others by means of singing, music of other kinds, and lofty sentiments.

If this be true, *sleep* has overtaken you. And if this sleep continues for some time, with unfailing certainty it will bring you into spiritual death.

Beloved, let us love one another: for love is of God;
and every one that loveth is begotten of God.

— 1 JOHN 4:7

IT is edifying to see how a person who is born anew is born into the family of God, into the communion of saints.

How grateful and happy did we not feel when the children of God received us into their fellowship and met us with love and solicitude! Oh, how we loved them and rejoiced every time we could be together with them privately or at meetings.

Do you love the children of God *now?*

I am not asking if you like those people to whom you feel yourself attracted. That the children of the world also do. I am asking you if you love the children of God because they are children of God, whether you feel yourself one in spirit with them or not.

Many of God's children have fallen asleep.

They do not feel at home in the fellowship of believers any longer. In many places believers do not go to prayer meetings or discussion meetings, not even devotional meetings, unless something special is offered them, a "great" preacher, a festive occasion, or some such diversion.

Satan is aware of the importance of the communion of saints. And therefore he seeks with all his might to destroy such fellowship.

He does this in two ways. Either by sowing factionalism and dissension among the children of God. Or by making them indifferent towards one another and by making them worldly, thus eliminating the warmth and power of true Christian fellowship.

Dear children of God, pray for the communion of saints, that it may be preserved in fervency, security, and purity. Pray that we may love one another with a love that is full of solicitude for one another, a love that is willing to serve others and to make sacrifices in their behalf.

> By faith Enoch was translated that he should not see
> death; and he was not found because God translated
> him: for he hath had witness borne to him that before
> his translation he had been well-pleasing unto God.
> —HEBREWS 11:5

WHAT was there about Enoch that was well-pleasing
unto God?

Verily, let none of us think that Enoch in himself had any
qualifications which made him well-pleasing unto God. We
are all by nature the children of wrath, the Scriptures tell us.
Also Enoch.

It is for this reason too that the Epistle to the Hebrews
emphasizes the fact that it was by *faith* that Enoch became
well-pleasing unto God. The sinner who believes in the salvation which has been divinely ordained of God is well-pleasing
unto Him, whether it be in the old dispensation or in the new.
Such a person is one to whom the Lord does not reckon sin.

However, it is clear from our text that there was something
about Enoch which made him especially well-pleasing unto
God. In Genesis 5:24 we are told what this was: *Enoch walked
with God.*

What does this mean? Well, that is not explained to us.
But I take it to mean simply and directly that Enoch walked
with God in the daily affairs of life. We are told that he lived
365 years. All these years he walked with God. In his home,
in his daily work, among the sheep-folds, on the long trips
between grazing lands.

This was what God prized so highly.

Love is that way. We too desire to *walk* together with the
one to whom our heart is attached.

Listen now, dear child of God! God is waiting for an opportunity to walk with you. To go with you in your daily life.
He feels disappointed that you pray to Him only two or three
times a day in your inner chamber. He would have you speak
informally with Him about all the affairs of your daily life,
just as a little child goes about all day long and speaks with
its mother. It is a great joy to a mother to hear her child
think aloud.

Lay not up for yourselves treasures upon the earth, where moth and rust consume, and where thieves break through and steal.

—MATTHEW 6:19

MOST people do not agree with these words of Jesus. They live their lives as though it were written: "Lay up for yourselves treasures upon the earth. There are no moths and no thieves in heaven. For there are no treasures there."

So they proceed to lay up treasures to the best of their ability.

Some lay up money. Some prefer things that are more substantial and certain, such as farms and other forms of real estate. Some desire comfortable homes. Some prefer adornments. Some are interested in art. Some seek knowledge. Some desire to participate in the rich cultural life of the age.

Some succeed. But many of them are not successful in laying up treasures of any kind.

Nor does their earthly poverty afford them any treasures in heaven. Their hearts cleave to the treasures they did not succeed in laying up. And they continue to hope, incessantly and untiringly, that fortune will some day favor them.

How does God look upon this?

Many think that He begrudges people the limited measure of success they achieve by their labors and their struggles here on earth, and that He stands ready to strip them of their possessions as soon as they have gathered a few of them.

No, He freely grants you all. He lets His sun rise on the evil and on the good; He permits it to rain upon the just and the unjust. It is He who has blessed your labors and given you all that you now have.

You have neither thought of this nor thanked Him for it. But He has done it notwithstanding.

God has done even more. He has sympathized with you in your *poverty* all the way. You have nothing but the treasures of this earth. He sees how unsound your joy is. Therefore He gives you this warning today.

255

> But lay up for yourselves treasures in heaven, where
> neither moth nor rust doth consume, and where
> thieves do not break through nor steal.
>
> —MATTHEW 6:20

WHEN Christ warns us against laying up for ourselves treasures on earth, it is not a warning against *saving*.

On the contrary. He admonishes us in His Word to practice godliness with *contentment*. A child of God dare never be wasteful, extravagant, or careless in the use of his worldly goods. By the miracle of the loaves in the wilderness Jesus provided food in an easy manner. Nevertheless He bade His disciples gather up all that remained over.

It is therefore not saving and laying aside for a rainy day against which Jesus warns us. Rather, he has in mind, here as elsewhere, our *attitude of heart*. What He is opposed to is the desire to lay up treasures for the sake of possessing them, for the sake of becoming rich, or in order merely to enjoy them.

Jesus makes very clear here and in other places in the Scriptures how persons with the right attitude should make use of that which they have saved and which they possess. We are to use our earthly treasures to lay up for ourselves treasures in heaven, He says.

He admonishes us directly to make use of our earthly means to win unto ourselves friends who will receive us in the eternal mansions.

Think of this when you meet a suffering and needy person. It will help you to make your sacrifice gladly.

According to my understanding of the words of Jesus, it is ordained of God that whatever you give *in love* of your time, strength, food, clothing, or money is noted in heaven. Even such a lowly deed as the giving of a cup of cold water, Jesus says.

However, Jesus cuts off very quickly any one who would speculate in these things. Those who give from selfish motives have already received their reward, He says. They have received their returns in cash. Nothing therefore is credited to their account in heaven.

The lamp of the body is the eye: if therefore thine
eye be single, thy whole body shall be full of light.
But if thine eye be evil, thy whole body shall be full
of darkness. If therefore the light that is in thee be
darkness, how great is the darkness!

—MATTHEW 6:22-23

J ESUS has placed this parable about the eye in the same
context as the laying up of treasures.

Here, as elsewhere, He goes to the heart, to the root of the
ailment. Your sinful relationship to earthly treasures is caused
by the fact that your *eye* has been ruined, He says. You have
an "evil" eye; you see wrong. The great things look small to
you and the small things great.

For this reason your mistaken attitude toward the treasures
of earth cannot be corrected except your eye be healed.

That Jesus alone can do for you.

He has a remarkable ointment for the eye. Yes, it is really
Jesus Himself who speaks of it in such terms.

Do you want some of this ointment?

If you will make use of it, you will begin to see aright. In
the first place, you will begin to see your sinfulness, your selfishness. All your laying up of treasures was, of course, nothing
but selfishness. In the next place, you will see your Savior.
And if you, in the light of the Spirit, see Him who went to
His death on account of your sins, you will have seen *the treasure*
which overshadows all others. All other treasures will pale in
comparison, and you will be willing to give them all up in
order to gain the one great treasure.

Then you will begin to look upon the treasures of earth in
their true light. You will see that you have received them all
from God. And you will begin to thank Him for them. For
money, and home, and farm, and knowledge, and art, and all
that makes for your own happiness and that of your dear ones.

Thereupon you will begin to see what God's purpose was
in giving you all these earthly treasures. You are simply a steward
of God. All that He has committed to your trust you are to
use to glorify Him in the service of others.

257

He entered into a certain village: and a certain woman named Martha received him into her house. And she had a sister called Mary, who also sat at the Lord's feet, and heard his word.

—LUKE 10:38-39

J ESUS comes to visit some of His best friends, the brother and the sisters in Bethany.

A conversation begins at once. The disciples sit in rapt attention. They know what these quiet hours afford them in the way of blissful nearness to the divine and of new glimpses into the mysteries of the kingdom of God.

Mary becomes occupied with the conversation at once, forgets everything and sits down as near Jesus as possible, in order not to miss a single word.

Martha, on the other hand, is conscious of her responsibilities as a hostess and occupies herself with serving. She, too, is vitally interested in the conversation, but is compelled to come and go. Therefore she hears only portions of it.

But every time she comes in and sees Mary seated, she becomes impatient. At last she can contain herself no longer. She goes directly to Jesus, interrupts the conversation and asks Him to tell Mary to help her with the serving in order that they may finish quickly and both sit down and listen to Him.

Jesus, however, does not upbraid Mary.

On the contrary, He rebukes Martha, mildly but very definitely.

He had observed how differently the two sisters received Him. Martha acted in a practical way, and did so very efficiently. It was her desire to honor her distinguished and beloved guest, and to please Him.

Mary, on the other hand, forgot everything, so absorbed did she become in the words of Jesus.

But *she* was the more well-pleasing unto the Lord. He said, "Mary hath chosen the good part, which shall not be taken away from her."

To Martha He says that among the many things, *one* thing alone is *needful:* to be still and listen when God speaks.

And behold, there was a man in Jerusalem, whose name was Simeon; and this man was righteous and devout, looking for the consolation of Israel.

—LUKE 2:25

WE are not told a great deal about old Simeon. But what we do hear is wondrously beautiful.

He was a God-fearing and righteous man who waited for the consolation of Israel. The Spirit of God was upon him. It moved him also on the day that he came to the temple and saw the new-born Messiah.

Whereupon he praised the Lord and prayed that he might depart in peace from this world, now that he had finished his course.

A blessed life!

It is not thus with all old people. There are many unhappy old folk. I am not now thinking of their poverty, their loneliness, or their helplessness. This is heavy enough to bear. But far worse is their restlessness, their lack of peace, the hard and rebellious attitude of mind with which they cling so tenaciously to life. Oftentimes also they are earth-bent and greedy.

My old friend, you who sit with this book in your hands, how have you fared in life?

Are you numbered among those who wait every day for the consolation of Israel and are led daily by the Spirit into the temple where they can with their own eyes behold their Savior? Or are you one of those who have never sought reconciliation with God, but continually hope for the best, vaguely trusting that God is merciful and will not cast out a sinful soul?

My aged friend! Take care! You are on the very brink of your grave.

Have you never heard of *dead* faith?

Pray God to open your eyes that you may realize your true condition and not give yourself peace or rest until you are in the right relationship with God and can say with old Simeon: "Now lettest thou thy servant depart, Lord, according to thy word, in peace; for mine eyes have seen thy salvation!"

> Now lettest thou thy servant depart, Lord, according
> to thy word, in peace; for mine eyes have seen thy
> salvation. —LUKE 2:29-30

IT is not easy to grow old.

Then one has reached the days of which it is written: "I have no pleasure in them." Old age is without a doubt the hardest class of all in the school of God. The trials of old age are both numerous and great.

My believing old friend, you who have reached this class, may I extend my good wishes to you? You have almost finished the course and kept the faith. What a victory!

Your life is moving in a small circle now, and your labors are not of far-reaching consequence. You are fortunate, you who have employed your powers unto the glory of God.

You are doubly fortunate, you who submit graciously to God now also, when He permits old age to deprive you of your physical and mental powers.

It is grace from God to be permitted to *use* one's powers unto the glory of God. But it is twofold grace from God to be able to *relinquish* one's powers in faith and to say gratefully: "The Lord gave, and the Lord hath taken away; blessed be the name of the Lord!"

There is a sacred halo of glorious beauty about *those* old folk who have gained the victory in the battle with old age and can pass their declining years in happiness. They have conquered! Not merely given in, resigned, to old age.

They are no longer offended when reminded of their age. Nor do they continually find fault with the times and with the young people. They realize that they cannot follow along with the times.

And still there is not the atmosphere of hopelessness about them.

They have been saved by the grace of God, and by the faithfulness of God they have been led from childhood to the gray hairs of old age. With courageous hearts they are prepared to meet the final enemy in His name.

And pass through death into life!

Pray without ceasing; in everything give thanks: for
this is the will of God in Christ Jesus to you-ward.
—1 THESSALONIANS 5:17-18

CHILDLIKE prayer for the Spirit of prayer will little by little
bring a change into our prayer life such as we had scarcely
thought possible.

Without our noticing the change, prayer will become the
unifying center of our busy and distracted lives.

All that we experience from day to day will draw our hearts
and minds quietly and naturally toward God. A desire to speak
with God about everything will arise from time to time.

The things we see and hear in connection with our dear
ones, our friends, our enemies, the converted, the unconverted,
in connection with things temporal and spiritual, little things
and greater things, the easy and the difficult—all the obser-
vations and experiences which give form and content to our
daily lives will begin in a natural and happy way to formulate
themselves into prayer.

Two people who love each other have not really *experienced*
the things of love until they have told each other of their
experiences. So also in prayer. The Spirit of prayer unites your
soul with God in such a way that you speak with God about
your experiences even before you are through experiencing
them, whether you do this only in petition, or in sighing,
grieving, fervent desire, or in thanksgiving and adoration.

You will experience it as blessed release thus to be able to
speak with God about everything in your daily life, especially
to be able to speak with Him about it at once, while it is still
warm with interest and of actual import.

It will dawn on you more and more that prayer is the most
important task in which you engage. And that you cannot
employ your time to better advantage than in prayer, either
while you are resting or while you are working.

Wherever you are!

> Now when he drew near to the gate of the city, behold, there was carried out one that was dead.
>
> —LUKE 7:12

BEHOLD, there was carried out one that was dead.

In a city sad sights such as these are a daily occurrence. But this does not in the least diminish the terror of them to the dear ones who are accompanying their dead to their last resting place.

This instance in Nain was a particularly sad one. The mourner was a widow who had previously accompanied her husband in a similar manner. Now it was her son, her only child. People were kind to her in her sorrow. But this did not bring her son back to her.

Then Jesus came.

He saw her and felt deep compassion for her, we are told.

He spoke to her: "Weep not." Thereupon He touched the bier, and the bearers stood still. Then He spoke the mighty words: "Young man, I say unto thee, Arise!" And behold, he that was dead arose! And his mother received him back again and took him home with her.

We can all imagine the jubilant joy which was hers.

But it was not only rejoicing at having received back her son which filled her heart. After all the pain and sorrow which she had experienced, her joy was no doubt a deeper one. Her greatest joy was that here in our world of sorrow and death she had met one who was as *strong* and as *good* as Jesus was.

Some day one that is dead will be borne out of our home also. At such a time it is good to have as our friend Him who is stronger than death.

He did not overcome death only in the city of Nain, at the bier of the widow's son. That was a great victory. But not the greatest. The boy had to die again, of course. Nay, His greatest victory was won when He conquered death for us all, once for all. By dying in our stead He conquered death and arose from the grave.

Therefore He can help His death-fearing friends even now. He does not remove death from us. But He does give us *inner* victory over death. He gives us courage to die.

262

Martha therefore said unto Jesus, Lord, if thou hadst
been here, my brother had not died.

—JOHN 11:21

LAST week, too, our text brought us into the peaceful little
home in Bethany.

At that time Jesus was a guest of the two sisters and their
brother. We also heard some of the things concerning which
they conversed.

Today we are afforded another glimpse into the same home.

Illness had come. Their beloved, gentle brother, Lazarus,
had become sick. The sisters had sent word for Jesus at once.
But He did not come. Then Lazarus died. The funeral was
already over. And still they had seen nothing of Jesus.

These two sisters are not the only friends of Jesus who have
had this experience. Since that day many a happy home has
experienced this same painful and unfathomable sorrow.

It was so bright and cozy in your home. Jesus was a daily
guest there. But then one day it came. Perhaps it was an illness.
Accompanied by many trials. The malady became worse and
worse, until death took your dear one from you. It was all so
terrible.

You, too, sent word to Jesus. You did so at once. But you
did not hear from Him. When your dear one died, you felt
about as Martha did when she said: "Lord, if thou hadst been
here, my brother had not died."

Why did not Jesus come to your assistance?

Yes, that question became almost more painful to you than
did illness, death, and sorrow.

Can He not help me, or will He not? Does it not help to
pray? Or is it only my prayers that he cannot hear?

My friend, wait for the Lord! His hour has not come yet.
You shall, however, as the sorrowing Martha did, soon see
His glory.

So then ye are no more strangers and sojourners, but ye are fellow-citizens with the saints, and of the household of God.

—EPHESIANS 2:19

To become a Christian introduces many blessed changes into our life. Among other things we become members of the *household of God.*

Through the blood of Christ we have received access to the very household of our heavenly Father, where we may go in and out from day to day. And through that same blood our great and holy God can enter into our small and sinful house each day.

This is the greatest honor and glory of our life, its indescribable bliss. To think that God goes in and out of your house—walks among the greater and the lesser events which constitute your daily life! What evil can befall the house in which God dwells?

However, much is expected of the members of God's household.

God expects a great deal. He expects to have the privilege of sanctifying our house and home by His divine presence. To fill it with a God-fearing, quiet, pure, and clean spirit, that all who dwell in the house may share in this spirit. Such homes and households mean more to God than many church buildings and more than many pastors and preachers.

But the world, too, expects a great deal from those who are of the household of God.

And the world has a right to do so. Let us pray that the world may know that God goes in and out of this home of ours.

Let the world know that we live our entire lives under the all-seeing eye of God, and that we therefore are equally conscientious whether people see us or not. Let the world see that we go in and out of the household of our Father with our joys and our sorrows. Let the world see that we are free citizens of the eternal realms, alive in this world, but not of it.

But I say unto you, Resist not him that is evil.

—MATTHEW 5:39

HERE Jesus speaks of the most difficult chapter in Christian life.

It is unspeakably hard to have some one offend us or hurt us, whether it affects our property or our good name and reputation. Something within us is stirred to remonstrance and we instinctively begin to think of revenge.

Jesus knows this and lovingly comes to our assistance, saying, "Resist not him that is evil toward you." Do not revenge yourselves, but give place to wrath.

This is good counsel indeed. Every time we follow it we experience how good it is.

When people are unreasonable and harsh toward you, be still and ask God for patience. Remember that as you do so you are doing something for your Savior with which your strongest words and greatest gifts cannot even be compared.

But will not the result of this be that those people who inflict injury in every way possible upon others and who are always pushing themselves forward will be strengthened in their unreasonableness? Will not a state of lawlessness be the result if we yield in this manner?

Jesus has given thought to this matter also. "Let anyone who would go to law with you, and take away your coat, have your cloak also." He presumes, of course, that you are in the right.

But even then He asks you for His sake, as a service to Him, to yield and let the other person have his or her way.

He did so Himself. He did not revile again when He was reviled. He did not threaten reprisal when He was made to suffer.

He has shown us that it is possible to leave vengeance to the Lord.

The righteous shall live by faith.

—ROMANS 1:17

MOST of us Christians are more occupied with dying from sin than with living for God.

As a result we do not succeed very well in the Christian life. It is well known that the more one fights with a chimney-sweep the blacker one becomes. Likewise one does not become holy simply by circling around in conflict with one's own impure desires.

Not until we center about our Savior and become occupied with Him will we be loosed from our self-life. We do not receive that willing spirit which inwardly renounces sin and which clings to the Lord until our eye of faith has been opened and we see Christ and all that we have in Him.

Not until then are we saved from our old "I"-life, which always centers about itself, into the new life which is centered in Christ.

As long as we, by our eye of faith, behold the glory of Christ, the glory of the world will not be able to entice us with its power. Faith's clear vision of the suffering and bleeding Savior makes us loathe sin. It makes us feel that it is a privilege to follow Jesus in the way of sacrifice which He trod.

To live by faith! This word opens to us a rich and mystery-laden realm with which most of us are but slightly acquainted.

To live by faith means to have one's connections with the invisible and heavenly realm in such order that eternal life flows quietly and uninterruptedly into one's soul, giving it a new content, new joys and new sorrows.

As we are lifted up into the invisible realm of faith, we see the present world in its true light.

It no longer becomes the *goal* of our life, but a means by which we can serve God.

Lord, are they few that are saved? And he said unto them, Strive to enter in by the narrow door: for many, I say unto you, shall seek to enter in, and shall not be able.

—LUKE 13:23-24

ARE they few that are saved?

This is, in truth, a pertinent question. Many in our day would answer at once: All. All are saved.

If any one dares to mention eternal perdition, they ask: Do you really believe that there is such a thing as eternal perdition? No educated person believes that any more. Would a good and merciful God do anything so brutal and senseless as to torture His opponents in all eternity?

I admit openly that no thought is as painful to me as the thought of eternal perdition. I am not able to think of it very long at a time.

But the time is past in my life when I permit my thoughts and my feelings to decide what is the truth. Jesus is my authority. I believe in Jesus Christ. Also when He speaks of eternal perdition.

But people say that it is not compatible with God's mercy.

Pause a little, my bold friend, before you upbraid Jesus for not being merciful. When you have walked the way *He* trod in merciful love unto death itself, then you can begin to speak of mercy.

None of us reaches the place of eternal suffering because God has ceased to be merciful. We do so because we have taken an attitude toward the mercy of God in which not even a merciful God can save us from eternal woe.

My friend, are you saved? Or are you also drifting along toward eternal perdition?

> Ye shall be sorrowful, but your sorrow shall be turned
> into joy.
>
> —JOHN 16:20

WE find these words in the midst of Jesus' "messages of comfort." They show us how Jesus both would and could comfort His people.

In the first place they show us how Jesus *sympathizes* with His friends.

What the disciples were to pass through during the hours immediately ahead of them was, comparatively speaking, not a great deal. It was in fact very little in comparison with that which was before Jesus. We might therefore have thought that Jesus would not have paid much attention to the lesser things which the disciples were dreading so much.

But Jesus entered into the very depths of their sorrow and anxiety as though He Himself had nothing with which to contend. The most important thing to Him that night was not what He Himself was about to suffer. It was the disciples of whom He was thinking and for whose welfare He was concerned.

Hear this, you who are a disciple of Jesus and who, at this very moment, perhaps, are in sorrow and distress, a dread of the future filling your soul. While others make merry boisterously and with shouts of laughter, you are weighed down with bitter sorrow. They do not understand you in your sorrow. Even if they did understand, there would be few who would take the time or would be willing to sympathize with you and enter into the real cause of your suffering.

But Jesus takes the necessary time.

Your distress is His distress. Notice that the disciples did not ask Him for comfort. That night they understood very little of what awaited them. Jesus, however, thought of their distress even before they themselves thought of going to Him with it. Such a friend is Jesus.

You fear oftentimes that your sorrow is of such a minor nature that Jesus is not concerned about it. But none of your sufferings are of minor importance to Him. He has purchased you with His own life-blood.

Every one that exalteth himself shall be humbled;
and he that humbleth himself shall be exalted.

—LUKE 14:11

JESUS had been invited to a social gathering. And He went
where He was bidden. But He was the same there as elsewhere.
On this occasion He noticed that the guests sought the chief
seats at the table. They were impelled by a desire to *make
themselves conspicuous.* Jesus sees a great deal of this wherever
He turns His eyes in this world.

Also among His own friends.

It manifests itself in various ways. It does not only seek the
highest places, but the *lowest* also, provided that the latter elicits
the most attention and receives the most praise.

Without any doubt, the desire to be noticed determines the
actions and the conduct of the great majority of people. On
the other hand, this desire keeps us from doing many a good
and necessary deed when there is no prospect of our being
noticed.

Many warm-hearted Christians have lost their zeal and fervor because their hearts, little by little, have conceived a desire
for the chief places, felt the titillating sensation of being noticed
and admired, perhaps by a large audience.

If they were not noticed, brought out, greeted, and if their
advice were not sought, then there would be one more offended
person in the group.

One can be saved from this sin *by coming down,* Jesus says.
Down to the foot of the cross where we receive forgiveness for
our exalted thoughts about ourselves. They who daily take
their place beneath the cross of Jesus will never demand a
prominent place among other people. To them it is life's greatest
mystery that God endures them. And the next greatest mystery
is that other people respect them and make use of them.

> And Jesus said unto them, Can the sons of the
> bridechamber fast, while the bridegroom is with
> them?
>
> —MARK 2:19

HERE we are afforded a very interesting glimpse into the feelings which Jesus and His friends aroused among their contemporaries. In this connection we have mentioned especially the disciples of John the Baptist and the Pharisees.

There was something about Jesus and His friends which their contemporaries could not grasp and at which they therefore became offended.

The interesting thing about our text is that it tells us that it was the *joy* of Jesus and His friends at which these other groups became offended.

This information is very precious to me.

Jesus was *glad*. And His friends were glad. The influence they had upon their surroundings was in accordance with this joy.

Obviously, this was as it should be.

Wherever He went, happiness and rejoicing went with Him.

In the home of the two sisters at Bethany, of which we heard last week, how completely did He not turn their sorrow into joy of the most wonderful kind! Or the widow of Nain! What an effulgence of gladness He brought into the loneliness of her sorrow! Or Zacchaeus. What a happy man Jesus made of this gross sinner!

Yes, we can understand why these people were happy. Verily, they had the bridegroom with them.

But it was this that caused offense.

People said that true seriousness was lacking. John the Baptist—what a different kind of prophet he was! He lived in the loneliness of the desert as a great ascetic. Jesus even went to weddings and other social gatherings.

Even today many take offense at the joy which Christian believers possess.

Are you among those who criticize the believers because of their joy, or are you one of those who have the bridegroom with them?

Why do John's disciples and the disciples of the
Pharisees fast, but thy disciples fast not?
—MARK 2:18

IT was the most religious circles among the people which
criticized the disciples, particularly those religious people who
did *not* accept Jesus. What they were offended at was the free
and spontaneous joy of the disciples.

This offensiveness has always been associated with Christianity. Even to this day. Now, too, it is oftentimes the very
religious people who criticize the disciples of Jesus the most.

Also in our day it is often the joy of the Christians for which
people criticize them. What a holy indignation is felt in the
circles of these religious people when believers say that they
are children of God. Immediately they speak about those who
are quick to judge and accuse the believers of considering
themselves better than others!

And when believers speak of their *assurance,* how are not
the religious folk wrought up over such *cock-sureness!*

When believers gather at their meetings to sing, pray, and
testify, the others remark about them that they are morbid,
over-excited, and fanatical.

The *sorrow* of the believers, too, causes offense.

When they are subject to deep-going doubts and terrible
suffering of soul, they are accused of cultivating religious brood-
ings which make people demented. These religious critics look
upon it as a national calamity that pietistic "revival-Christi-
anity" of this kind has become so powerful in the land.

Jesus, however, came to the defense of His friends, very
quietly and beautifully. I cannot read His words without feeling
that Jesus was particularly *happy* on this occasion. He was glad
because His friends were glad.

They had the bridegroom with them. It was therefore as
unnatural for them to sorrow as it would have been to fast at
a wedding.

But He knows too that *sorrow* will come also to them. When
the bridegroom is taken from them, then it will be natural for
them to fast, Jesus says.

271

But thou, when thou prayest, enter into thine inner chamber, and having shut thy door, pray to thy Father who is in secret.

—MATTHEW 6:6

Do you pray? Do you pray every day?

Is that necessary, you ask. Can God expect that? Does the Bible really say that we should pray every day?

My friend, deep within your own heart do you not think that it is a little strange that you do not pray, that you do not speak with your Creator and Father? You work and rest, sleep and eat, talk and write, read and listen, but never think of speaking with God. Never a thought of thanking Him! Never a thought of hearing what His mind and will is with respect to your life!

Do you not think that this is strange? And have you never asked yourself what the reason might be that you *refuse* to speak with God?

You do not believe in God perhaps? Then the matter is clear.

However, most people do believe in God. Many are even very orthodox and are alarmed at all the doubt, blasphemy, and denial of Christ which they hear.

This is good and well. But Jesus speaks today about praying. Why do you not pray when you believe that there is a God?

Jesus speaks here of the inner chamber. Do you go into your room to pray every day? Why do you not do it?

Now, what Jesus has been wanting to tell you today is this: You do not *love* God. That is why you do not pray.

He loves you. But you do not understand. You are afraid of Him when you feel that He is very near to you. And you are indifferent toward Him when he is far away.

You cannot change your God-estranged heart. But He can. Will you admit Him into your heart today and let Him perform the miracle?

He that believeth on me, though he die, yet shall he live; and whosoever liveth and believeth on me shall never die. Believest thou this?

—JOHN 11:25-26

THINGS were at a low ebb with Martha when she heard these words from the lips of Jesus. They had never been so low. Everything pertaining to God and faith had been so clear before. But now in her sorrow everything went to pieces.

And she who before had scarcely had time to sit down and listen to Jesus when He came on a visit now drank in every word that He spoke.

Martha has many sisters and brothers.

For a long time it was easy for you, too, to be a Christian. But then things went to pieces for you also. Now everything is such a burden, so difficult and futile. In fact, oftentimes you do not know whether you can consider yourself a child of God. It does not seem to you that your life is as it should be if you really at heart were a Christian.

Yes indeed, that is what always happens when the Spirit of God is permitted to shed His light upon that wretchedness which is called our daily life.

But do not permit yourself to be frightened! It is precisely now that you are to learn to *believe*.

Do note this: Your not knowing what to do and your helplessness are not a hindrance to Jesus.

On the contrary, God cannot bring His help in full to others than those who have become cognizant of their own helplessness. Through your painful mortification each day you are to learn that Christ not only puts to death but also makes alive. He is present with you each day to forgive you your sins, to make you happy and secure in Him, to put to death your self-life and raise you up to a new and ever freshening life in Him, that you may honor and serve Him better with each passing day.

"He that believeth on me, though he die, yet shall he live," Jesus says.

Do *you* believe this?

273

Repent ye, and believe in the gospel.

—MARK 1:15

Most people think that to ask an unconverted person to repent is as easy as slipping on a pair of hose. But let us for a moment think of how the Scriptures describe the unconverted.

"Every one that committeth sin is the *bondservant* of sin." Such persons are not "subject to the law of God." They are "born of the flesh, and are therefore flesh." And "the mind of the flesh is enmity against God." They are "dead through trespasses and sins."

How can any one then ask such a person to repent? Is not that as unreasonable as asking the lame to rise or the blind to see? Or as speaking to the dead?

Moreover, there is a great deal of evangelistic preaching in our day which is un-Biblical on this point. The unconverted are addressed as though they could convert themselves, yes, as though they desired to be converted.

My unconverted friend, permit me to tell you the terrible truth that you *cannot* convert yourself. You are a bondservant of sin. You are bound with shackles from which you cannot free yourself.

I have more to say to you. You do not desire to be converted either. You no doubt try to make yourself believe that eventually you will, but not just at this time. If you are honest, you will tell yourself that such talk on your part is pure falsehood.

But how then can Jesus say, "Repent"? Well, we are afforded here our first glimpse into the mystery of conversion as well as into the *gospel* of conversion.

We can repent when God speaks to us. When He has done this, something has happened to us. God has *spoken* to us.

Repentance consists in this, that a sinner chooses to *listen* to God when He speaks. Then the Word of God transforms this person into a new person.

Hearken to this, you who are still unconverted. Your only possibility of being converted is to give heed now while God calls you!

Him did God exalt with his right hand to be a Prince
and a Savior, to give repentance to Israel, and
remission of sins.

—ACTS 5:31

WE saw yesterday that we do not desire to be converted
and that we cannot convert ourselves. Our Word today tells
us that it is God who *gives* us repentance, just as He gives the
forgiveness of sins.

We are flesh; we love ourselves and feel an aversion to God.
We are the bondservants of sin. We cannot therefore change
ourselves. But God can change us.

He raises the dead. He sets the prisoners free. He transforms
hearts that are of flesh and at enmity with God.

And all this He does by a single word.

He *calls* the sinner. That means that He calls out to the
sinner. The word in the Old Testament which we have translated "to call" means simply to call out to or to call by name.

The call of God consists therefore in this that God calls
out to the sinner. Calls out in such a way that the sinner hears
and understands that it is *me* He is calling!

By this word, by this call God gives the sinner repentance.

One day Jesus met a man with a withered hand and said
to him, "Stretch forth thy hand!" And the man stretched it
forth, although it was so withered that he could not move it.
How then could he do it? In this way: With the words of Jesus
went the power to do what Jesus asked him to do. Herein lies
the *grace* of the call of God.

It does not of itself occur to anyone to repent. By His call
God works upon our mind, our feelings, and our will until we
freely choose to repent.

Wherein then does our choice consist? It does not consist
in our own decision to tear ourselves loose from sin, to love
God and to hate sin. For of ourselves we cannot do any of
these things. Our choice consists simply in deciding whether
we will hearken to God, who by His Word has begun to transform us, or whether we will close our ears and hearts to Him.

My sheep hear my voice, and I know them, and they
follow me.

—JOHN 10:27

Here Jesus tells us that He knows His own.

He knows whether or not all we who sit here together in
our home today are His.

Do you know if *you* are one of His?

Jesus knows. Would you like to know what Jesus thinks of
you and your relationship to God?

Listen here to the way Jesus describes those who are His
sheep!

They "hear my voice." That is the first thing He mentions.

Does that apply to you? Do you hear anything that Jesus
says from day to day?

Many will answer happily in the affirmative. Jesus speaks
and they hear Him. Every day. It is the joy of their life to hear
the voice of Jesus in the Word and in prayer, while at work
and at rest, every day, yes, sometimes even at night.

He speaks to them in many ways.

Oftentimes He speaks with harshness and severity, and they
become frightened at His words. But they know His voice also
when he chastens them for their unbelief, disobedience, and
unfaithfulness. Moreover, they thank Him when He, with the
voice of authority, puts holy fear into their lukewarm and
indifferent hearts.

They hear His voice when He comforts His weeping and
sorrowing children. A word from Him banishes all their sorrow
and distress and brings sunshine and joy into their grayest
week-day.

"They follow me." That is the other thing He says about
His own.

Yes, those who have seen the Lamb of God, those who have
been privileged to hide themselves with all their shame and
distress in His wounds and stripes, they follow Him. They never
feel happy within unless they walk in the footprints of the
Lamb. It is not *always* easy to walk in them. But all who love
the Lamb take up their cross and follow Him.

Him that cometh to me I will in no wise cast out.

—JOHN 6:37

J ESUS speaks here of those who *come* to Him.

They are never *many*.

Most people go *away* from Jesus. This is without a doubt the most terrible fact that we are called upon to face in this terrible world of ours.

Most people go away when Jesus comes.

Some hate Him; some blaspheme; some doubt; some are ashamed of Him. To all of them Jesus is immaterial. While not the least little thing can take place in town or country without their listening to an account of it, they can live weeks, months, yes, years, without thinking about Jesus.

Then there are those who come.

Before, they went away also. Yes, they ran away many a time when God came near to them. They fled from God and their own evil consciences.

But now they come.

Trembling and fearful. It is not easy to meet God when one has lived such a life.

Still, if they could only leave their old life behind, they might find courage to come. The worst is that they can never really cut loose from shore. They cannot put an end to their old life in sin.

Nor can they ever arrive at an understanding of themselves. One moment they hate sin and reach out after God. The next day they are indifferent and antagonistic toward God. Can God receive any one who is so helpless with respect to his or her own sins, who perhaps does not even really desire to be entirely separated from them?

Nothing is clear to you. One thing, however, you do know: I, who was blind, now see. Back to your old life you cannot go. You tremble at the thought of it, but you feel that you must come out into the light with all your sin and with all your shame.

Listen now to the words of Jesus: "Him that cometh to me I will in no wise cast out."

277

And the seed should spring up and grow, he knoweth not how. The earth beareth fruit of herself; first the blade, then the ear, then the full grain in the ear.

—MARK 4:27-28

IF we have by faith accepted Christ into our hearts, we have within ourselves the strongest power there is in life. This power operates within us constantly, day and night. There is continual activity in life's hidden workshop.

Always in accordance with a definite plan. If you have sown oats, then fully matured oats is the working model that is employed: first the blade, then the ear, then the full grain in the ear.

The strongest power that has ever been at work in our world is Jesus Christ. Now, I have received this Person, with all His liberating power, into the very center of my life. Beginning at this center and working out, He is to dispel sin from my whole being, from my soul and from my body.

The seed grows without our knowing how.

A profound mystery! Many children of God sit looking back upon their life with God; at such and such a time in the past you were more zealous, more spiritual, more useful to God, more circumspect with regard to sin, more strict with yourself. You see no growth! You have rather gone the other way.

My grieving friend, look at the shade trees. At this time of the year they stand there without a single leaf. Have they stopped growing? No, they have only shed last year's foliage.

It is hard when you and I must shed the old leaves. But the life is not in the leaves. The life is in Christ. His power, moreover, can work the more unhindered within us the more we feel our own impotence, the more dependent upon Him we become.

Remember how often His power has brought roses out of thorns!

Seek ye Jehovah while he may be found; call ye upon
him while he is near!

—ISAIAH 55:6

Here too we encounter some of the offensiveness of
Christianity.

We are told here that the call, the awakening, is connected
with a definite time. Our little minds feel constrained to ask
why God does not call a person just as well in every period
of life.

I do not know whether we will ever have that question
answered. Scripture and experience tell us that the call of God
is associated with *definite* seasons, in fact, with comparatively
brief periods in the life of a human being.

The time of our spiritual awakening has been prepared by
God through long periods of time, without our knowing it.
Prepared to the very minutest detail. Prepared through the
lesser and the greater events which God has ordained should
take place in our lives, in every moment of our lives.

Then, when the preparations have been completed, God
has intervened with that divine miracle which we call the
spiritual awakening: God draws us, suddenly but quietly, into
His holy presence.

But with it comes also the hour of temptation.

For you do not feel at ease in the presence of God; you are
afraid of Him. You would rather avoid Him. Therefore you are
tempted to say: "There cannot be any hurry about this, can
there? I will become a Christian. But just now it is not con-
venient for me. Later it will no doubt be easier to make the
great and final decision."

This is the fateful temptation that comes to all awakened souls.

Here, too, hell participates very actively. Satan knows that
at the time of spiritual awakening the Lord is near. He knows
that with the call follows a supernatural power which makes
it possible for the awakened soul to break with its former manner
of life.

Seek the Lord while He may be found, while He is near
to you!

279

Beloved, think it not strange concerning the fiery trial among you, which cometh upon you to prove you, as though a strange thing happened unto you.

—1 PETER 4:12

Yes, the same thing happens to us as happened to the believers of that day when the fires of trial came.

We think it strange.

Not only that. We are quick to mope and wail, to give up.

But it is at times such as these that we should be in earnest about standing the test of life. It is then that our Christian character should be strengthened and established. Such times should see our faith and our fear of God established upon a solid foundation.

First, look up to Him who sends you these difficulties!

It is not easy when the Lord lays His mighty hand upon us. But continue to look at that hand until you see that it is pierced. Then you will be inwardly emancipated, even though adversity continues, yes, increases outwardly.

Then you will see that the Lord always gives more than He takes.

It is easy enough to believe in God when all goes well. Then it is no art to thank Him for His blessings.

Not until adversity puts in its appearance does it become manifest how much of our gratitude was true and how much was merely sentimental phrase-making. Not until God deals with us in ways that we do not understand at all does it become apparent whether it was God in whom we put our confidence or the prosperity He sent us.

Tried and tested Christians also feel the pain of adversity and suffering. Nor are they afraid to tell God how deeply it pains them.

But it is this very sensitiveness and unwillingness to suffer from which they desire to be delivered. Therefore their constant sigh and prayer is that they may learn to suffer willingly and receive grace to *glorify* God in their tribulations.

The lamp of the body is the eye: if therefore thine eye be single, the whole body shall be full of light. But if thine eye be evil, thy whole body shall be full of darkness. If therefore the light that is in thee be darkness, how great is the darkness!

—MATTHEW 6:22-23

THE virus of sin has contaminated us throughout, from our innermost to our outermost being. Both soul and body.

As a consequence of this contamination our whole physical body and our entire soul-life function improperly.

In our text Jesus shows us how sin has destroyed the eye of the soul, our spiritual vision.

The eye does not produce light, but it does receive light for the whole body. If the eye is damaged to such an extent that it cannot receive light, the whole body is plunged into darkness.

That people walk about in spiritual darkness is not due to the fact that it is dark about them.

There is light enough.

But the eye, the eye of the soul, is evil, Jesus says; and as a result it cannot receive spiritual light, light from heaven.

Whereupon Jesus makes use of an illustration to show how evil the eye of the soul has become. It cannot distinguish between true and false values, between that which is temporal and that which is eternal, between heavenly and earthly treasures.

All people seek after "goodly pearls." We all try to secure the best we think it possible to get out of life.

But while heaven hangs over us, filled to overflowing with eternal, incorruptible treasures, all of which can and will be ours if we want them to be, we still dig in this old earth of ours to find our treasures.

Blind to the things which are *above* us, we gaze with desire upon the things which are *beneath* us.

For what are you living?

God give you courage to answer this question.

281

Ye therefore shall be perfect, as your heavenly Father
is perfect.

—MATTHEW 5:48

EVERY one who is familiar with the Bible knows that this
passage does not teach that believers here on earth are free
from sin. We all know that it is written: "If we say that we
have no sin, we deceive ourselves, and the truth is not in us."

None of us becomes a Christian until we have learned to
know the perfect requirements of God's law in Christ Jesus. It
is the attempt to fulfill these requirements which crushes our
hard hearts and transforms us into sinners who hunger for the
grace of God.

Moreover, sinners who have been created anew by God *love*
God; therefore we love also this requirement, that of perfection.
This brings us to the very essence of sanctification. In sanctification God exercises imperfect but regenerate human beings
in the art of living perfectly.

This is what imparts to sanctification the great *tension* that
is always associated with it. This is also what makes sanctification a *matter of faith*. Faith in this connection consists in our
holding fast without compromise the requirements of Christ:
I, the imperfect one, must do that which is perfect.

But here, too, is the great danger in connection with
sanctification.

When we see from day to day that it is not possible for
imperfect human beings such as we are to do that which is
perfect, we are tempted to follow the dictates of our own mind,
which say that the perfect is impossible to those who are imperfect. Whereupon we lower the requirements to that which
we think an ordinary person can attempt with success.

Faith, on the other hand, *believes* in the requirements of
God, even though they are unattainable. And does not give
up the requirement of perfection, even though it is aware of
its own imperfect fulfillment of God's perfect law from day
to day.

And as he passed by, he saw a man blind from his birth.

—JOHN 9:1

Yes, Jesus went from one sufferer to another. But also from one miracle to another. Here He restored sight to a man born blind.

"Why does not Jesus perform miracles now?" some ask.

Jesus does perform miracles now. Physical miracles, too. He would gladly do wonders. But it is now as it was then: There were places where He could do no mighty works. "And he marvelled at their unbelief," are the rueful words of the evangelist.

If you are in need of one of Jesus' temporal or physical miracles, ask Him with all boldness to help you. But in order to be safe add: "Only if it will glorify Thy name!" Then it will be still easier for Jesus to help you.

To perform a miracle in our souls is the greatest of all. What good would it do were He to heal everyone's bodies, if their souls were not healed?

Moreover, miracles such as *these* occur daily. God be praised! Not a day passes but that souls are saved in every part of the world.

Blindness is the worse disease of the soul.

For the reason, too, that we are *all* blind. We were *born blind,* all of us. This was an unavoidable consequence of sin.

How blind is not the criminal! Or the drunkard! Or the adulterer! Or the embezzler! They do not see the things that are to their own best interests.

But *all* are blind as far as God is concerned. They do not see their own Creator, Father, and Savior. Yes, a miracle must take place. Jesus must touch our unseeing eyes. Then we will begin to see. And the first thing that we will see will be our sins. To begin with, many see scarcely anything else but their sins. And become bewildered and full of despair. But this is not dangerous. Say as did the man born blind: "One thing I know, that, whereas I was blind, now I see."

Greater love hath no man than this, that a man lay down his life for his friends.

—JOHN 15:13

Nᴏɴᴇ of us is so poor that we do not own a friend.

We know that of all our temporal blessings, God has given us none more glorious than intimate fellowship with those we love.

But if it is so great to be a friend of a human being, what then is it not to be a friend of God!

Is that possible?

Yes, unto this end were we created. When we, by our sins, became enemies of God, He did everything in order to make us friends again. He left His own heaven and entered into human life. Yes, He permitted Himself to be put to death by His enemies in order to make friends of them.

And the friends He won can never fully thank Him for this incomprehensible friendship. Many have been enticed by all the honor and gold that the world can give, or have been threatened with punishment and death to make them give up their heavenly Friend. But they have bravely chosen death.

But why do the friends of Jesus weep and sigh so often?

Ask Peter, when he went out and wept bitterly. He did not weep because he was a friend of Jesus, but because he thought he could be a friend of His no longer. Ask the believers who grieve because of their unfaithfulness and disobedience toward their best Friend.

But note their joy also when Jesus speaks to their sad and bewildered hearts: "Ye did not choose me, but I chose you."

He knew beforehand what you were and is not surprised at your wretchedness. He loves you, not for your sake, but because He is love. None of your sins can nullify His love. Draw nigh to His heart again in all quietness and tell Him all your shame.

But I will warn you whom ye shall fear: Fear him, who after he hath killed hath power to cast into hell; yea, I say unto you, Fear him.

—LUKE 12:5

THE disciples needed an admonition to fear God.

We need it, too.

Yes, I often ask myself: Is there anything our generation needs more urgently than really to fear God?

There is fear enough otherwise in our day and age.

We fear illness. Oh, to what lengths cannot this fear drive a person!

We fear poverty. Many there are who because of this fear are driven to become rascals and criminals.

We fear people. There is scarcely any limit to the extent to which fear of others can make a coward of its victim. What will not people do to be counted among the "cultured"; what will they not do in order not to offend against "good taste"; what will they not do in order to gain the plaudits of others, or to avoid becoming the object of their smiles and their disdain?

Yes, there is enough fear.

Jesus tells us that this fear which stunts the growth of a person's character and contaminates the soul is all due to the fact that we do not fear the *only* one whom we *should* fear, namely, the living God.

Joseph feared God and therefore had the necessary strength to say "no" to that dangerous woman. Elijah feared God and as a result had the courage to stand before the mighty king Ahab and rebuke him for his sin.

Those who fear God do not need to fear people; nor need they fear misfortune, illness, or death.

God, give us grace to fear and love Thee above all else!
Amen.

> But all their works they do to be seen of men.
> —MATTHEW 23:5

JESUS here touches upon one of the weakest points in our lives, namely, our love of honor.

I know of no one sin which does as much damage to a person's character as this.

It permeates and poisons our whole daily life. If people could read on the outside of you how much you are occupied only during the course of one day with this, "to be seen of men," no doubt many would be amazed. Perhaps also think less of you than they do.

Added to this is the fact that this sin is exceedingly destructive to all life with God.

"How can ye believe, who receive glory one of another?" Jesus says.

If the judgment of others is all-dominating in our lives, then it is clear that we have not been laid hold of by God in our innermost being so that regard for what He thinks of us is above all else.

This sin becomes even worse when we would seek to win the honor and recognition of others by means of our own godliness and our own pious life.

Then this sin becomes *Pharisaism*.

It is this that Jesus so violently opposed in His adversaries and against which He so earnestly admonished His friends.

These words of Jesus give us all something to think about.

Let us go to the Lord at once, lay bare before Him our whole inner being and acknowledge our vanity.

He will understand and forgive us.

There is a fountain open to the house of David and to the inhabitants of Jerusalem, a fountain which cleanses from sin and *all* uncleanness.

Oh, God be praised!

> The thief cometh not, but that he may steal, and
> kill, and destroy: I came that they may have life, and
> may have it abundantly.
>
> —JOHN 10:10

J ESUS has many discouraged soldiers in His ranks. They fight,
but lose, lose again and again. And any one who is losing in
a struggle easily becomes discouraged.

There are more Christians devoid of hope and joy than we
suspect. For the little skirmishes of everyday life are the decisive
conflicts in every Christian's life.

Are you *willing* to fight?

Are you really willing to put an end to your old sinful habits?
Do you wage a life-and-death warfare against them?

Do you feel *sin* as your enemy? Not merely its consequences,
but the very thing itself, that of sinning against God? Do you
feel that sinning is like sending a dagger into the very heart
of God?

Do you believe in victory?

Do you have the *will* to conquer?

Think now of the sinful habits against which you are strug-
gling. You are perhaps quick-tempered. Or you are peevish and
contrary. Or self-willed and imperious. Or envious and slanderous. Or covetous and miserly. Or full of impure thoughts
and desires.

Would you really become the master of these sins?

Or would you rather fight and *lose?*

Enter with a sincere heart into the presence of God and
answer yourself, whether you would like to be victorious or
defeated in your daily struggle.

Be honest!

If you must answer that you have sunk down into lukewarmness and half-heartedness and that you no longer feel that
you *burn* yourself when you come in contact with sin, then
tell it in all candidness to your Savior.

He has life to give you, yes, life *abundant.*

> Each man is tempted, when he is drawn away by his
> own lust, and enticed.
>
> —JAMES 1:14

WE have what is known as *wish-thinking.*

By that we mean thinking which does not follow the laws of logic but the impulses of our whims and desires. To strengthen or defend our wishes we try to provide them with a foundation in logic.

There is a great deal of this kind of thinking in daily life. Undoubtedly it is *this* which makes many a private and public debate so spirited.

It is not so much a matter of ascertaining the *truth* but of defending one's own *wishes.*

In the hour of temptation wish-thinking occurs in its completest form.

If we cannot defend our actions from a *moral* standpoint, we become the more zealous to defend them on logical grounds.

The process of inner *corruption* sets in.

That *falsification* of character begins which consists not only in committing sin in the hour of temptation, but also in being untrue to oneself afterwards. In lying oneself away from one's evil *motive.* By saying that things went so badly in the hour of temptation, not because you *wanted* to sin but because of the circumstances, because of other people, or because of your inherent nature. You blamed it all to these things.

By so doing you lied yourself away from the deepest thing in sin, namely, its guilt; this that you sinned willfully, that it was *your* act.

The hour of temptation becomes the hour of our life's great *humiliation.*

No doubt we all have memories which cause our faces to blush with shame.

We failed. The metal in us was too soft. We were capable of longing, hoping, thinking, and talking, but not of *living.* For to live is to be tempted.

Come unto me, all ye that labor and are heavy laden,
and I will give you rest.

—MATTHEW 11:28

Souls who are earnest in their striving oftentimes cannot
believe that God can forgive their sins.

Why not?

Because they feel that they can never get into the right
relationship either to God or to their sins. They feel that they
do not love God and do not hate sin. That they are not truly
sorry for their sins. In fact, they feel that they do not do battle
against them as they ought.

Now listen to what Jesus says: "Come unto me!"

To come to Jesus is enough. If sick persons come to the
surgeon before it is too late they are saved. The sick can do
nothing themselves, either the one way or the other. Nor is
that necessary.

Jesus will save you. All *you* need to do is to turn to Him
and tell Him how bad your situation is in every way.

The result will be that you will find *rest*.

Yes, you say, but must not something take place in me?

Yes, indeed. Two things must happen. But they have already
happened.

In the first place, it was necessary for *atonement* to be made.
But that has already been done. Jesus made atonement in your
stead. Look now to Jesus and you will see something new. You
will see that everything that He did, He did in *your stead*.

In the second place, *acknowledgment* of sin must take place.
Unless you confess your sins, God cannot forgive.

Have I truly confessed, you ask.

Let me ask you a counter-question: Is there anything of
which you have any knowledge that you have refused to confess
to God? No, you say.

Well, nothing more is necessary. Yours is the *rest* of God.

Sit down quietly now and look to your Substitute. And
return thanks to Him!

But when the king came in to behold the guests, he saw there a man who had not on a wedding garment.

—MATTHEW 22:11

IN this parable Jesus tells us that God is preparing an eternal wedding feast and that he is sending out invitations to all the people of earth, but that most of them do not care about the invitation.

But the most serious thing in the whole parable is contained in our verse.

Among the few who accepted the invitation was one who was subsequently cast out. He did not have on a wedding garment.

To us this sounds harsh and unreasonable. But to an Oriental everything would be clear. At royal festivals it was the custom that all the guests *received* a festive garment as they arrived. It was an insult to the prince not to put on the princely garment provided for the guests at his festival.

That was what this man did. He despised the gift as well as the wishes of the prince. Therefore things went as they did.

Today Jesus would warn *us* who have accepted the invitation and started out upon the way to the eternal wedding feast. He bids us prove ourselves, whether or not we have on the wedding garment.

Will you heed the warning of Jesus today? Do you desire to know the truth about yourself, whether you are a Christian in *truth* or only in *name?*

The poor man in the text kept silence. You would perhaps *speak,* and say:

"But I am converted. Do you not remember that they prayed for me at that after-meeting? And since that time I have of course been a Christian. Everybody has confidence in me. I sing; I pray at the prayer meetings; I testify."

Suppose that the King should say: "I know all that. But I do not know you. You make use of my grace to excuse your sins. You do not give me an opportunity to speak out to you about your most cherished sinful desires. You have a name that you are spiritually alive, but you are dead."

But I made supplication for thee, that thy faith fail not.

—LUKE 22:32

HERE Jesus tells us that temptation has a heaven-side, not only a hell-side.

Heaven, too, plays a part in the hour of temptation.

Heaven puts at the disposal of the little human soul all the powers that it needs to effect its rescue from the attack of hell.

Jesus mentions here especially His *intercession* on our behalf.

This throws new light upon the hour of temptation. An intense battle is being fought, not only *within* the human soul, but also *for* it. Heaven and hell, God and Satan, are contending for the immortal human soul.

Jesus tells us this also in order to arouse us. We are often very indifferent.

We live very thoughtlessly, as though temptation were a joke or fun of some kind. The citizens of the eternal realms above, on the other hand, take it very seriously. They carry on a life-and-death struggle for the frivolous, thoughtless souls of human beings.

God help us to wake up and see the seriousness of life! Then our hearts will be filled with some of that holy fear of which the Scriptures speak. Such fear is not in conflict with the spirit of sonship. But it is in conflict with the plans of hell, the aim of which is to anesthetize us, that we may neither see nor sense the eternal risk involved in life.

"But I made supplication for thee, that thy faith fail not."

We have an alert and faithful Savior. He follows the flow of events in our little lives. He knows when the tempter is laying his snare. He sees also how heedlessly unprepared we are.

Then He intervenes. He does not prevent Satan from tempting us. But by His intercession He awakens us, that we may not only feel the temptation, but also behold our Savior.

The kingdom of heaven is like unto a treasure hidden in the field; which a man found, and hid; and in his joy he goeth and selleth all that he hath, and buyeth that field.

—MATTHEW 13:44

THE treasure was hidden. So it is also with the kingdom of God, Jesus says.

Yes, that treasure is indeed hidden from us!

Has God hidden this treasure? No, He has revealed it. He has revealed it as openly as it *can* be revealed.

But sin has drawn a veil over our eyes, and we do not see the treasure. "It is hidden from your eyes," Jesus said once to His own people. Indeed, He designated this as the great *tragedy* of human life. People cannot see the kingdom of God as a treasure.

And people today—do they look upon God and Christianity as a treasure, as something good?

And it certainly cannot be said that they do not understand the value of treasures. All they do is to search for treasure. It occurs to only a few of them, however, to search the Scriptures. Only a very few attend church to find treasures. Only a few seek God in prayer.

Most people do not even think about Christianity. It lies entirely beyond their spiritual horizon.

A few still have some contact with Christianity through relatives and friends. But it never occurs to them to look upon it as something good; on the contrary, they consider it *a necessary evil.*

They have an instinctive feeling that they too must some time become Christians if all is to be well. But they put it off as long as possible. They do not see the treasure.

O merciful God, almighty God, have compassion on our people!

And having found one pearl of great price, he went
and sold all that he had, and bought it.

—MATTHEW 13:46

OUR greatest misfortune is not that we sin and destroy both
ourselves and others by our sin. Nor that we, on account of
our sins, have incurred a debt that we cannot pay and that
has separated us from God.

Nay, our greatest misfortune is that we do not see our own
need nor our own salvation. We do not see our Savior. We
stumble over the treasure every day and still do not
see it.

Thus we begin to realize that salvation really consists in
seeing the treasure.

Yes, *that* is the miracle, the miracle of salvation.

No miracle is more unfathomable to me than this, that God
succeeds in opening our unseeing eyes so that we begin to look
upon God and His salvation as a treasure, as a great good.

But when this miracle does take place, the same thing
happens to us as happened to the merchant. We become willing
to give up everything in order to keep the pearl of great price.

Notice the people who through a spiritual awakening catch
a glimpse of the pearl. They do not haggle any longer for the
purpose of clinging to *sin* of one kind or another. Nay, the
prayer and the cry of their soul is that no sin may hinder them
from coming into possession of the pearl.

They no longer squirm away from making a *full accounting*
before God, which they feared before more than anything else.
Now they would gladly turn their hearts inside out in order to
be certain that there was no deceit anywhere.

They have only *one* sorrow: they cannot get possession of
the pearl.

Now and then it seems that they have really found it. They
become as happy as children. Then it slips out of their
grasp again.

My friend! You *have* the pearl.

Blessed are they that *hunger* and *thirst!* Blessed are they who
mourn.

> There was a man that was a householder, who planted
> a vineyard, and set a hedge about it, and digged a
> winepress in it, and built a tower, and let it out to
> husbandmen, and went into another country.
>
> —MATTHEW 21:33

WE too have received a garden to cultivate.

It was given to us as a gift at our birth. A sound body and the faculties and powers of our soul. A loving mother and a good father. Many brothers and sisters and good companions. A good home. A good bringing up and instruction in many useful things, both at home and at school.

In the midst of this beautiful garden God planted the tree of life. At our very birth God met us in holy *Baptism*. Our soul was small, but the triune God nevertheless found room there. In the bright spring morning of our life many a blessed heavenly seed was sown in the little garden of our heart.

Then He set a hedge about it. A remarkable hedge. For many years—how many I do not know, but for many years—nothing could harm the little garden. Not we ourselves; we were still too small. Not any other person, either. No, not even the devil.

We lived a few happy years in our garden. And God garnered fruit there. We prayed our childhood prayers, which made glad the heart of God. And we struggled with our childhood sins. True, we often fell. But when we turned to God and asked His forgiveness, God received again the fruit which He sought. We ourselves received the most. For we received power to uproot many a thorny growth.

But since that time? Since that time many have permitted the weeds to grow again. Thorns and thistles have choked everything that God planted.

However, they are not happy with the garden destroyed. They sit during hours of quietude, longing sorely for the faith and for the garden of their childhood.

> And a certain man was there, who had been thirty
> and eight years in his infirmity. When Jesus saw him
> lying, and knew that he had been now a long time
> in that case, he saith unto him, Wouldest thou be
> made whole?
>
> —JOHN 5:5-6

JESUS has many ailing friends.

They have once been healed. They have received the antidote to sin into their hearts, the unmerited grace of God, which is effective both against the guilt and the power of sin.

But little by little they have neglected to make use of this means of healing. And unless one's relationship to God is always right, peace with Him soon comes to an end, and one's old sinful habits, quietly but surely, resume their dominion again.

There will still be striving, but not with victory in mind. One loses faith in the ability to become victorious.

There are more people lying at this pool than we suspect.

With unnumbered and unheard-of sufferings, and, worst of all, with hopelessness hanging clammily and heavily over their longing souls.

While others observe a festive occasion and go up to Jerusalem, these people lie in hopeless agony.

But then Jesus comes.

Today He asks you: "Wouldest thou be made whole?"

Wouldest thou? That is the question, for most of the people at this pool do not desire to be made well. They will not enter upon a decisive struggle against their sins. That would involve too great an expenditure of honor, strength, time, and money.

Wouldest *thou*?

"Oh, it is impossible for me!" you sigh.

My dear friend, Jesus is not asking you if you can, but if you will. Jesus can if you will.

Tell Him the whole truth, how you have yielded and compromised until you have become the contemptible wretch that you are. Tell Him all, and He will forgive you all—without any merit at all on your part.

295

Try your own selves, whether ye are in the faith!
—2 Corinthians 13:5

Here, too, we notice the distinct line of demarcation which separates the righteous person from the hypocrite and the self-deceived person.

Hypocrite persons fear self-examination and avoid it at all costs. Gradually they acquire much practice in comforting themselves and defending themselves against the restless thoughts which the Spirit of God puts into their conscience.

The righteous fear self-examination also. But they desire it nevertheless; and seek it. They desire to know the truth about themselves, even though it results in the passing of judgment upon their Christian life.

The righteous permit the light of God to be shed upon all their sins and desires. They desire to know at all times whether they have entered into a compact with any sin as a result of which they may be excusing and defending sin in themselves.

They desire to know if there is anything in which they do not desire to know the will of God. They know that there are instances enough in which they are not able to do the will of God, but this does not disturb them as long as they are conscious of the fact that they are not seeking in wilfulness or love of ease to explain away the will of God.

Nor do sincere souls stop at this.

They have learned to have a holy lack of confidence in themselves, also in their own self-examination. Therefore they ask the Lord to try them. As the old psalmist did: "Search me, O God, and know my heart! . . . And see if there be any wicked way in me, And lead me in the way everlasting!"

And God hears their prayer and points now to one, now to another thing in their lives which is contrary to the will of God. The result is sorrow, distress, and shame. And the soul's hunger and thirst for grace is kept alive, yes, experiences a normal growth. Faith fights the good fight and keeps healthy and sound. The cross becomes a place of refuge.

Joy and sorrow, smiles and tears mingle there as they are mingled in life.

> The nobleman saith unto him, Sir, come down ere my child die! Jesus saith unto him, Go thy way; thy son liveth. The man believed the word that Jesus spake unto him, and he went his way.
>
> —JOHN 4:49-50

THIS is the account of an official in a little city. He had a sick child.

Comparatively speaking, this is, of course, a daily occurrence. It is strange that this incident should have become known throughout the whole world. But as we look at it a little more closely, it impresses us very deeply.

In the first place, we learn that it was distress which drove the man to Jesus. He had manifestly heard a great deal concerning this remarkable man. Now he came to Him personally. This was to be an event of decisive importance in his life.

That this was the case we can understand clearly from the fact that he was imbued with great confidence in Jesus. He was determined to have Jesus come home with him to see his son. But Jesus said, "Go thy way; thy son liveth!" And the man went home upon Jesus' word and nothing more. His associations with Jesus had made this possible.

It says that when he reached home and learned that his child had been healed at the very moment that Jesus spoke, he believed. He began to believe in Jesus as his *own* Savior, not only as his child's.

It says also that his whole house believed. Also his child who had been ill.

Think of what happened in that house that day!

Without a doubt they all thanked God for the illness which had brought them all this happiness and blessing.

The Gospel writer begins the account in this way: "He came therefore again unto Cana of Galilee, where he made the water wine." I wonder whether John would not thereby say: "Behold, this time, too, He made water into wine!"

Indeed, is not this what He has done here in our home also?

> And there was a certain nobleman, whose son was sick at Capernaum. When he heard that Jesus was come out of Judaea into Galilee, he went unto him, and besought him that he would come down, and heal his son.
>
> —JOHN 4:46-47

W E followed this man yesterday on his trip to see Jesus and found that this journey led to salvation for him and his whole house.

Since that day millions of people have gone to Jesus in their distress.

Have you noticed that it was illness that drove most of them to Jesus? Then as now. Sickness is like a herald which goes before and announces the coming of Jesus, opening hearts and homes to Him.

No doubt there is some one sitting here today who came into fellowship with Jesus through illness. Perhaps the same thing happened here as happened in the home of the nobleman of Capernaum; the whole household became believers during a siege of sickness. Perhaps here, too, it was a little boy. Perhaps that boy is sitting here now. And you are all thanking God for that blessed illness which led to such glorious healing.

But it is hard to think of the many who suffer distress, sickness, and other trials *without going to Jesus.*

I wonder if there are such persons here.

Was it a child that became sick in your home? You suffered terribly. It was all so devoid of meaning. You sighed and wept almost incessantly. You became tired and discouraged and lost all hope.

All this suffering! And still you have not thought of Jesus! Why have you not gone with your sick child and your ailing heart to the best Friend that you have?

Burn all bridges behind you. Go, as this nobleman did, directly to Jesus and lay before Him all your needs. Then you too shall experience *the miracle.*

298

Seeing ye have purified your souls in your obedience
to the truth unto unfeigned love of the brethren,
love one another from the heart fervently.

—1 PETER 1:22

Purify your souls!

Yes, that is needed. How unclean is not the soul which we
carry in our bosom. Egoism, love of self, vanity, a penchant
for criticism, envy, immorality. What a bottomless and boundless sea of unclean thoughts and fantasies there is in the human
soul!

Many pay no attention to the uncleanness, and let it pass.

Others have taken up the battle. They suffer under all this
uncleanness. They are repulsive even to themselves. Oftentimes they are at the brink of despair, for all seems vain,
regardless of how hard they struggle. It is like fighting with a
chimney-sweep; the more you fight, the dirtier you become.
Peter knew this, and shows us another way.

Purify your souls by love of the brethren, he says. The
unclean content of our souls cannot be attacked *directly*. To
get the air out of a glass is a very difficult task if I concern
myself directly with the air in the glass. But if I fill the glass
with water, the air will be forced out very easily.

We cannot drive the impure thoughts and fancies out of
our hearts by attacking them *directly*. The apostle says that we
should fill our hearts with a new content; then our evil thoughts
will be compelled to evacuate.

Confess your impure thoughts to God. Then listen to His
words: The blood of Jesus Christ, the Son of God, *cleanses* us
from all *sin*. Thus you become clean before God.

Then proceed in willing and self-sacrificing love to serve
all with whom you associate and you will notice that your soul
will become filled with pure and fervent thoughts toward those
to whom you are showing kindness. This is the most certain
antidote for impure thinking.

Do not be dismayed if you find that you fall back at times.
Remember Him who said: "They that are in health have no
need of a physician, but they that are sick."

Behold, I stand at the door and knock: if any man hear my voice and open the door, I will come in to him, and will sup with him, and he with me.

—REVELATION 3:20

THE friends of Jesus often experience difficulty.

They are of a noble family, with a great inheritance in prospect. Even here below they experience the powers of the world to come.

But they have their Treasure in an earthen vessel. Moreover, the vessel is exceedingly frail. Then, too, they are always in a dangerous environment. They are pilgrims on the way to their eternal home, passing through enemy country.

In the world ye shall have tribulation. This tribulation is never greater than when the atmosphere of the world settles down with suffocating effect upon our inner life. The "busyness" of the day would hinder us in our prayers and in meditation upon the Word of God. God becomes distant, the world near and very alluring. In an atmosphere of this kind temptations multiply and defeat follows hard upon defeat.

The worst aspect of it is that we ourselves are to blame for it all by our unfaithfulness and disobedience.

My weary friend, listen now: Jesus stands at the door and knocks. He would hold communion with you.

No, you say, He does not desire fellowship with me. Everything has become hopeless as far as I am concerned.

Yes, He does. With you in particular, because you need it so sorely.

Notice that it was to the church in Laodicea that He spoke these beautiful words. The church which was in such a bad way that it was neither cold nor warm. It is to this very church that Jesus speaks these comforting words: "Behold, I stand at the door and knock."

Open to Him at once! Confess to Him how your inner life has withered away and how impotent you are.

Then He will hold communion with you again.

Bless Jehovah, O my soul,
And forget not all his benefits.

—PSALM 103:2

THE greatest of all Jehovah's benefits is Christ, who by His life and by His death has received power to forgive sins on earth. "Be of good cheer, thy sins are forgiven thee," He whispers each day into hearts which are anxious because of their sins and seek God in all sincerity.

The receiving of this benefit is the condition upon which all other benefits become of eternal value to us.

If we would learn to bless the Lord for all His benefits, we must first learn to give thanks for the forgiveness of sins.

If you are desirous of exercising yourself in gratitude, then begin here.

If you would learn to give thanks, then do not thank God at random or in general, but thank Him for *definite* benefits. Then your gratitude will become natural and real.

Thank God when He has given you that for which you have made supplication.

Thank God when He gives you more than that for which you have asked.

Thank Him when He gives without your asking Him.

Thank Him also for not hearing all your prayers, for giving you gold when you ask for silver, as Luther puts it.

My soul, forget not all His benefits!

Let us give thanks to Him in our *hearts.* The apostle speaks of making melody unto the Lord in his heart. Yes, that is precisely what we should do. Every day.

Let us give thanks to God in words, that heaven and earth may hear that we are glad and that we give glory to God.

And let us thank Him in *deed.* By a life which shows others that we are grateful to our heavenly Father.

Lord, forgive us for our ingratitude and give us eyes that are open to see all Thy benefits toward us. And to thank and glorify Thee.

Amen.

But each man is tempted, when he is drawn away by his own lust, and enticed.

—JAMES 1:14

OUR soul life does not function normally during temptation.

Sin is not the normal thing in our soul-life. There is nothing so illogical, so meaningless, as sin. Yes, sin is the only meaningless thing within the confines of God's whole creation.

For there is no reasonable ground for sinning, for disobeying the good will of God. There is only *one* reason for sin and that reason is our own wicked will.

In the hour of temptation the abnormal part of our soul-life becomes most clearly apparent. In our feelings, our intellect, and our will.

In our feelings a burning desire for the forbidden thing is kindled. The object of our desires becomes for the time being more important and of greater value than anything else in the world.

Temptation affects our *intellect* by lowering our powers of judgment. It lowers not only our moral powers, but our intellectual powers as well. Our ordinary faculties for judging values cease to function, and sin appears less and less dangerous. The "braking apparatus" of our intellect is completely disconnected. People who are most intelligent can in a brief moment of temptation commit the most impossible follies, follies which they oftentimes are compelled to look back upon with regret for a whole lifetime.

Upon our *will* temptation has a most paralyzing effect.

The many good resolutions which we make between periods of temptation in the ordinary course of our life melt like wax in the heat of temptation and run off between our fingers. Temptation makes us weak and feeble.

We are like drunken people. We put forth great efforts to raise ourselves up, only to succeed in rolling completely over.

302

> Having begun in the Spirit, are ye now perfected in the flesh?
>
> —GALATIANS 3:3

WE all need this question.

There are many Christians who began promisingly, but who have little by little sunk down into a weak, soft, cowardly, and bungling life, with the result that their Christianity is only a shadow, yes, a caricature of what it at one time was.

Permit me to mention one of the most important causes of this degeneration of the Christian life.

We sin our daily affairs. It may be that we have a violent temper or that we are peevish, untruthful, or frivolous. Father, mother, spouse, brothers and sisters, children or servants see it. Here is where many Christians have lost their boldness, both before God and people.

They do not give up Christianity. That they cannot do. But they become defeated warriors. Unhappy and unmanly or unwomanly. With the pressure of a bad conscience to contend with continually.

The wounds of the soul will not heal.

True, they confess their sins to God and try to comfort their restless souls with the grace of God. But peace and joy will not return.

The simple and absolutely unfailing remedy for this cancer of the Christian life is this: Pray for forgiveness! I mean ask the people for forgiveness who have witnessed your failures. Tell them that you did not act like a Christian. Tell them how it hurts you. And you will experience the *releasing* effect of such confession.

The fact that it is exceedingly hard for all of us to ask for forgiveness shows how sin has ravaged our lives. We instinctively seem to think that we lose something essential if we ask for forgiveness.

Pray God for courage to do this, and you will see how you will succeed in your whole Christian life.

> And if thy brother sin against thee, go, show him
> his fault between thee and him alone: if he hear thee,
> thou hast gained thy brother.
>
> —MATTHEW 18:15

W HEN a brother or sister sins, it is not only the world which rejoices and blasphemes because of the hypocrisy of the Christians.

Many believers also sin against the unfortunate one who falls. First and foremost by Pharisaical, self-righteous slander. Then by the aloofness and suspicion with which they meet the person.

The most difficult of all these cases, however, is the one to which Jesus alludes here today: "If thy brother sin against *thee.*"

Do you remember what you did the time he offended you so grievously?

You have perhaps never sinned at any time as you did then. Do you recall all the evil thoughts that filled your mind at the time?

Moreover, when you met your friends, you told them not a little of what you had been thinking.

Afterward, when you went home and your conscience upbraided you for your slander, you perhaps even defended yourself by saying: "What I said was true nevertheless, every bit of it!"

Today Jesus asks you to go to this brother of yours.

In your best moments you have no doubt thought: "I am not unreasonable, either. If he will come and ask for forgiveness, I will of course forgive him!"

But listen now: Jesus says that *you* are to go to *him.*

"Yes, but it is he that has sinned. He will have to come to me," you say.

Jesus knows that it is he that has sinned.

He says: "If thy brother sin against thee."

But, nevertheless, He bids *you* go.

Will you do as Jesus tells you?

304

And if thy brother sin against thee, go, show him
his fault between thee and him alone: if he hear thee,
thou hast gained thy brother.

—MATTHEW 18:15

W E saw yesterday that Jesus bids us go to the brother or
sister who has sinned against us.

Many have gone. But they went and scolded all they could.

It is important therefore not to go until we are clear in our
own minds as to what Jesus would have us do *for her.*

Jesus bids you go and *win your brother or sister.*

It is for this reason that it is necessary for you to be clear
in your own mind as to what you are seeking to accomplish as
far as she is concerned. Are you going to see her to prove to
her that you are in the right? Or are you seeking to win your
sister?

If you will begin by praying that you may succeed in winning
your sister, then much in your attitude will be changed. Perhaps
some thing or other that you have done against her will bob
up in your consciousness.

Suppose you begin your conversation by asking her to forgive
you for this.

Am I to ask her for forgiveness who has offended me so
deeply? Why should I go to her?

Because you have a good conscience in the matter. And
because God came to us in this way when we had sinned against
Him. Suppose He had waited until *we* came to *Him?*

Nor should you go until you are certain that Jesus will go
with you, and will be the third *Party* in your reconciliation
meeting.

If He with the pierced hands is in your midst, you will
succeed without any doubt.

Then you will both become humble enough to extend to
each other the hand of Christian friendship in all love and
sincerity.

Behold, I stand at the door and knock: if any man hear my voice and open the door, I will come in to him, and will sup with him, and he with me.

—REVELATION 3:20

THIS is the message of Jesus to all fallen souls whose God-emptied hearts are full of painful restlessness and consuming longing. In our day we have in our midst many thinking, speculating, doubting, seeking souls. They know that it is the things of eternity alone which can fill the vacuum in their hearts.

They are religious and would continue to be religious. But all that they experience is their own thoughts and longings and strivings. They wait incessantly for God to become a reality to them.

"Thou art not far from the kingdom of God," Jesus said to a thinking and longing man nineteen hundred years ago. And these words assuredly apply to many today.

Jesus would no doubt add: "Behold, I stand at the door and knock! If any man hear my voice and open the door, I will come in to him." So near to the kingdom of God are you.

You have heard His voice. Your religious restlessness and longing shows that. You have heard well, too; for you understand clearly that you have not experienced God, only your own longings and strivings.

You need only open the door, Jesus says.

What does He mean by that? Simply that you are to tell Him the truth, also *that* truth that you are without God, notwithstanding all your religion.

Then Jesus will see to it that your religion becomes something more than mere longing and sighing. He Himself will come in to you and abide with you.

Then you will personally experience these things. True, everything will not always be bright and easy. He will tell you many a bitter truth. But even then you will feel that it is God who is speaking to you.

Love suffereth long, and is kind; love envieth not.

—1 CORINTHIANS 13:4

I F we would enter into the bright and happy realm of love, we must bear in mind that love is above all an attitude of heart, that is, a definite way of *willing.*

The vital factor in the relationship between two who love each other is not what is said or done, but the good will, the loving thought, which is back of the words and acts.

Even a cup of cold water is something that Jesus cannot forget when He sees therein a loving thought for Him and for His cause in this world.

This tells us something very important. To will well, to wish that which is good, is the first and most important element in all love. It is your attitude of heart that is important, what your *will* regarding others is.

You are often anxious about your words and your acts because they are not loving and kind. Very well, but the danger does not really lie there. The important thing is to have the right attitude of heart.

Give, therefore, this attitude of heart a chance in your daily life!

Wish that which is well, will that which is good in your heart as you go about your daily tasks. "Bless and curse not," the Scriptures say.

Bless every person you meet or who merely flits across your mental horizon.

Bless and curse not; envy not; do not become peeved; criticize not!

Moreover, send your good wishes up to the throne of grace and people shall receive the good things you wish for them.

What opportunities to do good, my friends! Make use of your time! First and foremost here in your home. It is of materials such as this that people build Christian homes, happy homes, strong homes, homes that will endure the strain and stress of both prosperity and adversity.

> Among them that are born of women there hath not arisen a greater than John the Baptist: yet he that is but little in the kingdom of heaven is greater then he.
>
> —MATTHEW 11:11

JOHN the Baptist stood high in the estimation of the people. But Jesus accorded him an even higher place. No one has been given as exalted a position as John: to be the herald to announce the coming of the Messiah.

And yet: those who are but little in the kingdom of God are greater than John the Baptist.

Thus Jesus evaluates people. He rates their great calling and abundant qualifications very highly—He Himself has given them all these things. But the decisive thing to Jesus is our relationship to Him.

Jesus can think of no higher honor and dignity for us than to be a citizen of the kingdom of which He is the thorn-crowned King.

Dear child of God! Let us sit down quietly at the feet of Jesus for a while and listen to what He has to tell us about our exalted estate and our position as children of God.

Our eyes become moist many a time when we look at our daily life. Our hearts shrink back when we feel the sin in our members and feel our impotence both with respect to loving God and to dying away from sin.

But do not forget now that you are a child of God *for Jesus' sake!*

It is for Jesus' sake that you are permitted to be His child, the one in whom He will glorify Himself in time and in eternity by forgiving you your sin, by wooing you away from the world, by hearing you when you pray, by sending you inner as well as outward difficulties in order that both you and the world may know what the power of Christ can do.

And at last you shall glorify Him by passing unharmed through the hands of the last great enemy and by entering into the eternal glory of God.

Not until then will you know in all its fulness what it means to be a child of God.

He himself knew what he would do.

J ESUS did not always perform miracles.

He did not always feed the people miraculously.

He accepted money from His friends to purchase bread. And He permitted His disciples to go and buy bread, even though they had a long way to go.

However, if need was present, Jesus did perform miracles, and did so willingly and gladly.

But even in need and distress Jesus desires to show us how helpless we are before He will intervene.

It was for this reason that He asked the disciples to find a way to feed the five thousand.

Not until they were agreed that such a thing was impossible out there in the wilderness did Jesus interpose His miracle.

Misfortune came to you one day. And Jesus asked you, as He did His disciples, what you would do now.

You thought and thought, night and day. But one thing seemed as impossible as another. Perhaps you have not found a way out yet.

Listen now: Jesus Himself knew what He would do also for you. He knew it before you suffered your misfortune. As a matter of fact, it was He who sent it. But He did not do so before He had thought of what He would do to help and bless you.

He waits now only for you to tell Him that you do not know what to do. Then He will perform the miracle that is needed, now as before. He will open a way for you in your temporal affairs. In spiritual things He will bless you with enlightened eyes, that you may see His goodness and greatness.

Yes, look at Him, how He stands there, calm and confident in the midst of His bewildered disciples.

Fight the good fight of the faith!

—1 TIMOTHY 6:12

To believe requires practice.

For faith is an art. The highest of all the arts in life.

And the practice consists among other things in distinguishing between what I am in *Christ* and what I am in *myself*.

I see my slovenly life, my worldly heart, my lukewarmness in prayer, my love of the world, my fear of renunciation, my lack of desire toward God and His Word. And I become restless; I become bewildered; yes, I become anxious.

This will be the case until I again agree with God that I in myself am helpless, but that I in faith, that is, in confidence in my Substitute, can stand before God as before.

It is what Christ has given me that makes me precious in the sight of God.

I am now a little more *thankful.* A little more *confident* in my Substitute. A little more certain of what I have in Him.

Thus I have had a little more practice in believing.

Fight the good fight of the faith!

Yes, here we have the decisive front in this fight. Paul says triumphantly at the close of his life: "I have kept the faith!" The very secret of the fight of faith is to keep *this* faith: that after I have failed or erred I give myself no peace until I again have recovered by boldness before God, in confidence in my Substitute.

This is the believer's best defense. This is the shield of faith whereby he or she may be able to quench all the fiery darts of the evil one.

> "Lord Jesus Christ,
> My Savior blest,
> My refuge and salvation,
> I trust in Thee;
> Abide in me;
> Thy word shall be
> My hope and consolation."

310

And he sat down over against the treasury, and beheld how the multitude cast money into the treasury.

—MARK 12:41

THEY were receiving an offering in the temple. Jesus sat and looked on.

He does that always. He sits and looks at us as we give. He does not see only *what* we give but also *how* we give. With what hearts we give.

Do you like to have Jesus looking on as you decide how much you are to give to the temple, to the many-sided work of the kingdom of God in the world? Are you one of those who are co-partners with the Savior and therefore never can give a gift before you have conferred with Him about the amount you should give?

Or are you one of those who *own* your means yourself, but out of the goodness of your heart share a little of it with God?

Ordinarily it is not easy for you to give a large gift. In fact, it is often difficult enough to give a small gift. You give it very unwillingly and think that it is terrible that so many offerings are being taken up all the time. You are even afraid that our poor people will be ruined by all the gifts that are pressed out of them, more or less voluntarily.

May I comfort you in your anxiety with regard to our national economic welfare. There is not as much danger connected with this giving as you think. Our nation spends many times more for liquor and tobacco, the theater, candy and gum than it does for the kingdom of God.

If you were concerned about the expenditures of our people for drinking, smoking, and luxury of all kinds, I would support you with all the power at my command. On the contrary, I thank God because our people still give as much as they do for God's cause. It holds out hope and promise for the future of our nation. For God says: "Give, and it shall be given unto you!"

311

> Verily, I say unto you, This poor widow cast in more than all they that are casting into the treasury: for they all did cast in of their superfluity; but she of her want did cast in all that she had.
>
> —MARK 12:43-44

IN our age of great economic pressure many have little to give. They feel that it is nothing short of embarrassing when an offering is to be laid upon the altar, that it is like going up and giving a demonstration of one's poverty.

My friend, you should not feel that way. Jesus sits down over against the temple treasury now also. He knows how little you have to give. Just as He knew that the widow had no more than she gave.

Notice how happy Jesus became. He called to His disciples that they too might share His joy. If your resources are small, then give your little gift and do it without being ashamed.

You, however, whose gift is small even though you have an abundance from which to give, you know, do you not, that Jesus sits and looks on every time you give? Your gift shows Him the condition of your heart. It shows that you *love* neither Him nor your neighbor. Your heart is closed to need. You live for yourself and your own.

You do not *believe*, either. You do not believe that God keeps His promises. That is why you are so afraid to give. You think that it is dangerous to give away money and therefore you give as little as you possibly can without losing your respectability.

The Word today speaks to you gently but earnestly. Not only must your *gifts* be changed, but your *heart* as well.

Pray God that you may see Him who gave and gave until He gave His last drop of blood for you. He will change your heart. And impart to you a mind to give, making you a cheerful giver.

Then you, too, will begin to gladden the heart of God—and many people—by your gifts. You yourself, however, will reap the greatest joy. For it is more blessed to give than to receive.

Thou wicked servant, I forgave thee all that debt, because thou besoughtest me: shouldest not thou also have had mercy on thy fellow-servant, even as I had mercy on thee?

—MATTHEW 18:32-33

THIS man was converted.

Jesus would have this fact emphasized. Nevertheless, he was lost because he would not forgive his brother.

As far as my understanding of the Scriptures goes, no sin is more dangerous as far as our relationship to God is concerned than implacability and hatred. Notice how often Jesus enforces the truth that God cannot forgive us our sins if we do not from our hearts forgive those who have sinned against us. Even among the few and brief petitions of the Lord's Prayer we find this reminder: "And forgive us our trespasses *as we forgive those who trespass against us.*"

Obviously, this is not more dangerous than other sins because it is grosser or greater than many others. Nay, it is because it, in a peculiar manner, imparts to our whole soul-life an icy frigidity.

A converted man lay at the point of death. A Christian friend of his came to visit him. He asked how things were with him as he lay there face to face with death. The sick man replied that all was well. "Then you have made up with your neighbor, with whom you have been on unfriendly terms?" said the visitor. "No," said the dying man, "I have not."

"Yes, but the Bible says that you will be lost if you refuse to be reconciled to your adversary. You are very sick and are about to die. If you so desire, I will go and get your neighbor at once," he said.

"No," said the dying man, "if it costs that much to get to heaven, I shall have to take my chances."

With these words he turned his face toward the wall and would hear nothing further of the matter.

Oh, how horrible, how terrible!

313

> After these things I saw, and behold, a great multitude, which no man could number, out of every nation and of all tribes and peoples and tongues, standing before the throne and before the Lamb, arrayed in white robes, and palms in their hands.
>
> —REVELATION 7:9

It is All Saints' Day.

The church of God militant today lifts its eyes toward the church triumphant.

We thank God for those who have overcome, who have the palms in their hands. No doubt all of us have some of our dear ones up there. We give thanks to God for them, even though our gratitude be mingled with tears.

We thank God because the multitude is so great that no one can number it. We are not accustomed to such great numbers. On *this* earth we are always the *little* flock. Not until we are gathered out of all the ages and every nation shall we see the great host arrayed in white "like thousand snow-clad mountains bright."

They have all come through the great tribulation.

But we have not. And today the Lord would comfort His weary pilgrims. Blessed are ye that mourn, for ye shall laugh! He says. Blessed are they that are on the way to the eternal banquet-feast, even though the way is narrow and steep and thorns prick their feet.

Blessed are ye who are loved of God, even though people smile disdainfully at you, blaspheme and persecute you. They who are up yonder have suffered likewise.

> "Despised and scorned they sojourned here,
> But now, how glorious they appear!
> So oft, in troubled days gone by,
> In anguish they would weep and sigh."

My weary friend! Sit down a little while along the wayside and rest your weary heart. Look up! And thank the Savior who opened a way for you through His blood. He rejoices at every step you take. And waits for the hour when you are to close your eyes here on earth, to open them again in eternal wonderment in God's heaven. Oh, God be praised!

> In nothing be anxious; but in everything by prayer
> and supplication with thanksgiving let your requests
> be made known unto God.
>
> —PHILIPPIANS 4:6

THIS is an apostolic admonition. We have many such. But few that are as difficult to obey as this one. It says: In *nothing* be anxious!

The greatest cause of anxiety to a child of God is *sin*.

Yes, my dear child of God! I congratulate you upon being sorry for your sins. May your sorrow not be merely worldly sorrow. We children of God very often and to a great extent grieve over our sins with a sorrow which is of the world. We are sorry because of the consequences of sin and not because of sin itself, the fact that we have sinned against God.

God would have us be *sorry* for our sins, but not *anxious* about them. He Himself has made full satisfaction for all our sins with His blood. Therefore He can say: Be not *anxious*!

But there are always many things which cause anxiety to a child of God. It may be illness, sorrow, financial difficulties, old age, or death. As a result our restless little souls suffer the most bitter agonies.

It says: "Be not anxious!" How can the apostle use such strong language?

Oh, he no doubt knows what he is saying. He is saying it only to the children of God. Not to others. He knows what it is to be a child of God.

God raised you up from your sins, washed you and made you white in His blood. Then He lifted you up into His lap and threw His eternal arms about you. And whispered into your apprehensive soul: "Now you are my child. And I care for my own. You shall receive everything that you need. Moreover, I protect those who are mine. Nothing shall come nigh unto thee without my permission."

When I think of this, I am ashamed of my anxious thoughts.

315

Blessed are the pure in heart: for they shall see God.
—MATTHEW 5:8

THIS passage has plunged many sincere souls into the depths of condemnation. For they feel, of course, that nothing in them is as unclean as their heart.

The pure heart, that must be one without sinful and impure desires.

No, it is not; for if that were the case, there would not be a single pure heart in this world of ours. Then not a single soul would ever see God in this earthly life. It is written: "If we say that we have no sin, we deceive ourselves."

Yes, but then the pure heart must be one that is filled with faith and love. Ask Paul. He says that he *is*, not that he was, but that he *is* the chief of sinners. And ask John. He speaks of his heart condemning him.

What then *is* meant by a pure heart, you ask.

Well, the word used in the original text, both in the Old and in the New Testament, does not mean sinless or perfect, but pure in the sense of unmixed, that is, without falsehood or guile. In many places the word is used in such a way that there can be no doubt but that it means sincere. Truth in the inward parts, the psalmist calls it in one place.

The pure heart is, then, a *sinner's* heart.

And therefore it is full of impure and sinful desires. Therefore, too, it is cold and indifferent. But this sinner's heart was pure because he would not conceal, nor excuse, nor defend the impurity of his heart, but would *see* the impurity and spread it out *before God.*

Blessed are such hearts, says Jesus, for they shall see God.

Yes, they see God on the cross; they see the Lamb of God. The Spirit of God makes this possible.

And yours shall be the privilege of seeing more. You shall see God in your daily affairs. In your daily work. In your daily struggles. And in your joys. You shall see God's way and His will.

Rejoice in the Lord always: again I will say, Rejoice!
—PHILIPPIANS 4:4

I T is as though Paul cannot find words that are strong enough to express to his friends this admonition to rejoice. He mentions his own joy several times in this letter.

This is indeed strange. For he was in prison when he wrote the letter. And he says himself that he does not know as yet whether his case will result in his release from prison or in his execution.

Many think that it is impossible for a Christian to be happy at all times and cite many good reasons in proof of their contention.

But it says nevertheless: Rejoice in the Lord *always!*

True, it says: "Rejoice in the *Lord.* And that is the solution of the problem. As long as I seek to find something in *myself* as a cause for rejoicing, it will of course be impossible to rejoice *always.* But as soon as I have learned to rejoice in the Lord I have found a source of joy which is equally rich with each passing day.

The apostle knows full well that there is not *only* joy in the heart of a child of God. He says that a child of God may be both happy and sad at the same time: "As sorrowing, yet always rejoicing."

Yes, the remarkable thing about the children of God is this very thing that they have a sorrow on account of themselves of which they can never rid themselves here below. But they have at the same time a joy in the Lord which does not cease as long as they continue to be sorry for sin.

Even more remarkable is this, that this joy and this sorrow fructify each other.

The more I see and regret my selfishness, my coldness, my worldliness, and my indifference, the more closely will I cling to the cross and the Crucified One.

And the more my heart is permitted to look into the mystery of grace, the greater and the more profound becomes my sorrow at grieving my Savior.

Teach me thy way, O Jehovah!

—PSALM 86:11

THIS is a humble prayer. The psalmist acknowledges that he does not understand the Lord's way with him.

God has a way, a plan for all of us. And this way is such that it corresponds exactly with our talents and abilities and our circumstances as a whole. If we will follow the way which God has appointed for us, we will live useful and fruitful lives because our capacities and powers will have been employed in the best possible way. This again will afford us the deepest and most abiding joy in life.

There are many unhappy people, more than we know. Many bear their misfortunes in brave silence.

Most people find the reasons for their unhappiness in the unfortunate nature of their outward circumstances in life: adversity, illness, sorrow, and evil people. Only a few see that their one great misfortune in life is that they did not follow the way the Lord appointed for them.

Even the prophet of old saw this: "It is thy destruction, O Israel, that thou art against me, against thy help."

Human happiness does not consist in avoiding adversity, suffering, sorrow, and bereavement, but in knowing that I am occupying the place in life which God intended for me and in being permitted to do my work and make use of my talents in accordance with the will of God, whether it be in serving or in suffering.

No prayer is as precious to God as this: "Teach me *thy* way, O Jehovah!"

Most people are very little concerned about God and His way. They follow their own. If they are in doubt as to the way they should choose, they take counsel with other people, not with God.

Therefore there is great joy in heaven when a soul begins to pray this prayer.

Has God heard you pray it?

I exhort therefore, first of all, that supplications, prayers, intercessions, thanksgivings, be made for all men.

—1 TIMOTHY 2:1

HERE we are told again about some of the uses to which prayer may be put.

We benefit so very few people.

To most of those we meet on our way we bring evil, more or less.

Both by what we say and by what we do not say.

Both by what we are and by what we do.

But the Lord is waiting for us to ask *Him* to do good to the many we meet in life.

We are to be permitted, if we will, to bring to all with whom we come in contact a blessing from the Savior.

Jesus would have me ask for a blessing for that person on the street whom I have never seen before and perhaps will never see again—and then send that blessing along with the person.

We are to be permitted, if we will, to bring a gift from the other world to the home we visit, the office we enter, the house that is under construction, the work that is being done, simply by turning in prayer to Him who waits for our supplications.

Friends, let us go to Jesus and tell Him how we sin against Him by the way in which we neglect to make use of the privilege of prayer.

And let us pray for the *Spirit of prayer!*

He will teach us to pray.

Teach us how simple it is to pray, for prayer is for those who have nought but their own distress and who do not even expect anything on the basis of their needs, but only for Jesus' sake.

Then is when we learn to pray *in Jesus' name.*

Lord, teach us to pray!

319

Neither doth any know the Father, save the Son.

—MATTHEW 11:27

GLORIOUSLY alive He stood there in the midst of the race, the God of whom the human spirit had had forebodings, the God whom this spirit had groped for in all religions and had speculated about in all its thinking.

This was the glad tidings which nineteen hundred years ago sped across the Greek-Roman world: God, not in heaven, but on earth. Not in divine splendor, but in a man of earth. Not as lord of heaven and earth, but as the willing servant of all.

How people have misunderstood God!

Of all the mistaken conceptions which people have, those about God are the worst.

That God is great, every one feels. But we feel only the greatness of His *power*. As a result God becomes a world-despot to us. The Unapproachable One, who does not concern Himself about the things of this earthly realm.

Not until God's own Son had lived a human life here among us on our own earth did we see the greatness of God.

God is great as a Creator. He is great as a law-giver in relation to His creation, both in the realm of nature and of the spirit. And He is great in the power which He exercises over His creation.

But He is greatest in His power over Himself, in making Himself a servant of all.

When Jesus was to tell us the name of God, He said: "Our Father, who art in heaven."

He is the Father of everything called father, of the lilies of the field, of the birds under the heavens. But first and last of all human beings.

"Praise to the Lord, who o'er all things so wondrously reigneth,
Shelters thee under His wings, yea, so gently sustaineth;
Hast thou not seen
How thy desires e'er have been
Granted in what He ordaineth?"

320

I glorified thee on the earth, having accomplished
the work which thou hast given me to do.

—JOHN 17:4

W E saw yesterday how the Son revealed God as the Father
who shares life so intimately with His children that not even
a hair falls from their heads without His knowledge and will.

This is great, but still not the greatest.

The greatest is that our great God suffers with His fallen
children. Suffers the boundless suffering of love, suffers because
He cannot reach His children with His love.

Whereupon He proceeds to perform the greatest miracle
known to heaven and earth. The Son, the Only-begotten,
sacrifices His divine existence in order to live His life throughout all the eternities as a man.

We stand amazed, and say: "That God *could* do this, that
He could choose to live His own life on a lower level, from
that of being God to that of being human!

In heaven they stand in wonder and amazement and say:
That God *would* do this!

He was His Father's Son on earth as in heaven. He asked
for nothing else but the privilege of serving, of imparting His
happiness to every heart and home.

But the race did not recognize Him. It demanded *proof.*
But he could give only one proof, the proof of love—love
unto death!

The death of the cross.

By His death atonement was made for our sin. That is, now
God could again reach His fallen children with His love.

Now nothing can hinder Him from making you happy
for time and for eternity *except you yourself.* No devil, no
human being, not your many and foul sins, not your contrary
and rebellious heart.

If you will, He will make you a child of God for the sake
of Jesus Christ.

Blessed are they that mourn: for they shall be comforted.

—MATTHEW 5:4

A SURPRISING word!

We usually send condolences to those who mourn. Jesus calls them blessed.

Why?

Because sorrow worketh repentance. It is God who works repentance. And He does it through sorrow.

This sorrow often begins quietly and almost imperceptibly as slight restlessness. And grows gradually into sorrow and anxiety.

To begin with we become restless because of our *thoughtlessness* and indifference. We feel that we are putting a low estimate upon our souls and thus injuring them.

Afterward we become restless because of the *lassitude of our wills*. We see what is right and what we ought to do. We intend to enter in through the *narrow* gate of which Jesus speaks and to which we have now come. But we never take the matter seriously. We think, hope, and long. But we never act.

Now we become anxious also because of our *cowardice*. We see now that it is fear of others that keeps us back.

Thus God works repentance.

It becomes very hard to sin. We cannot go on without peace with God and with our own conscience. Thus we are inwardly liberated from our old life until we freely forsake it all and go to God.

Yes, blessed are they who mourn!

Hearken to this, you who mourn. You despair because you do not succeed in becoming repentant. You can find no peace, no joy, no assurance. Since you began to seek God in earnest you have scarcely experienced anything but sorrow, distress, and anxiety.

Listen to Jesus' words today: "Blessed are they that mourn." God has begun His work within you. He has begun it in you in the same way as in the rest of us, through *sorrow*.

But He says: "You *shall be* comforted."

Blessed are they that mourn: for they shall be comforted.

—MATTHEW 5:4

W E considered yesterday the blessed sorrow which leads a soul to repentance.

But this sorrow does not cease with repentance. And those who mourn are just as blessed whether they mourn during or after their conversion. Even you who have been given an insight into the mystery of the Gospel, that God justifies the ungodly, even you often feel sad, yes, restless and anxious. Your daily life is to you a daily sorrow. You experience defeat more than victory. Your sins of omission are more numerous than those of commission. Your heart is the worst of all. It is worse than all your words and acts put together.

And like so many other children of God you think that this constant grief and restlessness is *dangerous.* You are afraid that there is something wrong with your relationship to God, that you are deceiving yourself. You think that if you were really a child of God, the condition of your heart would not be what it is. But in this, fortunately, you are mistaken. "*Blessed* are they that mourn," Jesus says.

For sorrow works repentance. Also in you. And this is the work of God. If He is to succeed in preserving and furthering that life which He has created within you, then He must work in you daily repentance toward your sins. This He does through sorrow.

But *am* I converted, some ask.

The surest indication that you not only were converted once upon a time but that you are living today the life of a converted soul with God is precisely this mourning for God. That mourning which never finds peace in sin but which goes to God with everything, great and small.

You are blessed, Jesus says. He says even more: you shall be *comforted.* God will comfort you. That is what He has already done. What else has He really done but comfort your sorrowing soul? Also today He comforts you.

Him that cometh to me I will in no wise cast out.

—JOHN 6:37

HERE we have a description of God's children which is very clear and very profound.

You who doubt whether you are a child of God, examine yourself on this point, for here we have one of the most distinctive marks of a child of God. A child of God is a person who *comes* to Jesus. A person who not only has come, but who *comes* to Jesus. Every day, yes, every time he becomes convinced in his conscience that he has sinned.

Here is the real difference between a converted and an unconverted person. Both sin. And both are convinced of their sin by the Spirit of God. But the unconverted *go away* from God with their sins. The converted *come to* God with them.

It is not always easy for a child of God to come to God with her sins. It was not easy when she came to God the first time, but to come *every day* is more difficult. If she did not have the consolation of the Gospel, she would not dare to come, so disheartened is she oftentimes.

Therefore you shall hear the Gospel today also, my dear child of God. And today it reads like this: Those who come to God are never turned away. Never. As long as you come and confess your daily transgressions and your sins of omission, so long are you a child of God.

Do not be anxious if you find that sin cleaves to you.

You have not as yet been discharged from the great hospital of grace. If you suffer a relapse in your illness, simply call the great and good Physician. Remember His words: "They that are whole have no need of a physician, but they that are sick."

Be of good cheer! In a short time you will be discharged from the hospital. This service also death will render you. Not until then will your soul be fully made whole. From then on you shall never in all eternity grieve your Savior any more.

But when these things begin to come to pass, look up, and lift up your heads; because your redemption draweth nigh.

—LUKE 21:28

J ESUS spoke often of His coming again. It is clear that Jesus rejoices at the thought of the day of His return.

When He speaks to the disciples about this day, He does so in order to comfort them and to make them glad.

Here in this chapter He tells them of the world events which are to usher in the Day. He says expressly that He does this that they may lift up their heads toward that Day, the World-Day, after the long and dark night through which the world has lived.

On another occasion He designates His return as a *rebirth of the world.* He sees it clearly as the World-Spring, to be heralded by the mighty spring break-up which at that time shall occur throughout the whole universe: "There shall be signs in sun and moon and stars; and upon the earth distress of nations, in perplexity for the roaring of the sea and the billows."

But at that very time the disciples of Jesus shall experience the goal of their desires, *the day of their redemption,* as it is significantly designated in the Scriptures.

Then shall they be released from sin and all its consequences in soul and body. Then shall they be lifted up from sorrow and tears, from doubt, fear, and spiritual danger. They shall not taste death; they shall be clothed upon, not unclothed. They shall meet their Friend in the skies.

And they shall experience the greatest thing that anyone can experience: They shall *see Him as He is.* Him in whom they had believed but whom they had never seen in the way that their yearning souls longed to see Him.

"Oh, hasten Thine appearing, Thou Bright and Morning Star!
Lord, may we soon be hearing the trumpet sound afar;
Thy people all are yearning to be Thy raptured bride,
And at Thine own returning be caught up to Thy side."

325

Come unto me, all ye that labor and are heavy laden,
and I will give you rest.

—MATTHEW 11:28

E VERY sincere soul has been endowed with a *holy suspicion*
of himself and is therefore frequently afraid of deceiving himself.

His soul asks: "Can I *rest* in the grace of God when I do
not improve? Is not this to sin against grace? My daily life is
a daily condemnation of myself."

My friend! Do in all calmness what Jesus tells you to do.
That is never dangerous. He says: "Come unto me, all ye that
labor and are heavy laden, and I will give you rest."

It says: *All.*

And it says: "Those that come to me, I will in no wise
cast out."

Of course you are mistaken if you think that you can come
to Jesus and find rest daily *without becoming better.* That is
absolutely impossible.

On the contrary, the fact of the matter is that if I do not
get better, if there is no growth and progress in my daily life,
it is because I do *not* come to Christ that He may give me *rest.*

For there is no other way to progress in sanctification than
by the way of *forgiveness,* the way of the free *grace* of God.

She who comes to Christ every day and confesses and receives forgiveness of her sins cannot avoid growth and progress.

Inherent in the forgiveness of sins lies *concealed a power*
to oppose that sin for which we have received forgiveness.
God has put tremendous moral power into confession and
forgiveness.

The *humiliation* connected with confession and forgiveness
is a hidden antidote to the lust and power of sin.

Come unto me, says Jesus. That is the panacea.

All day long.

Thou has been faithful over a few things, I will set thee over many things.

—MATTHEW 25:21

ALL human beings, even though not highly gifted, have within themselves great possibilities.

But, as is well known, only a few people utilize these possibilities.

Some do accomplish a great deal during their lifetime, both by mind and by hand. But most of those who *do* great things *are* not great themselves. As characters they are often small of stature, dominated by the meanest considerations of honor, power, gain, or enjoyment.

Among the children of God, too, we find something similar. The number of those who *do* great things is greater than those who *are* great.

There are many people who have etched their names indelibly into the history of the kingdom of God here in our country. They have made a great contribution of time, strength, thought, initiative, and money.

But many of these people diminish in size when one comes in closer touch with them personally. They are oftentimes vain, covetous of honor, opinionated, and difficult to work with.

One does not very often meet the truly *great* Christians, those who are humble of heart, not only of mouth, those who are patient, forbearing, considerate, and careful, who acknowledge their own mistakes and excuse the mistakes of others.

Jesus tells us here today why so many of us fail in this.

We are not faithful in little things.

This way to true greatness is so plain that not even a fool can mistake it. Great ability is not required.

It is the little things that count.

But the way is narrow and steep. And for that reason there are few who, in all earnestness, are willing to follow it.

327

Ask, and it shall be given you; seek, and ye shall
find; knock, and it shall be opened unto you!

—LUKE 11:9

W HEN I read what Jesus and His disciples said about prayer,
then I understand how little most of us have learned to pray.

Jesus expects us to come to Him and to tell Him what we
need. The oftener we come, the more He likes it.

When I err during the day, He expects me to come to Him
at once and ask forgiveness. He longs to impart it to me.

As I day by day feel the power of sin in my life, He expects
me to tell Him about it in order that He may impart to me
from on high the power which I need in order to combat my
super-powerful foes.

When my dear ones, or I myself, are in difficulty and distress,
Jesus expects me to come and tell Him what the trouble is.
He longs to help His poor friends, this rich Friend of ours!

When it is a question of God's cause, with its many tasks,
both new and old, its opposition from the world and the indifference of so many believers, then Jesus expects us to come
to Him and tell Him what our feelings in the matter are, to
ask Him what it is necessary to do in each particular case.

He has never intended that His cause should be furthered
without our coming to Him each day and availing ourselves
of the power which He will supply and which no opposition
can withstand—the holy power of prayer, which moves both
heaven and earth.

Jesus expects that we who have received His own permission
to pray for whatever we desire should go our way through this
world's barren desert like streams of refreshing water.

Every one that cometh unto me, and heareth my words, and doeth them, I will show you to whom he is like: he is like a man building a house, who digged and went deep, and laid a foundation upon a rock.

—LUKE 6:47-48

THESE are the concluding words of Jesus' Sermon on the Mount. He closes by describing two kinds of hearers: those who *do* what they hear, and those who do *not*.

This is therefore a text that is precisely suited to us who are now to hear the Word of God.

Jesus speaks first of those who do as He says. It seems to me that we can hear Jesus' joy through His words.

Today, too, He rejoices when He looks upon you who have built your house upon a firm foundation, enabling it to stand in storms and floods, in life and in death.

How did these people go about building their house upon a rock?

There was a time when things *went to pieces* for them.

We usually speak of that as their spiritual *awakening*. What individuals experience during their awakening is that the foundation upon which they have been building fails.

The person of whom Jesus speaks *digged deep*.

Yes, that is what these folk did too. Ordinarily we speak of that as *conversion*. Those who turn to God are those who cannot be satisfied with fraud or half-way measures. There is darkness and there are dismal depths in the human soul. But they dig deep—all the way to the bottom. All sin must come out into the light of God, old and new, small and great, open and hidden.

But the more they dig, the more everything gives way beneath them. They are given a glimpse into a heart which is permeated through and through with sin. At last they sink down in exhaustion and despair. But discover then to their own amazement and joy that they have sunk down upon the firm foundation: Christ.

And when a flood arose, the stream brake against that house, and could not shake it: because it had been well builded.

—LUKE 6:48

W E spoke yesterday of those fortunate people who dug deep and built their houses on a firm foundation. Are they then through digging?

No, they have learned that nothing is more deceitful than the human heart. Their hearts are full of holy fear and trembling. They search themselves. They make inquiry continually to see if their faith is dead, if they are sinning against grace, if they have the appearance of godliness but lack its power, if they have forsaken their first love, if they have their lamp in hand but have no oil.

They pray God also to try them: "Search me, O God, and see if there be any wicked way in me."

And God hears their prayer.

He sees the many dangers that confront us. Also the danger of beginning to have faith in our own faith instead of faith in Christ. Of beginning to rest in our own Christianity instead of in God.

Then He takes away from us the kind of grace that we can *feel.* Our foundation is tested. What do we have left when we can no longer *feel* the grace of God? All we feel then is the mind of the flesh. Our heart is worldly and earthbent; sin plays with us and entices us; we have no desire to read the Bible or to pray, no love of the saints. Everything is muddled, devoid of interest, hopeless.

Some deep digging has been done. Now I see with new eyes what my Christianity was worth. My self-confidence has been trimmed down very thoroughly. Boastful speech and haughty demeanor are gone. Now I see that Christ is my only salvation. He is my heart's only hope. It would break, were it not for Him.

Then shall the kingdom of heaven be likened unto ten virgins, who took their lamps, and went forth to meet the bridegroom. And five of them were foolish, and five were wise.

—MATTHEW 25:1-2

J ESUS speaks often of His return unto the final judgment.

In this parable He would tell us what a *dreadful* surprise it will be to those who at last shall see that they are forever excluded from the kingdom, that they are eternally lost.

Five of the virgins had never thought that this would happen.

I ask myself: I wonder if anyone will reach eternal perdition without feeling that it was something they thought would never happen, yes, could not happen?

If we could ask all the people who today are unconverted whether they are afraid of being lost, no doubt we would receive about the following answer: "Are you beside yourself? *I* be lost? Never!"

And they mean it in all sincerity, without a doubt.

How can they be so certain in the matter? Jesus speaks to them, too; He includes them also in His admonition.

Yes, He does. But many of them live in *false peace*. Admonition is ineffective. They are always positive of themselves.

Others, again, acknowledge, willingly enough, that they do not live as they ought and that their relationship with God is not as it should be. Nevertheless they do not think that they will be lost. They intend to be saved, and they do *plan* to repent. There is no doubt in their minds about that. But they cannot do it now.

Likely it is this type of thinking which gives them the necessary boldness to postpone their conversion.

Yes, we can understand full well that it will come as an unexpected surprise when they open their eyes in perdition.

O God, help the unconverted to heed Thy word.

331

> Afterward came also the other virgins, saying, Lord,
> Lord, open to us. But he answered and said, Verily
> I say unto you, I know you not.
>
> —MATTHEW 25:11-12

Today we hear of an even worse surprise on the last day.
Jesus tells us that many of those who have been converted and
are recognized as God's children will at last see that they have
deceived themselves and must enter into eternal perdition.

It is clear that Jesus desires to show us how much *alike* they
were, the wise and the foolish virgins. They all waited for the
Bridegroom. They went forth to meet Him. They all had their
lamps. They were in the same company. The wise virgins had
no idea of how terrible the condition of the foolish virgins was.

Notwithstanding this similarity, five of them were lost.

But this is impossible, someone says. If it is like this, then
none of us here on earth can with certainty know anything
about our eternal fate.

Yes, God be praised, we can. The way to heaven is so plain
that not even a fool can mistake it. It is revealed even unto
babes, Jesus says.

Why did the five fare so badly? How does it happen that a
watchful Christian slips into self-deception?

Well, that is a sad story. The Spirit does not neglect to
remind and admonish. All self-examination, however, is hard
and painful. As soon as the heart begins to enter into a compact
with sin, one begins to *fear* self-scrutiny.

When the Spirit of God under such circumstances seeks to
point out the weak spot, we begin to defend ourselves and say:
"I am converted. I have the confidence of the Christians. I
take part in Christian work, and with success."

And if we nevertheless become a little restless occasionally,
notwithstanding our self-defense, we are quick to comfort ourselves with the fact that fear and trembling are a part of the
believer's lot. This is the way a wise virgin becomes a foolish
one, the way which leads from a watchful Christian life to a
life of self-deception.

And while they went away to buy, the bridegroom came; and they that were ready went in with him to the marriage feast: and the door was shut.

—MATTHEW 25:10

How does it affect you when you hear this parable of the virgins who deceived themselves and were lost?

"I am so afraid that the same thing will happen to me too," you say. "Oftentimes I seem to notice things in my life and heart which indicate deception in me also."

Thank God for this fear! It shows that you are not as yet a foolish virgin, but one who submits to the discipline and heeds the warnings of the Spirit. The wise virgins have several characteristics which are easy for the spiritual eye to see. They have an inherent *distrust* of themselves. Therefore they give heed when the Spirit brings things to their remembrance and admonishes them. Yes, they are often struck by the truth, are often *terrified* by the Word of the Lord. They are frequently in *distress*.

Therefore they feel, as a rule, that they are poor and weak. They feel that they have too little sorrow because of sin and too little repentance, too little fear and trembling, too little faith and love; they feel that they pray too little, that they are not devoted enough and do not have a sufficiently willing spirit in the matter of serving the Lord.

Now note wherein they differ from the foolish virgins. They lay everything before the Savior. They cannot live without doing this. They would know what He thinks about them. They would order their lives in accordance with His will.

They who mourn shall be *comforted,* Jesus says. The Spirit comforts them daily. He points out the cross to them until *peace* and *assurance* settle down upon their souls. But they live from hand to mouth. Before long there is something which makes their hearts restless again. And they begin to examine themselves once more.

Yes, *self-examination* is the very means of saving us from self-deception and perdition. It keeps us awake, makes us feel the *need* of the cross and the blood.

333

Lift up your eyes, and look on the fields, that they are white already unto harvest.

—JOHN 4:35

THAT which is taking place these days in the Christian and non-Christian nations cries to high heaven the responsibility and obligation of the church of Jesus Christ.

Never have the doors been as wide open as now. Never in recorded history has the whole human race been as bewildered and uncertain as it is now.

Nor has there ever been such a determined struggle for people's souls and for the nations as there is now. Religions old and new vie with each other for the opportunity to satisfy the religious unrest and longing which quietly finds its way into human souls in spite of mammon-worship and the dance craze. Now it is a question whether the church of God is alive and is making use of the greatest opportunity it has ever had in our era.

My view is that nothing is so insistently urgent as that all the children of God throughout the whole world unite in child-like, definite prayer for a *world-wide spiritual awakening.*

We hear from all our missionaries, from all our mission fields, that the open doors we now have to the heathen nations will in a short time probably be closed by the anti-Christian culture and religion constantly being brought into these countries from Europe.

It is an established fact that the movements opposing Christian missions among the heathen come from Europe. The danger from this cannot be averted, therefore, except by a great spiritual awakening in Christian lands.

The thought of it overwhelms one. And many will smile at it. Others will not smile, but will relegate the whole matter to the limbo of other desirable but unattainable things. They, however, who have learned that the words of Jesus can be relied upon, will go to work. Did He not say: "Nothing shall be impossible unto you?"

Lord, teach us to pray!

Zacchaeus, make haste, and come down; for today I
must abide at thy house.

—LUKE 19:5

ZACCHAEUS had heard so much about Jesus that his thoughts
were occupied with Him continually. Now he had heard that
Jesus was staying in the city. If he only could see Him! But in
such a crowd it was no use for Zacchaeus to try; he was too
small of stature. Then he brushed aside all such considerations
and climbed up into a tree, even though he was one of the
prominent officials of the city. Today he was *determined* to
see Jesus.

What happens? Jesus sees him and stops. A few moments
afterwards Jesus is in his home.

The chief publican, who of late has been the city's most
despairing soul, now walks about his house completely transformed: Jesus is with him. Now people may say what they will.
He has received forgiveness for his sins. That is why he is
so happy.

This is perhaps what should take place in your home also.

There are so many things which should be changed here.
Perhaps you have already tried to change certain ones. But you
are beginning to realize that it is you yourself who must be
changed.

You too have felt a desire to have Jesus come into your
home. It is becoming so hard to sin away your brief little span
of years. So hard to sin against God, who has been so im-
measurably kind toward you.

"Make haste," Jesus said to Zacchaeus. He says the same
thing to you. Do not defer this important decision any longer.

"Come down," He said also. You too must come down and
take upon yourself the reproach which has always been the lot
of Jesus and His true friends.

But do not be afraid!

When Jesus enters your home, it means little to you whether
people smile contemptuously at you or not.

> For we are his workmanship, created in Christ Jesus for good works, which God afore prepared that we should walk in them.
>
> —EPHESIANS 2:10

THIS matter of work is a difficult one in Christianity.

It is easy for us to go from one extreme to another, from laziness to outward hurry and hubbub. It is difficult for us to achieve the proper balance between work and rest.

Our text today puts both rest and work in their proper place. If we do not get our rest, we become tired workers. I think that we Christians in this day and age have too little rest. By that I do not mean to say, however, that we work too much. But that our Christianity is strained and labored. We carry Christianity as though it were a heavy burden instead of letting it carry us.

Here in the Word for today we are told what *God* does. It is a message of quietude and rest.

To be a Christian means to permit oneself to be cared for by God. Like a little child. What does the child *do?* Oh, not much. The chief thing that it does no doubt is this: It allows itself to be loved by father and mother.

You who are a child of God, do not forget that, after all, you are a *child* of God. Let yourself be loved and cared for by your heavenly Father. It is a joy to Him to manifest His love to you. Just as it is a joy to you fathers and mothers to love and care for your little ones.

We are His workmanship, it says. This piece of workmanship is not finished. We are like children, not yet mature.

Do not be discouraged, therefore, when you experience how *immature* you are. How you err. How unwisely you can act. How you can fail.

No, do not be discouraged. Simply heed God when He speaks to you! Let the Spirit of God tell you the truth! Let Him impart forgiveness to you! Let Him explain Christ to you! And, above all, let Him love you!

Having begun in the Spirit, are ye now perfected in the flesh?

—GALATIANS 3:3

THERE are many paths that lead from a promising beginning in the Spirit to a dismal consummation in the flesh.

You made a good beginning. God overcame your old, passionately self-loving ego. You surrendered without condition to God, and your heart was filled with the love of Christ.

You lived for God and your neighbor, following Christ uncompromisingly and fearlessly.

Then a change occurred, during a period of spiritual weakness, perhaps as a consequence of spiritual undernourishment. You began to listen to the tempter's words: Spare thyself.

Now you discovered many valid reasons for allowing yourself more consideration.

That was all that was necessary. You became solicitous about your own person. You provided minutely for your own comfort, your own advantage, your own enjoyment.

However, now, too, you would be a Christian. Therefore you want to do something for God and for others. But always in such a way that you can make proper allowances for yourself.

It is thus that the pampered and unreal type of Christianity of which there is so much in our day develops, both in city and in country. A passive type of Christianity, without sacrifice, brings the soul neither joy nor sorrow but only that lukewarmness which the Lord spews out of His mouth.

My unhappy friend, would you be healed of this, then take up your cross again, enter into the *service* of the Lord once more and begin to make *sacrifices* for Him!

But now do not try to think of something great to do! Begin with lowly forms of service, those in your own home above all. This will bring about a definite break with your old nature every day.

But when the Son of man shall come in his glory, and all the angels with him, then shall he sit on the throne of his glory: and before him shall be gathered all the nations.

—MATTHEW 25:31-32

In this parable Jesus tells us a little about the last of all our days.

We know none of the days that are to come; we do not even know what the end of this day will bring.

But Jesus knows all the days that lie before us, also the last one. Here He tells us that this last day shall be our final and decisive day of reckoning.

Before that day we shall all have had many days of reckoning. But the characteristic thing about all the other days of reckoning will be that they were not the final day of reckoning. If we were willing to be reconciled to God in those days, He forgave us our debt and we began anew.

But when the last day of reckoning comes, nothing can be changed any more. Then the result of our lives will be determined for all time to come.

We need this reminder about the final reckoning because we are all thoughtless and indifferent. Jesus reminds us today that all of us, without exception, must give a very accurate and detailed account of everything in our life, even the most insignificant words that we have spoken.

He would let us know that *nothing of all that we have done is forgotten.* We forget quickly. But in heaven nothing is forgotten.

Is it to frighten us that Jesus comes to us with this earnest message?

Nay, any one who knows Him knows that He does not come to frighten anybody. But among the many things He has to tell us, He has to leave with us a word also about the seriousness of life.

Today He asks all of us the serious question: Are you prepared to give an account of the life you have lived?

338

And the man and his wife hid themselves from the presence of Jehovah God amongst the trees of the garden. —GENESIS 3:8

ANXIETY at the thought of meeting God is common to all the children of Adam and Eve. If we were permitted to pursue our own unsaved course, none of us would seriously seek the face of the Lord. But God in His mercy sees to it that none can forever depart from the presence of the Lord without first having stood face to face with their God.

This we are accustomed to speak of as spiritual *awakening.* The essential *grace* of God in connection with our spiritual awakening is that we are brought face to face with God, regardless of the fact that we neither desire it nor have asked for it.

As is well known, spiritual awakening is always accompanied by tremendous *anxiety,* whether the awakening leads to conversion or not.

This anxiety is no doubt caused by the fact that we are compelled to stand before the face of the Lord, and our whole past life is revealed by His penetrating light.

We love sin and cannot think of living without it. But in the nearness of God it is terrible to commit sin. In this glaring light one can see the fearful consequences and eternal risk of sin. Now comes also the fear that one must give up one's life in sin.

Finally, we have this anxiety in connection with the *decision* we must make.

As a result of the awakening the soul is *compelled* to make a decision. We are not compelled to repent, but we are compelled to decide one way or another.

We may decide which ever way we will. But this is the very thing that gives rise to the deepest anxiety during the time of spiritual awakening. We see with a clearness that renders us uncomfortable that the decision which our spiritual awakening is now forcing us to make will in itself show clearly what we do will.

What then is *your* decision?

Simon, Simon, behold, Satan asked to have you, that he might sift you as wheat: but I made supplication for thee that thy faith fail not.

—LUKE 22:31-32

HERE Jesus tells us how hell itself reaches into time. Hell is the steadily flowing spring from which comes temptation.

It is this that Jesus desires to point out to those who walk thoughtlessly and indifferently along the pathway of life with the dizzy chasm of eternal hell running directly along the wayside.

We have no doubt all felt or at least have had an intimation of these invisible powers from hell which project themselves into our little lives. When the joy of living is changed into the seriousness of living. When we feel like a chip in a plunging torrent.

It is as though we are in a mighty maelstrom of *lust*.

Or in the horrible undertow of *events*. Events which we have not ordered and for which we have not planned. Events over which we have no control.

Events are, as we all know, more potent than thoughts or ideas.

Judas received the purse.

Peter was given access to the courtyard of the high priest. He was the one whom the high priest's servant asked if he too were not a Nazarene.

We experience somewhat the same also.

Suddenly a succession of events confronts us with terrific, tempting power.

The finest and most sensitive organs of our soul feel instinctively the grip of the hand which invisibly reaches out after us from hell.

Even the youngest of us sitting here today has felt this to some extent.

No man can serve two masters. . . . Ye cannot serve
God and mammon.

—MATTHEW 6:24

No one can serve two masters, Jesus says.

And yet this is the very thing that everybody is trying
to do.

All people, even the most ungodly, have a religion, a secret
place of refuge, that compact with God which they depend
upon to save them when the hour of need comes. That minimum of religion which they seldom reveal to others, but which
is the haven of refuge to which they always repair when the
storms of life are let loose upon them or the earnest warnings
of conscience threaten their poise of mind.

Most of us do not desire to live our earthly lives, with all
their uncertainties, entirely apart from God.

It may be possible to find a few who after due deliberation
have torn away from all religion. But it is certain that many
of those who by word of mouth deny God in their hearts are
convinced that there is a God and secretly reserve for themselves some mutilated little portion of religion.

Fallen humanity *would* serve two masters.

We would serve ourselves. We would make use of this world
as a great, varied place of amusement where we can go from
one form of diversion to another as we become bored in turn
of the various types of entertainment.

But at the same time we want a return ticket.

For the day will come when we will have passed by all the
amusement centers.

And, worst of all, when the capacity to enjoy pleasure is
gone, when body and soul are a burden to ourselves and others.

This is why we want to have a God in reserve.

My son, give me thy heart!

THEY had just had family devotions. The father had just read the very same words from the Scriptures that we have just heard. Little Randi was not more than eight years old, but she was a thoughtful little girl. However, she could not understand what her father had read that day. When the devotions were concluded, she went over to her father and said: "What do we do when we give God our hearts?"

"That I shall tell you; but first go and get your little purse."

Randi was very willing to do that because every time her father asked her to go and get her purse he put some money into it. When Randi returned with her purse, her father put a whole dollar into it. Randi beamed with joy. At that moment she probably forgot her question completely.

But her father had not forgotten it. Now he spoke up: "You asked me just now how we give God our hearts. Then I asked you to go and get your purse. You did, and gave it to me. It was empty and I put a dollar into it. That is the way we give God our hearts. It is empty of all that God would have it contain. But then God takes our empty hearts and fills them. And do you know with what He fills them?"

Randi sat and looked at her father with her large eyes. She really did not know what she should answer.

"Well," said her father. "He puts Jesus into our hearts. Remember that you received Jesus into your heart when you were a wee little child. When you were *baptized*, Jesus came into your heart."

"And will He never leave me?" asked Randi.

"No," said her father. "He does not *want* to leave you. But He must depart from many hearts. For if we do anything that we know is sinful and we refuse to ask Jesus to forgive us, then Jesus cannot stay in our hearts any longer."

Randi understood this. And she was glad that she, too, could give her heart to Jesus.

> The trumpet shall sound, and the dead shall be raised incorruptible, and we shall be changed. . . . Then shall come to pass the saying that is written, Death is swallowed up in victory.
>
> —1 CORINTHIANS 15:52, 54

HOPE sheds its beneficent rays also upon our bodies.

If we live long enough, we shall have to be witnesses of their approaching disintegration, inch by inch. Our powers will lose their edge; our limbs will become stiff; our senses will become weak.

Our bodies become more and more useless to us. At last we must give them up completely. Then they will be in such a condition that our dear ones who are left with them will have no choice but to bury them as quickly as possible, six feet beneath the sod.

But:

> "I know of a morning bright and fair,
> Where tidings of joy shall wake us.
> When songs from on high shall fill the air,
> And God to His glory take us."

Then we shall receive our bodies back again. Forever made whole of all blemishes and weaknesses. Forever as beautiful as God's own thoughts regarding us.

Then all the powers which we here *began* to employ in His service shall forever be in the service of the Lord.

There are many and various kinds of powers residing in us. We see this best in that Man who used all His powers and used them in the right way, namely, Jesus.

In us lie many *unused* powers. We are not in a relationship to God in which it is possible to make full use of them. But on resurrection morning we shall be able to make use of all of them.

And, in addition, we shall employ all the *new* powers which God shall give us, when all the virus of sin shall have been eliminated from our bodies. And all shall be put at the disposal of the Lord!

What a glorious hope!

I am ashamed that I at times can live in dread of death.

Now is my soul troubled; and what shall I say? Father, save me from this hour. But for this cause came I unto this hour.

—JOHN 12:27

WHEN God created the teeming multitudinousness which we call the universe, He sat quietly upon His throne and spoke the word by which everything came forth, quickly or gradually, as He willed it.

And in governing and preserving the mighty universe, from the greatest planets and solar systems to the smallest bacilli, He also sits quietly upon His throne.

But when He was to save the fallen race, then he could not sit upon His throne. Then He had to descend. He had to come down from heaven. God had to become human, yes, had to humble Himself and become obedient unto death.

The passion history of Jesus extends from His birth to His death.

None of us was so poor but that a cradle or a crib stood in readiness for us at our birth. When Jesus was born, no little bed was waiting. He was wrapped in swaddling clothes and laid in a manger.

And when He was to die, there was no bed. You and I hope that we can be in our own beds when the day comes that we are to die. Jesus had to die on a cross.

Crucifixion implies, as we know, that crucified persons are so accursed that they are not even permitted to lie on the earth and die. They must hang between heaven and earth.

From His birth in poverty to His ignominious death His life was one of continual suffering. It was worst toward the last. In our text we are told that His suffering was so terrible that He did not know what to say.

My precious Savior, grant me a period of quiet contemplation, that I may follow Thee in Thy sufferings and behold Thee in Thy boundless love. Permit me to behold anew the price that it was necessary for Thee to pay for my salvation. Amen.

Thou sayest that I am a king. To this end have I
been born, and to this end am I come into the world,
that I should bear witness unto the truth. Every one
that is of the truth heareth my voice.

—JOHN 18:37

IT is not really to be wondered at that the Roman official,
seeing Jesus in His deep humiliation, should ask "Art thou a
king then?" To which Jesus answered: "I am a king. To this
end have I been born, and to this end am I come into
the world."

Ordinarily kings require that their servants shall be willing
to die for them. But this King dies for His friends, yes, even
for His enemies!

Never has any king gained a victory like the one which
Jesus won, without power, without sword. His is a greater and
more glorious kingdom than those of all the kings of earth. It
is not limited by national boundaries or racial differences. Every
one that is of the truth hears His voice in every part of the
earth, among the black and the white, the yellow and
the brown.

And in every land it is the best who belong to Him: those
who are of the truth, those who were unable to withstand the
truth, and humbled themselves when Jesus began to testify to
them about their sin and their untruthfulness. Then they saw
their King, thorn-crowned, crucified, slain for all their sins.

Today you are meeting your King. Today He is testifying to
your conscience.

Behold, thy King!

Your suffering, bleeding, dying King! The chastisement of
our peace was upon Him. Today you may find peace, peace
with God. And with it you will be given victory over your
sins. Your enemies are His enemies. He will fight for you and
with you.

> "On my heart imprint Thy image,
> Blessed, Jesus, King of grace,
> That life's riches, cares, and pleasures
> Have no power Thee to efface."

345

To this end have I been born, and to this end am I come into the world, that I should bear witness unto the truth. Every one that is of the truth heareth my voice.

—JOHN 18:37

J ESUS had often shown His kingly power.

He rebuked the winds and the sea, and there was a great calm. He healed the sick with only a word, and drove the demons out of those that were possessed. The dead arose at His command.

Today we meet Him at the bar of justice.

Never have we seen Him more kingly than He is as He stands there before His earthly judge. He could have had His servants fight for Him. Indeed, He could have commandeered twelve legions of angels to protect Him from His murderers.

But that power He did not use.

He had an even greater power. He had power, not only over wind and wave, over sickness and death and the hosts of the devil.

He had power over Himself.

He had the strength to stand without counsel and without protection in the very midst of His murderers. To let the highest court in the land pronounce judgment upon Him and declare Him to be a criminal who was dangerous to the whole country. To permit His opponents to have the last word. Yes, to speak the word which they were to seize upon at once and for which He was to be condemned.

And the man who in a few moments, in cowardice, was to condemn Him to death, him He sought to save by a quiet appeal to his sense of truth and justice.

Such power over Himself, power to humble Himself, our King had to have in order to save us.

> "O sacred Head, what glory,
> What bliss, till now, was Thine!
> Yet, though despised and gory,
> I joy to call Thee mine."

> Now there was . . . a devout man, and one that feared God with all his house.
>
> —ACTS 10:2

IN this chapter we get a glimpse of a good home. As we read, we sit wishing that it might be thus in our home.

Yes, home is a wonderful gift from God. *That* at least all are agreed upon. Through all ages and among all peoples, home has been praised in the most beautiful words that language possesses and in the finest tones of which music is capable. In all languages people say as with one voice: "There is no place like home." Memories of home alone have a wonderful power, even over the hardest and vilest of individuals.

The highest and the most profound happiness that we are capable of enjoying is imparted to us in our homes. At home we are loved, understood, and forgiven. This is the great secret of domestic happiness.

Home is ordained of God as the place where our life is to take root. The protected place, where our little life is to grow strong enough to endure the pressure and the blows of the great world outside. Strong enough to stand in the storms of life and strong enough to bear life's rain and sunshine.

And who of us has not experienced the quiet joy which was ours when we could withdraw from the drizzle of life into the shelter of our home and draw the curtains down between us and the world.

Home is a *gift*, but also a *task*.

It is not given us in a completely finished state. Not even our parental home. All of us should have a part in building it. Home is the finest and most difficult human craft.

And the *Christian* home, built upon the Chief Corner-Stone, with an open heaven above and an altar unto the Lord in its midst, is in all likelihood the most beautiful fruit of Christ's salvation to be achieved in the vales of earth.

347

> For God gave us not a spirit of fearfulness; but of
> power and love and discipline.
>
> — 2 TIMOTHY 1:7

THIS verse speaks to us about a matter that is pertinent to us all, large and small.

How discouraged cannot a child feel! It may be a difficult lesson that causes it to lose courage, or it may be a quarrelsome playmate. And from this *one* source of difficulty the discouragement spreads until it seems to the child that *everything* is impossible.

Young people, too, are not unacquainted with discouragement. Indeed, perhaps no other age feels inhibited by discouragement more often than youth. In so many ways they feel inadequate to the complex life into which they have been projected as adults.

And who does not feel the crushing sense of discouragement even in adulthood's strongest years?

Our text today tells us that discouragement does not come from God. If we will remember that, it will be easier to orientate ourselves when discouragement comes.

God is not opposed to our seeing our own inability and impotence. On the contrary, *that* is what the Spirit of God is seeking to impress upon us day by day. But not to make us discouraged. He would much rather give us courage, that courage which we receive when we believe in God.

This courage, born of faith, is also known as boldness in the blood of Christ. And therein lies its secret. Those who look to the blood of Christ do not lose courage, even if Satan accuses them and their hearts condemn them. If God has died for my sins, then I can defy all things, as Luther says.

Behold, here is the spirit of *power* of which the Word speaks today. Here is also the spirit of discipline that is mentioned. The calm and poised mind which, in the midst of adversity, waits for the Lord. Yes, which desires to be weak and powerless in itself "that the exceeding greatness of the power may be of God, and not from ourselves."

> Repent ye therefore, and turn again, that your sins
> may be blotted out, that so there may come seasons
> of refreshing from the presence of the Lord.
>
> —ACTS 3:19

CAN any friend of God hear this Word, "seasons of refreshing," without having her deepest longings touched thereby?

"Seasons of refreshing" here in our dear *home!* Do we not all need to be renewed? Some of us also converted? O Lord, we wait upon Thee!

"Seasons of refreshing" in our *neighborhood,* in our community! So often everything seems hopeless. The worldly-minded will not hear the Word. At their gatherings the young people are engaged in drinking and dancing. The believing Christians, moreover, are slothful; nor are they of one mind. O Lord, we wait!

"Seasons of refreshing" for our *country!*

Slavery to mammon, consumerism, pleasure-madness, immorality, drinking, lawlessness, and disrespect for the Word of God are among the sins that are in the process of permeating our people, in city and in rural community.

If this unholy development is to be arrested and our beloved nation prevented from sinking down into atheism and moral and national disintegration, we must have a quiet, strong, and sound spiritual awakening, reaching all classes of our people, in every city and country community. O Lord, we wait!

"Seasons of refreshing" for the *world!*

Is there anything that the whole sin-sick world needs more today than a spiritual awakening? To what will it lead, this bitter racial hatred and racial struggle, this plunder-made strife among the nations for wealth and power, this private and public disrespect for God's law and gospel?

To what will it lead if we do not have a spiritual awakening so far-reaching and so deep that it restrains sin in every part of the world and gives the gospel new opportunities to do its work in the bold and reckless generation which today peoples the earth?

349

And he shall be like a tree planted by the streams
   of water,
That bringeth forth its fruit in its season,
Whose leaf also doth not wither;
And whatsoever he doeth shall prosper.

—PSALM 1:3

WHAT an advantage to be planted in the garden of God,
where every shoot grows with the certain hope of maturity!

In the story about King Midas we are told that everything
he touched turned into gold. Everything that you, my brother
and sister, set your hand to shall *prosper.* "Whatsoever he doeth
shall prosper."

Do you hear this, you Christians who have given up hope?

Prosperity in all things! *All* things. "Only goodness and
lovingkindness shall follow me all the days of my life." "To
them that love God all things work together for good."

Has God exaggerated? Or has He made a mistake?

Not in the least, not even when it was said, and you yourself
thought, that fortune was against you; prosperity was still with
you. Some day you shall recognize this: to sin is the only thing
that is hopeless.

God's plans for my life shall be realized. That hope was
given to me by my Savior, in the washing of Holy Baptism.
The faint beginning of a human being which I am today shall
become fully developed and mature.

In spite of everything! In spite of all my inherent and in-
dwelling sinfulness. In spite of my personal disobedience. In
spite of the allurement of sin and the enmity of the world. In
spite of Satan's cunning.

In spite of all, I shall in a very short time stand in the
presence of God with rejoicing. Exactly as God intended that
I should when He from eternity decreed that I should be
a human being.

"Thy loving heart so faithful,
O Father, knoweth well
The needs of all Thy children
Who in Thy shadow dwell."

But watch ye at every season, making supplication, that ye may prevail to escape all these things that shall come to pass, and to stand before the Son of man.

—LUKE 21:36

J ESUS speaks to us today about the last great move that we shall make.

He looks forward to that occasion with joy.

He looks forward with joy to bringing His redeemed bride from the old sin-cursed earth over to the new earth where God and we shall dwell together like a great happy family throughout all eternity.

But most people do not care to hear anything about this moving.

They prefer to dwell here.

But Jesus tells us today that this moving-time is coming to all of us. God never intended this earth as an *abiding* place for us human beings.

It is to be burned.

Therefore we must all move. Those who desire to do so and those who do not.

But only those who have made ready to move shall be permitted to dwell on the new earth, Jesus says. The others will be forever homeless and must stay outside in the dark, where there shall be weeping and gnashing of teeth.

Are you ready to move?

Are you ready today? Jesus says that we must be ready at all times and seasons. For He is coming in an hour that we think not.

Suppose the Son of Man came today! Would you be ready to meet Him? Would it be the happiest day in your life? Or the most terrible day you had ever experienced?

> "Lord, obediently we go,
> Gladly leaving all below;
> Only Thou our Leader be,
> And we still will follow Thee."

351

Therefore be ye also ready; for in an hour that ye
think not the Son of man cometh.

—MATTHEW 24:44

J ESUS looks forward with joy to the day of His returning.

But a shadow falls across His rejoicing. He fears that His
friends will not be ready when He comes.

And, indeed, He has reason to fear.

Many of His friends are weighed down, by the cares of this
life or by the deceitfulness of riches, and as a result the day
will come upon them as a snare.

Here and there some awaken from their spiritual sleep and
ask in bewilderment: "What should I do in order to be ready
to meet Jesus?"

Listen now: what do you think you would do if you were
informed that Jesus would be coming before the evening of
this day?

You would no doubt find much to do. You would have to
be reconciled to God, perhaps also to some people with whom
you are living on unfriendly terms.

If so, I would advise you: do it *immediately*. For Jesus says
that we should be ready at all times and seasons, for we know
not when He will come.

Be thus reconciled; then you will be ready to meet the Son
of Man. For it is only the precious blood of Jesus that can give
you boldness to meet the Lord. Whether you live a hundred
years or you meet Jesus today, it is only the blood of Christ
that can cover your sin and save you in the judgment.

Many believers pass their time in fear lest they should not
be ready when Jesus comes.

This fear is an unfruitful one, and is contrary to His will.

I am not to think of whether I shall be ready to meet Jesus
tomorrow. I must make ready to meet Him *today*.

That is the secret, Jesus says, of being ready *when he comes*.

Amen, yea, come Lord Jesus!

But take heed to yourselves, lest haply your hearts be overcharged with surfeiting, and drunkenness, and cares of this life, and that day come on you suddenly as a snare.

—LUKE 21:34

NEARLY every time that Jesus speaks of His coming again He admonishes His friends frequently and earnestly against the dangers which they will encounter in the world.

Here he warns them against surfeiting and drunkenness. And since it is the surfeiting of the heart of which He is speaking, it must be that He has in mind the danger of *hyperspirituality*.

He has made mention of this in other places also. "Many shall come in my name, saying, I am he; and, The time is at hand: go ye not after them." "For there shall arise false Christs, and false prophets, and shall show great signs and wonders; so as to lead astray, if possible, even the elect."

All who use their eyes can see that this danger is upon us. False prophets there are a-plenty. They calculate the day and the hour. They show signs and wonders; and many people permit themselves to be led astray.

Let us be sober and keep to the clear Word of God, and not be swept away by the floods of hyper-spirituality. No human being knows when Christ will come again. He has, however, told us what signs shall precede His coming. To these we should give heed, and be ready at all times.

But let us not by calculating the times and seasons seek to acquire knowledge which God has deliberately hidden from us.

Jesus points further to the danger of *worldliness*.

This danger is always at hand. But toward the end of time it will be more dangerous than ever. Then love will grow cold among most people, and unrighteousness will prevail.

Can Jesus understand from our life and from our work that we are *awaiting* Him? Or are we among those whose hearts are overcharged with surfeiting, and drunkenness, and the cares of this life?

353

For in that he himself hath suffered being tempted,
he is able to succor them that are tempted.

—HEBREWS 2:18

I THINK we all carry with us memories from times of temptation which cause the blush of shame to suffuse our faces.

We were incapable of withstanding. We were able to long, to hope, to think, and to speak, but not to *live*. For to live is to be tempted.

At such times fearful discouragement settles down upon those who dare to look themselves in the face. Especially is this true of young people. They begin to despise, even to loathe, themselves. They feel that they are entirely inadequate to the demands of life. It seems to them that they can succeed only when there are no temptations.

Not only do they feel that they are sinful, but dangerous and harmful as well. Both to themselves and to others. They feel that they do not only degrade themselves, but others also. That they destroy that which is finest in others, and draw out the evil rather than the good that is in them.

Then in the minds of these young people who cannot with complacency look on while they sink down into such humiliation and degradation there arises the burning question: How can I *overcome* in the hour of temptation?

No longer do they inquire about cleverness and ability to balance one desire against another, or how to evade the dangerous consequences of sin.

Not at all. What they are asking for now is *victory*, ability to meet temptation without yielding.

Thirty years ago I was occupied with this question to the exclusion of all others. I found the answer, and I am now happy to comfort you with that comfort wherewith I myself was comforted.

I say therefore to you at once: There is one, and only one, who can help you. You may travel the world over and listen to as much counsel as you will. There is only one who can help you. His name is Christ. He has raised up from the mire both old and young.

> The fruit of the Spirit is love, joy, peace, longsuffering, kindness, goodness, faithfulness, meekness, self-control.
>
> —GALATIANS 5:22

In this verse the apostle tells us that love is followed by joy.

To will that which is good is not only the *nature* of love, but also its *joy.*

Walk among God's creatures, wishing them that which is good and blessing them, and you will be filled with a quiet, peaceful joy which will lift you as high above the joys and sorrows of this earthly life as God would have you live as a Christian.

Your life will become richer. A new and wonderful world will be opened to you. Your eyes will see, your ears hear, and your heart experience things you have never known before. The music of heaven will begin to resound in your soul. It will be as though heaven itself had come down to you and filled you with an unspeakable joy.

You will feel as though you were just beginning to live.

And you will be endued with new power to serve God, to say No to sin, to endure opposition, and to suffer evil. Power of which you never had any idea before.

"Longsuffering, kindness, goodness," the apostle calls it.

And this mind, which wills to do the good and does it, is invincible. Therefore the apostle says: "Overcome evil with good." Indeed, there is no other way of overcoming evil. Not even God Himself has any other means. He overcomes His *enemies* by His suffering love alone, and by it transforms them into His friends.

I do not have this love, someone may say.

That is not the worst. God does not expect that you and I, of ourselves, should have it; He expects rather that we should acknowledge that we do *not* have it. And that we should pray God for forgiveness for this terrible sin, that we do not love God. And then pray for the Spirit of God, who will work in us that love of God which we do not have of ourselves.

355

And he spake a parable unto them to the end that
they ought always to pray, and not to faint.

—LUKE 18:1

WE long for spiritual awakenings, we speak of spiritual awakenings, and we work for spiritual awakenings.

Yes, we even pray a little for spiritual awakenings.

But most of us will not enter into that work of praying which is the essential preparation for all spiritual awakenings.

Many of us misunderstand the work of the Spirit among the unconverted and think that it is limited chiefly to the seasons in which the awakening is taking place. We seem to think that the unconverted are not worked upon by God during the intervening periods.

But this is a misunderstanding.

The Spirit works unceasingly, during spiritual awakenings and between awakenings, even though His work differs in kind, and therefore also varies in its effect upon people's souls.

The work of the Spirit resembles mining operations. The hardness of heart of sinners and their reckless opposition to God must be blown to pieces. The spiritual awakening may be likened to the time when the explosive materials are set off. The periods between the spiritual awakenings correspond to the time when deep holes are laboriously being bored into the hard rock of the mountain.

To bore the holes is a task that tries one's patience. To light the fuse and fire the explosive is, on the other hand, work that is both easy and interesting. Then one truly sees *results* of one's labors. Moreover, it takes skilled workers to do the boring. Any one can light a fuse.

Let us enter upon this quiet, difficult, patience-trying task and by our daily prayers bore holy explosive materials into the souls of the unconverted. Yes, let us take up *this* work of prayer, and let us not grow weary.

As for me and my house, we will serve Jehovah.
—JOSHUA 24:15

M ANY are the homes that have begun as Joshua here indicates.

The two loved each other; they shared everything, including life in God. They prayed, they read the Bible, they sang, they conversed about God and their life in Him. But, in so many instances, it all went to pieces.

Domestic egoism made its appearance. It was easier to be loved than to love. It began with a small measure of ingratitude in little things and from there it went on to impoliteness. They began to be more courteous to strangers than to each other. The next step was sulkiness, silence, surliness, obstinacy.

Love is a tender and fragile plant which withers and dies without constant care. It is not enough to *have* love in our hearts; we must *show* it. People of a reticent nature are especially tempted on this score. Their unyielding and studied natures are such that their feelings die within them unexpressed. Especially is this true of some men.

O husband, whoever you are, do not be afraid to show your wife that you love her. Not only on formal occasions, but also in your daily life. That is when she needs you most. That is when she appreciates it most also. Nor should you be afraid to let others know that you honor and esteem your wife very highly.

Love's great test comes when we begin to realize that our loved one has failings and shortcomings. Because of the intimacy of home life we also *feel* these defects.

I, too, have failings and shortcomings, but the desire of my heart is that I may be loved in spite of these, yes, that I may be wooed away from my failings. And if I take offense at the failings of my dear ones, I reveal the extent to which my love is mingled with selfishness.

True love bears with and forgives the failings of the loved one. More than that, it sees that our dear ones need love even more because of their very failings.

Now when John heard in prison the works of the
Christ, he sent by his disciples and said unto him,
Art thou he that cometh, or look we for another?

—MATTHEW 11:2-3

ONLY a few months before, John had stood at the Jordan
pointing out the Messiah, the Lamb of God, to the multitudes
that were surging about him.

Now the situation was changed.

There were no multitudes about him. John the Baptist was
in a lonely cell in a fortress, away from his own. Here people
were few, but thoughts many. He had once said: "He must
increase, but I must decrease."

I do not know whether John had thought of it in this
particular way.

And yet it was not John's personal troubles that had brought
him into the gloom of doubt and despair. His spiritual conflict
began when he, in his lonely cell, heard that all Jesus did was
to continue John's own work, that of preaching and baptizing.
Jesus, too, preached only that the kingdom of God was at hand.

It was then that John began to doubt. Was I mistaken? Is
Jesus also only a forerunner?

There is always some friend of the Lord in the prison-house
of doubt. It is not long since all was well with you, too. You
beheld the Lamb of God who took away your sins. You were
courageous; and you testified, as John did, in the presence of
others. But now your courage is gone. You cannot find the old
paths. Both the Bible and prayer are as if closed to you. Doubt
has made everything seem empty to you. You have not invited
doubt, but it has come nevertheless.

John went to Jesus with his doubts. Do likewise. Tell Him
what your thoughts about Him are. And confess your sins to
Him. You, too, like John, will receive a word from Jesus which
will cause your doubts to disappear.

He must increase, but I must decrease.

—JOHN 3:30

J ESUS says of John the Baptist that he was the greatest of all the prophets. And the little that we are told about him reveals him as a monumental figure indeed.

He was great as an *ascetic*, subsisting in the loneliness of the desert on locusts and wild honey.

He was great as a *revivalist*. Remarkable indeed, for he did not go forth to the people; they streamed out to him, away there on the edge of the desert. Even the capital city came out to hear him.

He was great as a *witness to the truth*, with fidelity proclaiming it to both the Pharisees and the publicans, even to the rulers, one of whom he rebuked for immorality.

He was great when they came from the capital city to acclaim him as the *Messiah*. I am so insignificant in comparison with the Messiah, he said, that I am not worthy to render Him the service which the most menial of all servants performs, that of unloosing the latchet of His shoes.

But he was greatest of all when he spoke the words contained in our text. His disciples had come and told him that Jesus, whom he had recently baptized, had now begun to preach and baptize farther down the river. And now every one was going to Him, they said.

Then John answered: "He must increase, but I must decrease." He is the Messiah, and the people should follow Him. I am only the voice which preceded Him and called upon the people to gather about Him.

John was indeed permitted to see the fulfillment of his prophetical words. He was in truth to decrease. First he was torn away from his God-given task and thrust into a lonely prison-cell. Then he was hurled into the darkness of doubt and uncertainty.

But John was great also in his doubts. He took them to Jesus and was saved from them. Then he died for the sake of his faith and his God. After honoring God by his ascetic life and his brief but mighty labors, he was permitted to honor God by a martyr's death.

359

> Now when John heard in prison the works of the
> Christ, he sent by his disciples and said unto him,
> Art thou he that cometh, or look we for another?
> —MATTHEW 11:2-3

IT was what John *heard* that cast doubt into his mind.

It is thus now, too. Even during their school days many hear things which cast doubt into the little world of their childhood. And who can read a newspaper these days without having the subtle seeds of doubt sown in heart and mind. Who does not have friends and companions who amuse themselves by hurling burning bombs of doubt into the hearts of their believing comrades.

Oh, how it hurts! What a painful thing doubt is to both old and young. Not least to the young! What a spiritual shock we receive when the simple, shell-proof faith of our childhood is pierced to the depths and the cold waters of doubt begin to seep into our souls.

Many pride themselves on their doubts and think that all that they have now learned about the superstition and ignorance of the church and of the ministry is interesting in the extreme. But others suffer year after year. Is it all imagination, that by which father and mother and they themselves have lived? What can they then depend upon in life? Everything is in a flux. They are in a daze.

Added to this is something which is even more painful. The finest and most sensitive young people, those with the most tender consciences, feel that their doubts are *sin* against the God who has purchased them and received them in holy Baptism and been with them throughout all the years of their life, ever since their baptismal hour.

My friend! Doubt is not sin. Whether you sin or not depends upon what you do with your doubts, on whether or not you use them as a shield for the sins which you love.

Do not permit yourself to be frightened! Do as John did: go to Jesus yourself with your doubts. Tell Him about the thoughts which come tumbling in upon your soul. Above all, confess your *sins* to Him. Jesus Himself will set you free from both your sins and your doubts. Even as He set John free.

360

But while he was yet afar off, his father saw him,
and was moved with compassion, and ran, and fell
on his neck, and kissed him.

—LUKE 15:20

How the human mind works!

At all times.

But it has been occupied with nothing so much as with
God. What a literature about God we have in every language!

Yes, what have not people in every age and in every clime
thought, and longed, and hoped, and spoken, and written with
regard to God!

Still people do not know God, Jesus says.

"Neither doth any know the Father, save the Son, and he
to whomsoever the Son willeth to reveal him."

That is what Jesus does here. Yes, here in this most glorious
of all His parables Jesus would reveal the Father, the *unknown*
God, to us.

When we read this parable of the prodigal son, none of
us can doubt that it is the *love of God* that Jesus would
reveal here.

But does not every one know about the love of God?

No, it is precisely *that* which they do not know. When our
missionaries come out and tell the heathen that God *loves*
human beings, the first and most immediate thought of the
heathen is this: "If God loves us, then, of course, we do not
need to worship Him!"

And that is the way most people think also in our country.

It is a long time now since the gospel of the love of God
was brought to our country. What conclusion have the majority
of the American people drawn from this message? This, that
they can leave God out of consideration. They do not need
to bother their heads about God.

The way they *live* shows that this is the way they think.

361

For the time will fail me if I tell of . . . the prophets:
. . . who through faith subdued kingdoms, . . . turned
to flight armies of aliens, . . . and . . . were tortured,
not accepting their deliverance.

—HEBREWS 11:32-35

THIS chapter of Hebrews might rightly be called faith's song of songs. Here the aggressive, conquering, victorious power of faith is extolled in mighty, impressive words.

Christ has not only enjoined us to *defend* ourselves against our enemy, though many of us never get farther than to put up a weak defense.

He has charged us to take the *offensive* also, to go forth to conquer.

To make the greatest conquest that can be imagined, that of the whole world. All nations.

His army is small, but it has superior equipment.

We know from the World Wars what it means to have weapons of which the enemy has no knowledge, and which it therefore cannot use. Such a weapon the hosts of the Lord have in believing prayer.

The world cannot make use of this weapon. Therefore the world cannot prevail against the little flock of Christ, provided only that we have learned to make use of the weapon of prayer.

Those who have learned the secret of prayer and who, with the hand of faith, touch the arm of the Almighty shall not only be victorious over kingdoms and stop the mouths of lions; they shall even turn others unto God.

The greatest miracle of all!

Believe, and thou shalt see the glory of God!

Friends! The world expects a great deal of us. But heaven expects even more.

What do we ourselves expect to accomplish, in the power of Christ, unto the salvation of souls, that Christ may soon come in the clouds?

According to your faith be it unto you!

He who converteth a sinner from the error of his way
shall save a soul from death.

—JAMES 5:20

THE context shows us that the soul-winning work of which
James here speaks is *intercessory prayer.*

This brings us into the most secret chamber in God's great
workshop.

Think only of the fact that most of us who have been
converted have had some intercessor or other who faithfully
brought us personally to God in prayer during the time that
we lived in our unconverted state.

It seems to me that no one is poorer than those who have
no one who intercedes for them, no one who perseveres in
remembering them before God.

I think that we should arrange our work of praying in such
a way that we pray regularly for certain individuals, permitting
the Spirit to assign to us those persons for whom it is His will
that *we* should pray.

If all believing souls would do this, the Spirit could apportion
the unconverted people in our community among the believers
till at last there would not be a single soul without a consecrated
and faithful intercessor.

Then it would be hard for the unconverted to continue
in sin. Holy explosive materials would be bored into their
souls, and the ground would be blasted from beneath their
impenitent lives.

Spiritual awakenings will come to those cities and communities in which the believing Christians enter into this holy
work of prayer.

Awakenings cannot be brought about by *force;* neither can
they be called into being by *magic.* The Lord sends spiritual
awakenings in grace and mercy as answers to the prayers of
His children. In some places the struggle is hard and long. And
the opposition is not overcome save by prayer and fasting, as
Jesus says.

Do not become weary of praying, dear friends of God. You
shall see that the Lord keeps His promises.

But the witness which I have is greater than that of
John.

—JOHN 5:36

JESUS had just performed one of His mightiest miracles.

But it was on a Sabbath. And the Jewish leaders made use
of this as an excuse for not believing in Him.

When Jesus showed them that He had the right to do this,
they seized upon certain things that He had said and used them
as an excuse for their unbelief.

Then Jesus pointed to the fact that they themselves some
time ago had sent word to John. And John had told them
plainly that Jesus was the Messiah, the Lamb of God who bore
the sins of the world.

And now He added in lofty and holy self-consciousness:
"But the witness which I have is greater than that of
John: . . . the works which the Father hath given me to
accomplish."

However, they would not believe in Him. And they stood
there and disputed with Him in order to excuse their deliberate
opposition to Him.

Some *blaspheme* now, as they did in the time of Jesus.

Others *deny* Him: He is not the eternal Son of God, not
born of a virgin, not dead for our sins, not bodily resurrected.

Others do not deny anything. They simply *doubt*. As long
as the scholars are not agreed, we ordinary folk cannot, of
course, be certain, they say.

Others cross themselves at the thought of doubt or denial
of any kind. They are orthodox! But do they really believe!
No; they curse, swear, lie, and deceive.

Others are decent and good. But do they believe? No; they
will have nothing to do with Christ. They never read the Bible
and they never pray.

My doubting friend, if you are *determined* to doubt, you may
doubt to your dying day.

But if you want to be set free from doubt, Christ will convince you. He will *do* something to you that will convince you.

Will you consent to that?

364

Jehovah bless thee, and keep thee:
Jehovah make his face to shine upon thee, and be
gracious unto thee.

—NUMBERS 6:24-25

CHRISTMAS will soon be here.

But first comes the "Christmas rush." To most people that is the ushering in of Christmas. And when Christmas finally does come, many are too tired to observe it.

"But, dear me, is that a time for scolding?" you inquire wearily.

No, I certainly do not desire to add a single stone to your burden. But permit me to send you a greeting now, while your burden is heaviest. At Christmas time, when your burden has been lightened, you will receive so many greetings.

A hearty greeting to you as you carry your burden. It is heavy enough ordinarily; and it does not become any lighter toward Christmas, when the days seem long and the nights short, when sleep is scarce and your body is tired.

We see how heavy-eyed and pale the courteous sales people in the stores are these days, how ready to sink from exhaustion our kind and diligent workers are.

And parents! Well, they must have everything done in good season, everything pertaining to the house and the children, to the cleaning and the baking, to the Christmas tree and the gifts. We notice, of course, that they are tired, even though they do not mention it. And those, who toil from early morning until late at night—they breathe many a sigh on their way home from their labors. How will they be able to make both ends meet? They would so much like to gladden the hearts of all in some measure at Christmas time.

I do not really know why it is this way, why we must go through the "Christmas rush" in order to get to Christmas. But I suspect the hand of the enemy back of it all, the hand of him who cannot endure to see Christmas on earth.

But since it seems that we must go through this tension before Christmas, permit me to express the wish that the Lord might bless you and keep you during these days.

365

Jehovah bless thee, and keep thee.

—NUMBERS 6:24

Yes, may the Lord bless you as you go about your work, striving to make others happy at Christmas time.

God grant that both you and I may wear ourselves out making things pleasant for others. That is what He did, born yon Christmas night. Think of Him when you feel tired and weary!

As you go about your tasks washing, and dusting, and polishing, and decorating for Christmas, may the Lord bless your work!

But do not forget yourself!

There is no doubt a great deal of dust in many a corner of your heart. A Christmas housecleaning! A general accounting before God toward the close of the year. Then the old Christmas Gospel of the Savior who was born will fill your poor soul with the glorious music of Christmas.

And then a word to you, you who go about your work making things ready for Christmas for yourself and your dear ones without a thought of Him who brought Christmas to this earth of ours. Perhaps you, too, will sing Christmas carols, and perhaps you also will read the Christmas Gospel together with your dear ones after the tree has been lighted. Perhaps you will feel that the rusty strings of your soul have been touched again. But a longing, a sigh, perhaps a tear—and you lay aside both the Book and the "Child."

My friend, there was nothing festive about being born in a manger and dying on a cross.

But He could not endure to think that your life should be filled with empty joys and real sorrows and that you should at last pass on into unfathomable and endless woe.

However, after He has made ready to celebrate Christmas with you, you push Him quietly out through the door. You feel that your Christmas joy would vanish if Jesus should remain.

Be converted to God now, and yours will be a new joy and a new Christmas.

And it came to pass, while they were there, the days were fulfilled that she should be delivered. And she brought forth her firstborn son; and she wrapped him in swaddling clothes, and laid him in a manger, because there was no room for them in the inn.

—LUKE 2:6-7

CONDITIONS were such in the Orient that travelers with scant means frequently had to sleep over night with their animals. So undoubtedly not many who were in the city took any notice of the young couple in the stall.

But *heaven* followed the two with divine eagerness. At the very instant that the Child was born the heavens were opened and the plains of Bethlehem were suddenly flooded with celestial light. People, generally, did not see it. They slept. Only a few shepherds who were awake saw it. They stood spellbound in the midst of the heavenly radiance of that night. Then a beautiful angel came and said that they should not be afraid. For now had been born the Child whom God had promised, the Child for whom they had been waiting so intently during days that were long and nights that were dark.

The shining angel had scarcely spoken before the heavens were filled with angels without number, singing a celestial anthem in honor of Him who now was born.

It was earth's first Christmas song. The angels sang it. And the shepherds learned it. And soon it went from neighborhood to neighborhood, from country to country, from generation to generation. Today it is sung by five hundred millions of people in five hundred different languages.

This song about the Child in the manger touches the tenderest heart-strings of childhood and of old age, of men and of women. Even today heaven is never so near to us and never so gloriously beautiful as when we hear the Christmas carols sung around the Christmas tree.

"Thy little ones, dear Lord, are we,
And come Thy lowly bed to see;
Enlighten every soul and mind,
That we the way to Thee may find."

367

Be not afraid; for behold, I bring you good tidings of great joy which shall be to all the people: for there is born to you this day in the city of David a Savior, who is Christ the Lord.

—LUKE 2:10-11

J ESUS was born on a dark winter night.

Yes, since the day of the fall, it had been one long night. Without light from heaven, the souls of humankind groped their way toward the grave, generation after generation. Without hope and with fearful forebodings.

However, some stars did light up the darkness.

They were the promises God had given the little, despised, and now so grievously oppressed, people of Israel. And there were some righteous and devout people looking for the consolation of Israel.

The darker it grew, the more precious the stars became.

And one winter night, while some shepherds watched their sheep outside of Bethlehem, the light for which they had been waiting finally came. The glory of the Lord shone round about them.

And they were sore afraid.

But the angel understood them and said: "I bring you good tidings of great joy. A Savior is born to you this night. Enter into the city and you will see Him yourselves!"

Thereupon he drew aside the veil and the heavens were filled with angels who sang the joys of Christmas into the hearts of fearful human beings.

Christmas fear and Christmas joy—the two have gone together ever since the first Christmas here on earth.

We all become fearful when the celestial light shines upon us and we see how little Jesus means to us, how occupied we are with ourselves and with our own affairs.

Let us now go hand in hand to the manger and tell Him the truth, how full of fear we are and what it is that we fear. And then let us ask that heaven may be opened a little also unto us, that we may join in the heavenly song of praise: "Glory to God in the highest!"

There was the true light, even the light which lighteth every man, coming into the world.

—JOHN 1:9

A DAY was to dawn upon the dark and sinful earth.

Thus God had spoken.

But years passed by, centuries, too, even thousands of years! It is not easy to wait. Many grew weary. But some held fast to the promises and awaited the consolation of Israel. The quiet people, they were called.

Then one dark night those who sat in the shadow of death saw a great light. The true light, even the light which lighteth every one, was coming into the world.

The Messiah was born.

The true light! Yes, now we know what God is like. So unbounded in His goodness that He could not remain in heaven while His fallen children were perishing on earth. But at the same time so consuming in His wrath toward sin that he could not touch His unclean children until the Son was willing to make atonement.

Note here what sin implies: The all-loving Father cannot spare His only begotten Son from any suffering whatsoever. If the race is to be saved, the cup must be drained in its entirety.

From the tree of Calvary now shines forth upon all the sinners of earth the true light of God's grace.

Now we see what God has done to save sinners. He laid upon His Son the iniquity of us all. And as many as received Him, to them gave He the right to become children of God. Then there was light.

Lord Jesus! Give me courage to pause each day in the true light, that Thou mightest reveal to me the secret thoughts and counsels of my heart. But give me grace to see *Thee* in the midst of that light, that I may receive courage to speak the truth unto Thee and rest securely in Thy finished work. And sanctify Thou me in Thy truth, until I stand before Thee in the eternal light. Amen.

> Master, we toiled all night, and took nothing: but at thy word I will let down the nets.

> —LUKE 5:5

TOILED all night, and took nothing!

Then it is not easy to work. This did not happen only to Simon Peter. In our service for the Lord we all experience it, at least now and then.

We experience it occasionally in our homes. Everything seems onerous and hard to do. Daily devotions become a burden, prayer grows cold, and the Word seems closed. Our fellowship becomes worldly, with little love. We are afraid that we hurt rather than help our dear ones.

In our Christian organizations it is perhaps no better. Little interest and much criticism. Little willingness to sacrifice and no progress.

In the neighborhood it is the same. Worldliness is on the increase and ungodliness waxes bolder. Meetings are poorly attended. The young people are occupied with their gatherings, mostly with dancing. The Christians are discouraged, lukewarm, and weary.

My dear friend, let us do as Peter did: tell Jesus exactly what the situation is. We have toiled all night and taken nothing.

Then let us listen to what He tells us: "Launch out upon the deep!"

That is without a doubt what Jesus would tell His people today. We are living in difficult times. There are many things which would discourage us and make us weary in our labors today. We have very few great spirit-inspiring and spirit-renewing experiences in our day.

But these days also have their quiet message to us. And it is this: Launch out upon the deep. Upon the deep of prayer. Seek to get away from the tumult and to find quietude. That is where preparations are to be made for the great catch. Jesus is with us in our boat today as He formerly was with Peter. He wanted to glorify Himself in the presence of Peter. He would glorify Himself now also, in the presence of His weary but obedient and believing friends.

Where thy treasure is, there will thy heart be also.
—MATTHEW 6:21

W E all seek treasures.

And there are many kinds of treasures.

One strives for wealth. Another cares little for money if he can only have fun and amusement. A third cares neither for fortune nor for pleasure if she can only gain the honor and the fame for which she hungers. A fourth cares neither for money, pleasure, nor honor, if he can only acquire power. A fifth cares neither for money, honor, nor power, if she can only live in ease and comfort.

For what are *you* living?

If you have no higher goal in life, if you are not seeking other treasures than those you can find in *this* world, acknowledge it openly to yourself and to God. He has been waiting a long time for you to face the truth.

Then remember, my earth-bent and world-loving friend, that it is not you who are to make yourself love God and the heavenly treasures. For that you cannot do.

You are rather to acknowledge the truth that not God, but the world, is your treasure.

And then pray the Savior to make whole the eye of your soul, that you may once again *see* the heavenly treasures.

If you only get a vision of them, they will become *your* treasures. They will capture your heart so completely that your whole life will become wrapped up in them. It will become the one thing needful to you each day to take the place made ready for sinners beneath the cross of Jesus, there to breathe in His life-giving grace and to live unto His praise and glory.

Then you will learn also how to make use of the treasures of earth. You will learn that if they are to be *yours* you must give them back to God.

Blessed is he, whosoever shall find no occasion of stumbling in me.

—MATTHEW 11:6

NONE of us can avoid feeling the offense which is inherent in the person of Jesus. Sooner or later we are confronted with this enigmatic, inscrutable aspect of His person which even John the Baptist experienced and by which he was tempted.

Look! Yonder sit a father and a mother, one on each side of a little bed. Their child is in convulsions. On their knees they have prayed God to heal their little one. But nay, God does not heal. They have prayed imploringly that God would spare the little one from the cramps. But nay, the little one continues to lie there in its pains until death comes at last.

This seems hard to bear. And Jesus cannot say more at the time than He said to John the Baptist: "Blessed is he, whosoever shall find no occasion of stumbling in me."

See, a little group of people is making its way home from the churchyard. It is a father and five children. The two youngest children were too small to go along today; they are at home. The others have accompanied mother to her last resting place. The father is a believer in God. But now rebellion steals into his heart. How could God make them motherless, all these little ones?

And for the time being Jesus cannot answer otherwise than he answered the Baptist: "Blessed is he, whosoever shall find no occasion of stumbling in me."

To be God, our God must also be inscrutable. None of us have therefore learned to know God until we have become aware of His inscrutability.

Not until then is our faith really tested. "Blessed are they that have not seen, and yet have believed." This is "blind" trust. However, no faith sees more than blind faith. It sees and knows God so well that it relies upon Him notwithstanding His inscrutability, notwithstanding that aspect of Him which is an occasion of stumbling.

"*Blessed* is he, whosoever shall find no occasion of stumbling in me."

Today is salvation come to this house.

—LUKE 19:9

No Christian work is more difficult than that of building a Christian home. However, many do not realize this. Their Christian work is directed toward things outside, toward meetings and organizations. They do not put any *work* into the building of the Christian home. At least no planned work, no work with a conscious objective.

A home is not brought into being simply by the marriage of two people. Not by luxurious furnishings and a great deal of money for extravagant living and social functions. Not even by the fact that the two are personal Christians.

The home is wrought by the way these two succeed in living together. By the candid, intimate, patient, and forgiving love which exists between them. This is the vitally important thing in all home relationships, the relationship to the children, to friends, and to guests.

The secret of a Christian home is *to be Christians together.* And therefore we must look upon the achievement of this as a part of our Christian work from day to day.

We should have a meeting with God together each day in family devotions: prayer, reading of the Bible, and singing. Yes, let us sing together. Singing unites us in a mysterious way. And let us help each other to make family devotions a festive occasion in our homes each day.

This will make it necessary for us to pray for the devotional periods. We pray for meetings that we attend. But no meeting needs preparation in prayer more than our daily family devotions. Otherwise they will degenerate into the driest sort of routine.

O Thou good God, we thank Thee for the home Thou hast given us. First, for our parental home, with all its childhood joys. And then we thank Thee for the home that we have been permitted to establish. Lord, preserve us from those sins which would destroy our home! Amen.

Blessed be the God and Father of our Lord Jesus Christ, who according to his great mercy begat us again unto a living hope by the resurrection of Jesus Christ from the dead.

—1 PETER 1:3

CHRISTIAN faith has always been synonymous with the hope of glory.

As yet we have only been invited, have barely started out upon the way to the great eternal supper. The eternal feast of life has not begun as yet.

Hope has, therefore, from the very beginning, imparted to Christian life its loftiest tone. Indeed, even during the preparation, in the Old Covenant, it was thus. The harps of the ancients never sounded more gloriously than when they touched the strings of hope.

If heaven is thus on the *wrong* side, what must it not be on the *right* side, said a reflective Christian as he stood looking up at the star-strewn heavens.

We human beings are created to hope. To such an extent that we cannot live without it.

The decisively important thing is not, however, *that* we hope, but that *for which* we hope. Most people hope in such a way that the very ability to hope dies within them.

But praise be to God who begat us again unto a living hope! A living hope!

Peter no doubt means by this a hope that is fulfilled. Yes, perhaps he means even more: a hope which constantly gives rise to new hopes, which does not extinguish our faculty for hoping.

Hope is like the holy star which shone unto the Wise Men. It showed them the way and at the same time gave them courage to continue. Hope shows us the way in the darkest hours of life. We know that the sufferings of this present time are not worthy to be compared with the glory which shall be revealed to us-ward.

Therefore we go through life confidently—onward toward death.

Blessed be God!

374

Tell ye the daughter of Zion,
Behold, thy King cometh unto thee,
Meek, and riding upon an ass.

—MATTHEW 21:5

IT was a remarkable royal procession that made its way that Sunday toward the capital city.

The King did not appear very kingly as He sat there on His lowly mount. His servants had no shining armor nor gleaming swords. They were all poor fishermen. And they came from despised Galilee, both the King and His servants.

His following was large, but not imposing: a crying multitude, mostly women and children. And they cried with full throats today: "Hosanna!" Tomorrow: "Crucify!"

Now the procession stops. The King weeps! A king who weeps? Yes, the King of all kings! He dares to weep when there remain to Him no longer any means of helping His misguided people.

Whereupon He rides on toward the city. Is it David's old royal fortress that His eye is seeking? Nay, *His* royal fortress is outside the wall. On a little hill. It is called Golgotha. That fortress is not an easy one to take. Still, with courage true, He will go to meet His enemies.

As He rides along, He sees in the Spirit the *throne* which awaits Him. It is not the gold-adorned one from the time of the kings of Judah, but a bloody cross, an accursed tree.

The royal robe, too, awaits Him. Not the ancient one of purple: nay, the robe of mockery which the soldiers throw about Him. Nor is the scepter forgotten: a stick which a soldier happens to have in his hand. A donkey for a charger and a stick for a scepter—how appropriate they are to each other!

Now all that is lacking is the crown, the crown of thorns; and the race, without knowing it, will have crowned its King.

But even now God cries out to us all: "Behold, thy King!"

> With desire I have desired to eat this passover with
> you.
>
> —LUKE 22:15

HOLY Week was one of the most restless of all the weeks
that Jesus spent here upon earth, full of struggles, temptations,
and sufferings of the worst kind.

But also during this restless week He had one brief hour of
quietude. It was Communion hour on Thursday evening.

Jesus loved this hour very much. He had looked forward to
it with joy, as He Himself says: "With desire I have desired to
eat this passover with you."

Here is the climax of His giving of Himself for His friends.
Here is love's most exalted mystery. With body and spirit He
gives Himself in the Supper. Unites Himself with His own as
the vine with its branches.

Rejoice therefore, dear child of God when you partake of
the body and blood of Christ. He gives you more than your
mind can grasp. However, you can experience its power in
your daily life.

Do come to the Table of the Lord! He waits for you. You
feel weary, empty, dry, and worldly. And you are not certain
whether it is right of you to go to the Lord's Supper as long as
you feel that way.

But listen now. It is the empty and hungry and those who
thirst who need to sit down to the table, is it not? Jesus longs
to satisfy your hunger and to quench your thirst. Indeed, there
is something about Holy Communion which is an invitation
especially to the weak and weary.

If I would be blessed by the Word, I must follow along
carefully, in order that I may grasp what is said. But in Holy
Communion the Lord enters so deeply into my innermost being
that neither my mind nor my feelings can follow Him.

I have nothing more to do in the matter than to obediently
do as He says: "Take, eat!" and "Drink . . . all of it!" The
Lord Himself performs the miracle of communion in both my
soul and my body.

Behold, the Lamb of God, that taketh away the sin
of the world!

—JOHN 1:29

W E cannot fully understand the sufferings of Jesus, neither
His anxiety of soul in Gethsemane nor His experience of being
forsaken by God on the cross.

We *read* what the Scriptures tell us about the most terrible
thing that has ever happened here on earth. We *worship* in
silent impotence this most incomprehensible aspect of our
inscrutable God. We *stammer* out our thanksgiving as best
we can.

But most important of all is that which our text bids us do
today: *"Behold!"* The Israelites who had been bitten by poi-
sonous snakes in the wilderness had only one thing to do: look
up at the serpent of brass. Then they were healed. They were
not to creep over and touch it; nor were they expected to
understand this miracle of salvation. Nay, only behold!

Hear this, restless soul, you who can no longer live in sin,
but nevertheless cannot extricate yourself from your sins: Behold! Behold, the Lamb of God!

Do not permit yourself to become bewildered because you
cannot understand it. You do not have to understand it. Only
behold!

Do not permit yourself, either, to be hindered by your many
restless thoughts about not being able to believe, not being
able to lay hold of Christ, not being able to appropriate unto
yourself the grace of God.

Behold the Lamb of God, thou soul. No Israelite died of
the bites of the fiery serpents provided he looked up at the
serpent of brass. And no sinners can be lost as long as they
look to the Lamb of God.

Turn your tear-filled eyes toward the cross. You will never
see Christ more clearly than through your tears.

All the workings of salvation in our souls and in our lives
are a fruit of beholding the Lamb of God. Never does sin appear
so foul, never does sorrow because of sin become so great as
when we behold how much Jesus had to suffer on account of
our sins.

> Who was delivered up for our trespasses, and was raised for our justification.
>
> —ROMANS 4:25

EASTER Sunday records the greatest event in the history of the world.

Made alive in the Spirit, Jesus breaks the portals of Hades and opens the way from the dark valley of death to the fair land of life.

The power of death is now broken. The powers of death must surrender also the body.

That is what happened on Easter Sunday, when the *body* of Jesus was raised from the dead.

This is wonderful.

But the Easter Gospel has a still more glorious message to us who are not only marked by death but are also in ourselves death-sentenced criminals. It proclaims to us that the bodily resurrection of Christ is God's own signature affixed to the letter of pardon which Jesus applied for on our behalf.

When God ushered Jesus out through the portals of death and brought forth His body from the tomb, He made it clear to heaven and earth, yes, to hell also, that He had put His seal of approval upon that reconciliation with the race which was effected by the death of Jesus. Therefore the apostle says: "Raised for our justification."

Here we have Easter's most joyous message: my acquittal papers with God's own signature affixed thereto have been ready and waiting for me since Easter morning. If I stand beneath the cross of Jesus, I can read the charge that was against me; but I can see also that it has all been transferred to my Savior's account.

In His open tomb I find again my God-given proof that Jesus has paid for my sins, and I am free.

Who is he that condemneth? It is Christ Jesus that died, yea, rather, that was raised from the dead, who is at the right hand of God! Alleluia!

ASCENSION DAY

Lo, I am with you always, even unto the end of
the world.

—MATTHEW 28:20

JESUS added this glorious promise to the missionary command.
And there is a secret connection here. The whole history of
missions tells us that Jesus has never revealed Himself to His
church more gloriously than in her missionary endeavors.

It was for this work that He was given all power. Never
therefore do we see Him *use* this power as he does in missionary
work. He waits only for disciples in whose lives He is permitted
to reveal His omnipotence.

The great joy which missionaries experience in the midst
of their privations and sufferings is the consciousness of being
very near to the omnipotence of Jesus, the joy of feeling that
they are being used by the all-powerful Christ.

Even you and I who have not been chosen of the Lord to
labor out there but here at home, even we experience some
of the same joy in our missionary work, especially in our intercession for missions. Never do we experience so many answers to prayer as then. For we never pray more assuredly in
accordance with the will of the Lord than when we pray for
missions.

Jesus waits for your prayers in order that His omnipotence
may flow through them out to the missionaries and to the
heathen nations. When the missionaries go out into all the
world, enter then into your secret chamber. The Lord will also
now work with you and confirm the Word by the signs that
follow.

Besides the Scriptures I know of nothing which makes Jesus
greater to me than the history of missions.

"See heathen nations bending before the God of love,
And thousand hearts ascending in gratitude above;
While sinner, now confessing, the Gospel call obey,
And seek the Savior's blessing, a nation in a day."

PENTECOST SUNDAY

And suddenly there came from heaven a sound as of the rushing of a mighty wind, and it filled all the house where they were sitting. And there appeared unto them tongues parting asunder, like as of fire; and it sat upon each one of them.

—ACTS 2:2-3

JESUS said upon one occasion: "I came to cast fire upon the earth; and how would I that it were already kindled!"

That fire began on Pentecost Day. It has been burning ever since and shall continue to burn until Jesus comes again.

But it was a serious matter for Jesus to start this fire upon the earth. He had to permit Himself to be consumed by it.

Getting in touch with this fire becomes a matter of serious import to us also.

That is why so many people will have nothing to do with Christianity. They will oftentimes respect other religions, but they will not endure Christianity. In it the Spirit of *truth* prevails, the Spirit which convicts of sin.

And all those who will not permit themselves to be convicted of sin will flee from the Spirit of Christ, from the consuming fire of the Spirit in their conscience.

Are you fleeing from the scorching fire of truth?

Cease your flight today! You can no doubt flee from the truth, but never from the scorching fire. You will flee into that fire which can never be extinguished, either by God or human beings.

Turn to God today and tell Him the truth. The truth shall make you free. The holy fire of God shall burn away the bonds which hitherto have bound your immortal soul.

The Gospel of Pentecost proclaims to us that we can now be filled with the Spirit of God. This is the greatest thing that we human beings can experience on this earth.

For this we have been created.

MEMORIAL DAY

And I saw a new heaven and a new earth!
—REVELATION 21:1

JOHN had seen many terrible things in his visions out there on the island of Patmos. Now he was permitted to see the goal of it all. That which was the aim and the object of creation and redemption. That for which life and death, sorrow and tears, pains and cries are preparing us.

He saw the new earth under the new heaven.

And behold, the tabernacle of God is with humankind! This is the first and greatest thing of all. For the real misfortune that occurred when humanity fell was this: heaven and earth were separated. God could no longer dwell on our earth. Therefore, too, it became unbearable for us to dwell here.

But now the consequences of the fall have been removed. On the new earth God and humanity shall dwell together in all eternity.

We are hearing the highest note in our song of hope. The bridegroom is more to the bride than all that the bridegroom has and gives. The Lord cometh! From the very beginning that has been the heart of the Christian hope.

But you and I are still on this old earth. Oftentimes we feel pains both of body and soul. And we hear the sighs of others who suffer. It becomes unbearably hard at times. But then we hear Him say quietly: "I see your eyes, weary of the strain, wet and disconsolate with tears. But look to the fair shores of the New Jerusalem. As you do so all your woe will vanish!"

It has never been God's intention that we should be able to cope with the tribulations and the stress of this earthly life without our *hope*. Even Christ Himself, as He bore His cross, looked to the joy which awaited Him.

Perhaps you have only a few steps left of the journey. And lo, He shall wipe away all tears from your eyes!

MOTHER'S DAY

Even so let your light shine before men; that they
may see your good works, and glorify your Father who
is in heaven.

—MATTHEW 5:16

TODAY I have a word to you grown-up children who live at
home with your parents. Especially to you who desire to live
your lives for God.

May I ask you first: How much Christianity do your parents
see in you from day to day? Must your mother stand on pins
for you, now to sew, now to mend something for you? If she
does not have things ready for you when you want them, do
you become angry and sullen? And you perhaps speak harshly
to her at times also?

Do you ever think of your father's and mother's lot in this
world? No, you only want them to think of you. If you have
planned to visit some of your friends or to attend a meeting
of one kind or another, you never change your plans, even if
by your going you hinder your mother from going out the few
times she desires to do so.

Have you ever asked your father and mother for forgiveness
for all the self-love and wilfulness with which you have repaid
their gentle love and solicitude and willingness to sacrifice?
Think of how they have watched over you, have worked and
saved in order to make life pleasant for you!

Have you begun to be a help to your father and mother?
Have you begun to lighten their labors, to do the heaviest
work for them, to forego your own wishes in order that your
father and mother might be encouraged and made happy?

If you knew how they look for these things in your life!

And why? Is it because they have become weary of sacrificing
and working, of enduring hardship for their dear children? Oh
no, they will do that as long as they live. But they are so afraid
that your Christianity might be nothing else than *meeting-*
Christianity, Sunday-Christianity.

If you knew how happy they become when they see that
the Christianity of their children is real *everyday-*Christianity
which comes to light in their daily living, then you would pray
God more for this than for anything else. And God hears prayer.

FATHER'S DAY

A devout man, and one that feared God with all his
house.

—ACTS 10:2

Home is life's highest school.

We have schools of many and various kinds. Some train
teachers; others, craftspeople or business leaders. But the home
trains us to become adults.

The home is also God's school, the place where the Spirit
can most readily show us how sinful we are. For at home we
are ourselves much more than we are among strangers.

In the next place, the home, with its close contacts and
its constant dependence upon others, affords us the most practical opportunity of practicing the mind of Christ.

It is in the home, therefore, that our Christianity is put to
its most reliable test.

The progress we have made *at home* in self-control, in sacrificing our own advantage, in doing good, in making life
pleasant for others, in forgiving their failings and bearing with
their weaknesses, that progress we have made as Christians.
And not a bit more.

There was a funeral in a certain community. A believing
Christian man was dead. He was well known, and a large
number of his many and good friends were gathered for the
occasion. At his bier many had expressed their gratitude
to God for all that this servant of God had been and had
accomplished.

Finally his oldest son arose and thanked all present for the
love they had shown his father in life and for the honors they
had paid him at his funeral. And then he added:

"I too feel a desire to say a few words about father today.
Father was a Christian *at home*. To me that is greater than all
the other good things that have been said here today about
my father's life and work."

I cannot imagine a more glorious tribute.

THANKSGIVING DAY

My spirit hath rejoiced in God my Saviour.

—LUKE 1:47

TODAY read Mary's entire song of praise.

It has a beautiful melody. See if you can learn it. Your whole life in God would become the richer for it. And there would be greater joy in heaven. For nothing makes the heart of God rejoice more than songs of praise.

With most of God's children *prayer* undoubtedly constitutes their chief means of holding communion with their Lord. Thanksgiving occurs but seldom, and then in a low voice. The *singing of praise* is perhaps unknown.

Those who have not learned to give thanks have not yet learned to pray. Their prayer becomes a frightened cry of distress, not the child's confidential speaking with its Father about its recurring needs.

Thanksgiving is the joyous expression of the fact that one has not only received the benefits of the Lord but also *seen* them. And to see what God has really given us, imparts new confidence.

But the *singing of praise* sounds even a higher note than that of thanksgiving. In thanksgiving I am still circling about myself, giving thanks for what God has done for me. In the singing of praise, on the other hand, I thank Him because He in Himself is good, because His mercy endureth forever, and, most of all, because He is so good that he sent His Son to suffer in our stead.

My dear child of God! Bring your complaints to God and pour out your woes, yes, make supplication and pray! He rejoices in you and hears you graciously for Christ's sake.

But thank Him also!

He waits for that. You make His heart glad, you honor Him by so doing.

But praise God also! Sing praises unto Him in your heart and with your lips.

That is the best atmosphere in which your soul can breathe.

And your life shall bring quiet healing to the joyless hearts which you meet upon your way.